THE MONEY LORDS

THE MONEY

The Great

 Weybright and Talley · New York

LORDS

Finance Capitalists 1925-1950

MATTHEW JOSEPHSON

To my sons,
Eric Jonathan Josephson
and
Carl Phillip Josephson

Published in the United States by
WEYBRIGHT AND TALLEY, INC.
750 Third Avenue
New York, New York 10017

Library of Congress Catalog Card Number: 72-84210
Printed in the United States of America
Designed by The Etheredges

FOREWORD

On many occasions I have been asked how, in my judgment, our present-day money lords compare with the old-time "robber barons" of the post-Civil War era. This book attempts to answer that question.

It is composed of a representative selection of finance capitalists who were leading figures in the moneyed world during the period between the nineteen twenties and the nineteen fifties and whom I observed, sometimes at close hand, and wrote about at that time. The materials of this book were drawn in part from a number of extended "profiles" of these personages that were published in the *New Yorker* and the *Saturday Evening Post,* and in part from my own recollections and notes, including facts that were not previously published. This later breed of money lords, in effect, have been reconstituted and placed within their historical horizon.

My acquaintance with the world of Wall Street dates from the early nineteen twenties when, after World War I, we could see clearly the process of rapid change going on, as the simpler Victorian form of capitalism assumed its vast modern scale; the gigantic corporations raised up by men like Rockefeller, Carnegie, and Morgan were seen enduring, despite political attacks increasing in geometrical progression, and becoming in old age, pyramidal institutions. Or, as one commentator on our social history has pictured it, our American society was rebuilt as a series of free-standing "big business pyramids . . . very broad at the base and uncomfortably pointed at their tops. . . ."[1] Up their slopes the organization men were to be seen elbowing each other to reach the paneled offices, from which the fortunes of those giant corporations were directed; and down the slope went the others.

I begin with some recollections of "the way we were then" in the Wall Street of fifty years ago. From the vantage point of the world's most important financial center, one may enjoy quite a prospect of the movements of world history. I worked within the financial establishment for several years and came to know it well. I was in it and yet not of it. I felt that my real vocation was that of a writer and that my ruling interests were very different from those of the stockbrokers and addicted speculators—many of them likable human beings—with whom I worked every day. It was as if I were "a stranger come to spy out the land." My sense of being an outsider may well have reinforced my disposition to observe men and events with detachment.

MATTHEW JOSEPHSON
Sherman, Connecticut

ACKNOWLEDGMENTS

I wish to acknowledge the courtesy of Atheneum Press in granting permission to quote passages from pages 153–54 and 157–58 of Theodore H. White's *The Making of the President: 1960,* published by Atheneum Press, New York, 1961. A passage has also been quoted from General Joseph Stilwell's *The Stilwell Papers,* edited by Theodore H. White, page 15, by permission of the publisher, Macfadden, New York, 1948. I am also indebted to Harper & Row, publishers of Russell Lynes's *Confessions of a Dilettante,* New York, 1957, for according permission to quote a passage on pages 145 and 146. And, from the author's own book, *Infidel in the Temple: A Memoir of the 1930's,* passages have been quoted from pages 349 and 351 by arrangement with the publisher, Alfred A. Knopf.

CONTENTS

ix

PROLOGUE: THE WAY WE WERE THEN

The half-mile-square segment of New York City's acreage that lies between Fulton Street and Bowling Green, encompassing its old financial district, has been long known to all the world as "Wall Street," and still today holds an unending fascination for millions of people. Nowadays Wall Street reaches to midtown Manhattan along Madison Avenue and also extends to the business districts of North America's principal cities, State, La Salle, and Montgomery Streets, and, in fact, to the metropolitan centers of virtually all the more or less capitalist nations. In Europe some cities have old and important Bourses of their own; yet all dance to the tune played on the trading floor of the New York Stock Exchange. As long ago as the eighteen nineties, when much of Europe's capital was invested in our railroads, this had grown to be one of the world's richest securities exchanges. After World War I the

1

United States, long in debt to Europe, became the leading creditor nation.

The downtown financial district by then had become a region of high peaks and cliffs; among its canyons there were not only the brokers' offices, but also the headquarters of the money-center banks that held America's reserve funds and the giant insurance companies that were also pools of money. All roads, financially speaking, led to Wall Street, for it performed many vital services. There the varied units of commercial and industrial wealth, expressed in engraved paper as bonds or stock certificates, as well as contracts for stores of commodities, such as cotton, wheat, or metals, could be exchanged nearly instantaneously for coin, in small or huge sums, on the free and liquid market constantly maintained. In the wide trading room of the French Renaissance-style palace at Broad and Wall, whole fortunes changed hands at the mere nod or signal of members of the Exchange. Their transactions were indicated only by a scribbled symbol and some numerals on a slip of paper, then recorded and cleared by the marvelously swift-moving mechanism of the Exchange, and flashed by wire to the ends of the earth.

By the same token, reports of immense wealth and power concentrated here gave rise to fantastic legends about the half dozen, or fifty, or sometimes one hundred men who were said to "rule America" from their strongholds in downtown Manhattan. Local legend, preserved from generation to generation by old hands in the Street, dwelt on the perpetual warfare between the "bulls" and the "bears," or on the massacres of the "lambs" by the "wolves" of the district; or they recalled the old "battles of the giants," Jay Gould and Commodore Vanderbilt, Edward Harriman and J. P. Morgan. Sometimes they described the evildoings of powerful freebooters who wrought sudden ruin for the unwary, even precipitating money panics that affected the entire country. These legends gave Wall Street a sinister fame that in former years inspired fear and hatred among farmers of the West and South, who then composed a numerous debtor class. But the fabulous reports of fortunes swiftly won or lost also gave the place a special allure for many who were tempted to come and try their luck.

Why did the multitudes come here? Stock speculation had formerly been a game reserved for a select wealthy class and, in addition, a limited following of habitual gamblers. But of late, middle-class Americans in increasing numbers had begun to invest their savings in the securities of industrial and railroad corporations listed on the principal exchanges. During World War I, the United States Treasury had sold some forty billion dollars of war bonds to the public; thus many discovered the convenience of negotiable income-bearing securities as against savings bank funds or insurance policies. Learning something also of the sensational 1918–1919 boom in "war baby" stocks, such as Bethlehem Steel (up 1400 percent), or Baldwin Locomotive (up 360 percent), or General Motors (up 940 percent), a good part of the new-rich public entered the stock market. The old brokers used to say of this new public, "They all come here hoping to get rich quick, to win some 'easy money.' " The boom would be followed regularly by a slump—a season of expiation, as in the postwar recession of 1920; but soon afterward the troops of speculators would take heart again, for hope renewed itself eternally in their breasts.

How did I happen to turn up here? Did I too not hope to better my lot, to win fortune in some measure without great pains? I was probably less simplistic than other novices; I came to learn the ropes. In the autumn of 1923, at a time when the postwar industrial recovery was getting under way, I entered a Stock Exchange firm as an account representative and assistant statistician. At twenty-four I had had no business experience whatsoever, but had some training in writing prose and verse, and also as a newspaper reporter. I had begun to publish things and win some little repute, yet my earnings were so small that I grew desperately tired of my impecuniosity. One day I determined to strike out for Wall Street and try to win a grubstake that would permit me to return to my writing. In this limited objective I succeeded. The grubstake was not large, but allowed me time in which to start free-lancing in earnest. I was able to publish a first book in the field of belles-lettres with good results; thereafter I earned my living writing books and articles for magazines. Meanwhile Wall Street and its unending serial drama had got into my bones. I had survived a period of severe trial there, and in the process had learned a good deal about the market that I could not easily forget. In its successive phases of good fortune and disaster it reflected the unfolding economic history of our society. Eventually I was commissioned by magazine editors to write about the world of finance and certain of its key men; thus I maintained close contact with the world of big business and finance during a period of twenty-five years.

At the time of my initiation into the rough-and-tough markets of the early nineteen twenties, virtually all forms of financial skullduggery were permissible, and the rules of the game were utterly different from those of today—indeed there were virtually no rules.

I was never started at the bottom of the ladder but broken in at the top, as it were. A friendly newspaperman, who wrote a daily financial column, sent me with a letter of recommendation to the managing partner of a small, but long-established Stock Exchange firm. I was promptly engaged.

The firm of S. and B. was owned by four partners, two of them old grayheads, and the other two, brothers under forty and young in the business, who had recently bought a major share of the old firm by bringing in new capital. Their offices filled a whole floor of a tall building at Broadway and

Wall overlooking Trinity Church; its front section was a spacious room furnished in club-like style with places for forty to fifty customers. One wall was lined with a slate board where current market quotations were chalked up as they came in on the stock ticker, each of them under a column headed by a symbol denoting a corporate name, such as GE for General Electric and BS for Bethlehem Steel. From the opening gong at 10:00 A.M. to the close at 3:00 P.M., a spry young clerk trotted about chalking up prices on the board from the moving tape he held in his hand. Some three hundred stocks that regularly interested the firm's customers were listed on the board—with the opening, high, low, and last prices chalked up—so that the people gathered in the board room had a bird's-eye view of the whole market action. Around the room there were Edison telegraph tickers in glass domes clicking out the more complete market record on a tape that curled up in a wastebasket. One of the tickers reported the Curb Exchange stocks; another carried only Dow-Jones financial news dispatches; but all the tape was closely observed all day long by the inveterate traders in the room. Now the tickers are gone, and people watch an electronic screen and stockboard.

For a week or so I was shown around the back office where the paper work was done by clerks for the margin accounts of a thousand or so customers; they also had me look into the booth of the order clerk, fronting the board room, where orders were swiftly telephoned to our member on the floor of the Stock Exchange. The indentures on debentures and bonds and on stock certificates were explained to me briefly; and I was also told how trading accounts were established and credits allowed to clients for their purchases or sales on margin, under contractual agreements whose fine print seemed to convey virtually all rights in such affairs to the broker.

Soon I was posted up "front of the store," in the board

room beside a ticker and two telephones. "Here you can see what is happening in the whole market," one of the brokers said to me. "In fact your future is in the board room." The large room was generally filled with traders, big and small, scanning the market, occasionally placing orders to buy or sell. With the aid of a manual listing the abbreviated symbols for all listed stocks, I was able to follow their fluctuating price movements; and I also memorized the more active items, such as "X" for U.S. Steel, "GM" for General Motors, "S" for Studebaker, and "C" for Anaconda Copper. The firm's oldest partner, a pink-faced man sporting a waxed moustache and an Edwardian morning suit, had me assist him in preparing the weekly market letter, which furnished advice and comment to the customers. After a few weeks I was able to turn out a perfunctory two-page market review in a half-hour, using the market lingo and providing a scattering of information on various stocks (gathered from Poor's *Manual* and other financial media). Such information was declared by us to be "based on reliable sources, but not guaranteed." The firm's partners prepared me in a summary way for actual trading; they promised that they would cover up any deficiencies in my knowledge. I also watched how the habitués of the board room conducted their buying and selling operations.

These habitués, who came every day and from 10:00 A.M. to 3:00 P.M. ate, drank, and breathed only the stock market, were a knowing, sharp-faced breed somewhat resembling race-track followers. They invariably sat in groups by the stock ticker watching the proceedings closely, sometimes jotting down notes on a pad of paper. Some were of early middle age; others were older, or had prematurely white hair. I thought of them as old men with young faces. William Butler Yeats wrote perceptively in his memoirs that the gambler, like the hunter or the inveterate lover, appeared ever alert, ever eager for the chase. These people bought and sold securities on the move in one hundred or two hundred share

lots, which they held for a day or two, or a week, usually closing out their transactions before the weekend. (Brokers' fees
were modest then.) In a thousand such board rooms throughout America, they constituted the public of small traders,
then an important fraction of the market, as apart from the
professional brokers trading for their own account on the
floor of the Exchange. As they sat, without ever taking their
eyes from the moving tape, they exchanged brief, often jocu-
lar remarks, in the slang of the Street. From time to time one
or another would quickly leave off his watchful waiting and
become galvanized; he would rise from his chair, rush to the
order clerk, and blurt out an order, writing it down as well
on a slip of colored paper.

What was their "science?" I wondered. What inspired
their sudden choices or decisions? They had no science, but
lived in a world of myths ruled by the gods and demons of
the marketplace. They had their memories of the corporate
stocks they followed, bits of news from the financial service
or Dow-Jones news ticker in their heads, and their own way of
correlating changes in the news, or in the position of the market, with the habits of stocks of interest to themselves. A rise
in one of the Texas oils might suggest that another oil company in the same region was behind the market and should be
bought; rumors of certain strong interests, such as the Van
Sweringens buying a certain railroad in Ohio, would lead
them to believe that the Wabash, a railroad in Indiana, would
also become more attractive. They watched, too, for signs of
"accumulation" and movements of prices above or below
"points of resistance."

A handsome, reserved old gentleman who used to sit
quietly beside me might suddenly become a picture of ill-
contained excitement. He would then bound up out of his
chair to place an open order "at the market" for an odd lot of
Consolidated Gas. We had been watching it rise gradually all
day. Why had he waited until almost closing time and then

hurried in with an "open" order, which might cost him an eighth of a point or a quarter of a point more than a limited order at a fixed price? I could see from the man's worn yet carefully brushed clothes that he was not rich but perhaps had known better days. I asked him why he made his move at that moment; and he muttered out of the corner of his mouth, above the din of voices, telephones, and tickers, "I spotted *accumulation.*" And why had he not bought it earlier in the day? No, he preferred to wait until a sudden buying movement confirmed his suspicion, and was willing to pay a higher price. Was Consolidated Gas a "good" stock, I asked, like Union Pacific, or U.S. Steel, the sedate blue chips of that time? "What does that matter, anyway," he exclaimed. "Stocks go up when people want them enough, whether good or bad." A "bad" stock that was badly wanted was good enough for him. Look at Piggly-Wiggly Stores, that rose recently from 40 to 120; or Stutz Motors, cornered by a pool, and forced up to 1000 a share. But who, I went on, was accumulating Consolidated Gas?

The old man lowered his voice to a whisper and said: "*They.*" That was how the old habitués reasoned: stocks did not just go up; *They* put them up. And who were *They?* The Big Fish, controlling the corporations or with inside knowledge of their affairs, who swallowed up the ignorant small fry from time to time. (The corporate insiders were not then required by law to share their knowledge with the public.)

Plainly the quick-trading fraternity gave no thought to economics or science, but guided themselves by intuition derived from a faith in demonology.

Wall Street was a great whispering gallery echoing with rumors and the denials of rumors. These rumors always treated of "secrets," that is, secret intelligence affecting the corporate securities we traded in. The directors of such companies, as insiders, and the large brokers or investment bankers handling the big orders running to millions of dollars had advance intelligence which gave them a tremendous advantage over the small fry in timing their actions. (Did not old Nathan Rothschild steal a march on all London in 1815 with his early news of the Battle of Waterloo brought by his own fast boat?) Secrets, and even false secrets, had a market value; and both kinds were for sale.

There were also the "mystery stocks." We could see that strong interests were bidding for certain railroads, but few knew who they were or why they were interested. Throughout 1924 we watched how a certain automobile stock, Maxwell Motors, rose week by week from 14 to 50, then later to above 100. No one knew why it became so dear, though rumors circulated that the wily Bernard M. Baruch was directing the pool in the stock. When the secret was finally revealed that Maxwell would become the nucleus of the new motorcar giant, Chrysler, it was too late for us to do anything about it. The price was too high.

Sometimes "mysterious selling" would develop in certain stocks, while the rest of the market was rising. Large blocks were thrown on the Exchange floor and prices would plunge downward. The rumor would circulate rapidly that one of the great bears was selling the stock short, that is, maneuvering to force a decline. In short selling you sold so many shares of American Can or U.S. Steel at the current price, let us say one hundred dollars, borrowed the stock certificates for delivery temporarily from brokers who had it in their own names, and later bought back the same stock at ninety or eighty dollars, returning the borrowed certificates and keeping the difference as profit. With such episodes rumors regularly associated the name of certain famous professionals, such as Jesse Livermore, "the white-headed boy," who had repeatedly won fortunes before World War I by selling the market short. His operations were always artfully concealed, being spread among many different brokers, including several large houses that maintained scores of branch offices all around the country. Livermore himself remained "a man of mystery," never appearing on the floor of the Exhange in person, but secluding himself with a number of trusted assistants in a suite of rooms uptown whose address and telephone were unknown to all but a few. Bernard M. Baruch in his memoirs has repeatedly laid stress on the importance of secrecy in market maneuvers. In the days when he used to manage trading in copper-mining shares for the Guggenheims and Lewisohns, he would insist that they promise not even to tell their wives what was being done.

A couple of Big Fish traded through our office (as well as through other brokers) in what we then considered large lots of five hundred to a thousand shares, but efforts were made to keep us ordinary folk from knowing what they did. One clerk was engaged all day long reporting the market quotations by telephone to a company director whose name was kept secret. Another had an agent posted in our board room, who waited by a telephone all day, all week, all season. He was a big operator's Man Friday, bland of manner but closemouthed. Suddenly after a long interval of waiting, his telephone would ring; he would receive his orders and would spring into action, executing various transactions at the order clerk's window, of which he told us nothing. Thus agents of the pools or syndicates were placed here and there about the Street, and it was difficult to determine just what they were doing.

In all stocks that offered the slightest chance for profit through manipulation, as James R. Keene once said, "There were always pools buying on the decline, selling on the advance." Our group of day-to-day traders, watching the tape constantly, were trying to pit their intuitive sense of the market against the sure intelligence of the insiders. They would make attempts to time their moves in the interval between "accumulation" and "distribution"; yet the arts of deception long practiced here were so baffling that the most experienced of the small traders often met with failure, as I often heard them admit. If their ploys paid off, they would go up to the cashier's window and draw a check for part of their winnings, which they lived on. If they lost they would chew their fingernails ruefully and wait for another day.

Innocent though I was, I was soon encouraged by my employers to try operating in the market with my few small accounts. In the old Horatio Alger romances, a boy hired by a Wall Street firm would take ten years to climb the ladder, and gather a little wisdom of life in the process. But early in 1929 I began guiding a number of speculative clients—after only two weeks' preparation! A memoir of my experience (as published elsewhere some years ago) led a recent historian of the New York stock market to cite my case as evidence of the increased sales pressure exerted by brokers in the nineteen twenties.[1] Thus inexperienced personnel like myself were being employed all about the Street to draw the poor lambs into the market. The increased sales pressure was certainly visible, and it kept mounting up to the year 1929.

I had noticed that certain petroleum stocks had been fluctuating within a range of three or four points, from 33 to 36 per share, then drifting back to 33. With the approval of one of my clients, who deposited a little over a thousand dollars as margin, I purchased three hundred shares of Marland Oil for his account at 33. Within a few days, perhaps a week, the stock moved up to the higher point of its range, and we sold it at $36\frac{1}{2}$. Broker's commissions then were $15 per 100 shares; the interest charges against my client's debit balance amounted only to less than $10, so that the trade netted a profit of $950 after deducting commissions and interest. With a net gain of more than 95 percent within five days my client now had nearly twice as many chips to play with! I had also put two other accounts into Marland with the same happy results. It looked like a beautiful sort of game, and it impressed me as the most painless and quickest way of making money I had ever heard of. I found it even more beautiful when I was able to repeat the process with another well-behaved oil stock.

We were enjoying boom times under the benign administration of President Coolidge. Spring was coming, and more and more gas buggies were driven on the new hard-surfaced roads being built all over America. A bull market was on, and there seemed nothing to worry about. To be sure a few of my clients were mired down in stocks that never moved, or drifted lower, but the luckier ones were raising their bets. Swayed by emotions of greed, they showed themselves vain about their own cleverness in getting at the easy money and brought me more clients, who were eager to emulate the success of their business friends.

"You are getting action," the firm's managing partner said to me. "That is the main thing here." "Action" meant that by keeping my customers churning over their holdings I was netting commissions in good volume. My salary was one-third of those commissions, and as I proceeded with growing confidence to take advantage of short-term movements, it was soon raised from a beginner's pay to a living wage; a couple of months later it was raised again.

The youngest partner, a personable man of thirty-five, who with his brother controlled the firm, favored me with his friendly interest and counsel. He explained to me how he gathered in new business: by dining out; going to clubs, parties, and theaters; meeting many people; and seeking new acquaintances. Often, upon learning that he was a member of the Stock Exchange (which then enjoyed prestige), the persons he met would ask his opinion of some security or other. He would furnish advice as one informed, and in judicious terms; when the talk verged on the current stock market he would quietly drop a "point" or tip (brokers were not supposed to be blunt in encouraging people to speculate). If that stock went up, the other man would feel chagrined at not having acted upon the broker's advice and would be more receptive the next time they met. If, however, the stock in question declined, the broker next time would speak of something else. Many well-to-do Americans had a marked appetite for gambling, and they apparently rose regularly to the bait discreetly offered.

But how could my boss feel confidence in his prophecies, I asked. His answer was that every stock had its sponsor or "daddy" who pulled the wires that made it dance, and he knew some of those people intimately. Then he went on to reveal to me in confidence that he had dined the previous evening with a certain industrial magnate, a director of several corporations, and had learned from him that Tobacco Products, at its next director's meeting two weeks away, was going to increase its dividend. I was enchanted at being entrusted with this inside information and promptly undertook a telephone campaign that enlisted the funds of about half my clients in shares of Tobacco Products. They were all much impressed at the hint that I was acting with advance knowledge. TP was at $60, paying $4 in dividends. If the dividend rate was raised to $5, as promised, the stock could be expected to go to between $75 and $80 from the current level of $60 to $65.

I had been told, casually enough, that even in a bull market stocks suffered recurrent setbacks but had had no experience of this. For five or six months we had seen nothing but a rising trend, and only smiling faces in the crowded board room. Without warning of any kind a heavy squall of selling struck the market. All the leaders, such as General Motors, General Electric, U.S. Steel, and the popular oils, went down sharply, as much as two or three dollars a share. The wire news services now reported that bears were raiding the market. I had no clear instructions about what I was to do in such circumstances, but I could see that all my accounts were very lightly margined—borrowing was usually from 85 to 90 percent of face value of securities, leaving only a 10 to

15 percent margin—and the customers' equities could be severely depreciated in a single session.

"Well, stocks will fluctuate" was a famous understatement attributed to the elder Morgan. We bulls and lambs waited for a rally; instead everything opened steeply lower and the downward slide gathered momentum. The third day was the worst and witnessed some frantic selling, with leading stocks down 6 to 10 percent from their recent levels. What was actually a moderate correction turned into a full-scale catastrophe for my thinly margined clients. I had hoped to sell part of their holdings, salvaging what I could, but saw to my horror that for most of them it was too late.

Worst of all was the action of that favored tobacco stock, in which half of my accounts were involved. On that black day of my little bear market, the wire service brought the astonishing news that the company's directors at their quarterly meeting had reported business reverses; instead of raising the annual dividend, they had ordered it *reduced!* The stock underwent an overnight collapse, opening a full 10 points below its previous close. It flashed through my mind that we had been gulled, that some conspiratorial fellows had planned it this way, and profited. When I sought an explanation from the partner of the firm who had so woefully misled me with his "inside" information, he could not look me in the face and brushed me off saying he was busy. On reflection I concluded that he had not deliberately deceived me, but that he himself had been double-crossed. Here "fair was foul and foul was fair." To circulate false rumors was a fraud, but very hard for a small man to prove in court; the perpetrators of frauds nearly always went unpunished. Some corporations never published any reports at all, and the Exchange authorities did not require that they do so. Thomas Fortune Ryan, one of the aged survivors of the "robber baron" generation, used to say that so far as companies he controlled were concerned, "we only give out reports at times and in ways suitable to ourselves." In 1924 the old wolf was still alive and well—he was one of the world's richest men—and was connected by Street gossip with the operations of pools in tobacco stocks, including our unfortunate choice, Tobacco Products.

On the third and blackest day, at the close of the market session, I gladly accepted the invitation of one of the older customers' men to join him at a downtown speak-easy, where we consoled ourselves with whisky highballs. "Well, it's *only money*," he said with a laugh. He was a gray-headed veteran, and remarked that several of his clients had turned to selling short. To be sure, while most of the people in the board room appeared to be frightened and tense, watching the tape in silence, a few had kept laughing and cheering as the market sank hour by hour, one of them crying out, "See how much faster they go down! I've been waiting for this day for twelve long months."

What a way of earning a living! I had been doing well for a season, but now the losses came thick and fast. Where could one turn for safety among all the snares in this jungle? Was it not a perpetual war of predatory creatures, with each man's hand turned against the other? Some years later I came upon an illuminating item in the diaries of Clarence Barron, published after his death. It described how the young Boston financier, F. H. Prince, had gone to see J. P. Morgan, seeking his approval for Prince's investments in certain Morgan-controlled railroads. Prince related:

> I shook Mr. Morgan's hand and thanked him warmly for the great interest he was taking in me as a young man and said I should never forget his advice. I knew at this time that he was doing everything he could to ruin me. . . .

The first bear market, like a baptism under fire for the army recruit, is the hardest. We small operatives worked with too thinly margined accounts in those days, moving in the dark, without sound information. Brokerage charges and interest costs helped raise the odds against the gambles of the small fry—nine out of ten lost money. A light squall in the market wiped out the people operating with 10 percent margins; their distress selling was so much gain to the well-informed insiders. Nor was there any Federal regulation or state surveillance worth the name (despite Blue Sky laws). In 1933 the U.S. Senate Committee on Banking heard testimony by Congressman (later Mayor of New York) Fiorello La Guardia giving the names of a dozen financial reporters for New York's leading newspapers who regularly received bribes from the publicity agents of pools manipulating stocks. The Stock Exchange itself was a private club, whose Board of Governors had authority to enforce rules of ethical conduct, but used this authority seldom and sporadically.

When I turned up at my office the next morning suffering from a headache, the managing partner and margin clerk were lying in wait for me, thoroughly angry. "Where have you been at a time like this? We tried to call you all afternoon and evening!" I had dined out with my wife, trying to forget my ruined clients. "Margin! Margin! They all need margin right away," said the manager. I ventured that perhaps it would be most tactful to wait and not trouble them for the moment, whereupon the manager turned purple and yelled, "Get out and see them right away. Bring cash, checks, securities, anything, or we'll sell them all out!" The fine print in our contract allowed the broker full liberty to protect himself from loss. If the accounts were sold out at these low values without giving my clients a chance to recoup, it would mean my own finish.

Although this break was only a brief pause in the gradual climb of the bull market of 1924–1925, the narrow margins then permitted made for a high leverage effect. My weaker clients who could not send in more cash lost their savings, and I had to endure their bitter reproaches. In the

Street this process of clearing out weak holders was called "throwing the corpses overboard."

As I looked rather blue, the older partner who had been tutoring me said to me gruffly, "You are very foolish to feel sorry for your customers. They only come here to get *something for nothing*." Remarking that my commissions had shrunk, he added: "You will need some new blood." One of the office clerks who overheard this remark explained to me later, "The old man means 'new suckers.' Anyway, they say there's one born every minute."

After several weeks the market began to recover. My luckier customers flourished again. I also gained some new accounts opened by persons who had not learned about my reverses. Moreover I proceeded with greater caution thereafter. In my memory were stored away facts about the history and business standing of the different corporations listed on the Big Board, and I tried to measure values by correlating annual (or anticipated) earnings with current market prices. Sometimes I also tried the bear side of the market, but found it dangerous and nerve-wracking to play for short-run movements, without real information and confused by false rumors. If you were "long" of a hundred shares of stock, it could only go down to zero; but if you were trapped on the short side, the sky was the limit. A few years earlier, Allan A. Ryan (son of Thomas Fortune Ryan) had carried out a "corner" against short sellers in Stutz Motors, driving the stock up from about 100 to 1000 in a few days. The trapped bears cried scandal; the Exchange's Business Conduct Committee struck Stutz from the list, breaking the corner, and young Ryan resigned from the Exchange.

A clearer picture of the financial complex within which I worked formed itself in my mind after a year had gone by. I really was functioning as part of an army of small and large speculators, whose combined operations helped to maintain a more or less fluid market for the equity shares of America's industries. But we speculators and our brokerage firms operated at the lower level of the elaborate financial structure. At the higher level were the investment bankers and underwriters, wholesalers in the securities field who performed the vital function of raising long-term capital for the nation's expanding industries by the flotation of new issues of stocks and bonds. That was the constructive side of the Wall Street operation, and there too was the cream of the whole business.

A classic example was the huge promotion of the U.S. Steel merger in 1901 by the House of Morgan, which involved distributing to the public new securities valued at approximately a billion dollars. Morgan's commission for the job was said to have amounted to $65 million for a few weeks' work—in which he engaged all his credit resources—and then he was free to use his own capital again in similar ventures. That was a splendid way to make money, as I could judge through a small taste of it that came to me late in 1924.

The commission house which employed me did not participate in more than a few underwritings of new issues during each year. The richest of these plums went to the investment firms with large capital of their own, such as Harris, Forbes; Dillon, Read; or Lehman Brothers. We looked on enviously as Mr. Clarence Dillon bought the Dodge Brothers Motor Company, a strong family-owned corporation, for $137.5 millon—the picture of the single check for that amount, largest in history, appeared on the front pages of the nation's newspapers—then gasped as Dillon, Read quickly recapitalized the company with debenture notes, as well as preferred and common stock, and distributed it all to the public for $175 million. The new common stock, which promptly doubled in value, was soon absorbed by the Chrysler company. In our board room I heard the veteran traders discussing the $37.5 million "whack" that had gone to the Dillon, Read syndicate, describing it as "pure water."

After a while I participated in my small way in a similar underwriting and distributing affair. One of the most daring financial operators of the twenties was Harrison Williams, a former bicycle manufacturer from Ohio, who after the war had turned his attention to electric utilities. There was a rush on at the time to combine small city lighting companies with large holding companies—as Samuel Insull of Chicago, and others were doing. Williams combined numerous Midwestern units into the North American Company, which he then controlled, and arranged to capitalize his acquisitions with a large new issue of North American common stock. This time my firm was permitted to subscribe for several thousand shares of the new issue underwritten by the old investment banking firm of Goldman, Sachs. The issue of $100 million of stock came to market carrying the aura of Harrison Williams's recent financial success in such affairs, and sponsored by a powerful Wall Street syndicate. Our office manager urged me and other account representatives to buy as large an allotment for our clients as possible. Having read of the record demand for electrical "juice," I concluded there was no risk in this expanding industry; and so I dragooned my clients into buying some two thousand shares at the established price of $33 before the market opened for trading in the new issue. (The firm as sub-broker benefited by a discount of about 6 percent.) There was high excitement at the opening bell as heavy orders accumulated for North American, and it began to sell at 36. The news wires had reported our firm as among those having bought large blocks of the shares, and the worried manager now gave me his broadest smile. We were enjoying virtually a "free ride"; under renewed waves of buying orders, North American rose within two or three days to 40.

"You may become a partner of the firm one of these days," the manager whispered to me encouragingly. This time I held on to our strong stock for a longer pull of a couple of months, closing out between 45 and 50. I was enjoying success of a sort, selecting the more solid "rich man's" stocks for my customers, stocks that no one was in a hurry to sell out, and holding them for the long term. I also built up a small account of my own (held in my wife's name) using a wide margin and holding my strong shares through a buoyant market during two years. Starting with a sum of $1000 loaned to me privately, I achieved an equity of about $4000.

A few of my speculative followers pyramided their gains on long-pull holdings in high-grade stocks and expanded their accounts even more extensively. However, it appeared that, while I was giving better service to the customers by using wider margins and holding for the longer term, I was earning less commissions for the brokers. Catering as they did to small holders, the firm depended on "churning" stocks for commission; the partners urged me to step up the quick trading. But my disposition was to slow down.

There was a novice working next to me who called up long lists of prospects hour after hour on the phone. Once he asked to speak to a man who had recently died. On learning this, any sensible person would have hung up, but this fool persisted; he asked for the heir of the deceased, gave him a sales talk, and brought in a new investment account. The manager bade me to go and do likewise. But the hard sell was not for me.

I had learned a good deal, however, about how to survive in the market, even through a second squall of selling in the spring of 1925; but my methods were more suited to a trust company than to a commission house. Meanwhile working mostly with small accounts was nerve-wracking. There were too many intangibles, too great risks of suffering deception, and too little likelihood of being able—like the pool managers, the rare Jesse Livermores, or Bernard Baruchs—to secure in advance the fulfullment of one's prophecies. Those people not only "anticipated coming events" in the marketplace, but were able by their own operations to make sure they would happen as foreseen.

The commission-house brokers rarely won great fortunes. If they behaved with prudence they earned no more than a comfortable living out of the capital invested in their Exchange memberships and business places. (When, twenty years later, I looked in on the two firms I knew well, they had survived, but changed little.) Most of the famous plungers, even Jesse Livermore, died broke. For myself the prospect was even poorer; I thought I would do well to resign and return to my chosen trade, which I did early in 1926.

Still the life of the Street fascinated me then and long afterward. "Wall Street" seen as a community embraced an enormous variety of people performing different and specialized functions. In the huge commercial banks and trust companies of the district, for example, you encountered one particular group who worked with masses of money, which they treated wholly as a "commodity." In those days bankers were highly esteemed; several of the more brilliant students among my classmates at college had gone to work for such giant organizations as the National City Bank or the Guaranty Trust, believing, as one said, that "the future is to the bankers." Bankers were actively expanding America's foreign trade and many believed, after the war, that this movement would foster world peace. The banks that had investment affiliates, such as City, Chase, and Guaranty (controlled by Morgan and Company), were taking over the principal family-owned businesses, recapitalizing them, and distributing their securities to the public. A considerable part of the Wall Street community consisted of corporation lawyers who worked night and day with the bankers and brokers. Some of the leading firms, such as Polk, Wardwell and Davis (who represented Morgan); Sullivan and Cromwell; and Root, Buckner and Ballantine, were veritable lawyers' factories. Their people, I found, knew more about what was going on than anybody else and they wielded great influence.

The typical stockbroker was well-spoken and very well clad in conservative style, but not oversupplied with brains: those attached to the older firms, such as Kidder, Peabody; Harris, Forbes; or Hornblower and Weeks, were products of the Ivy League universities and predominantly WASP. They generally discriminated socially against Catholics and Jews, though not when it came to doing business for profit. Some of the oldest and strongest investment firms, however, were of German-Jewish origin, like Speyer's; Seligman's; and Kuhn, Loeb; which had all been established in New York since the eighteen thirties or eighteen forties, a generation before J. P. Morgan and George F. Baker arrived on the scene.

I encountered brokers who were learned and liberal in their politics, as well those who were narrow reactionaries. ("I read the *New Republic* every week," I remember one of them saying to me, "and especially Walter Lippmann.") But many of the old-line brokerage firms were staffed by the sons of the rich—to give them something to do during the mornings—and this sort often impressed me as both pretentious and shallow.

There was also a strange breed of deadbeats circulating through the board rooms of the financial district in those days: old men who might once have been well off, but who had suffered ruin, or sometimes disgrace or imprisonment for wrongdoing of some kind. These threadbare old men in their senescent years haunted the Street, drifting in and out of numerous popular offices and living on handouts; they knew the ways of the marketplace, and they purveyed tips or gossip of indeterminate value, constituting a sort of lower-level grapevine. One of these, called "Jimmy the Scout," was a small, fat old fellow with a fine large head and lined features—you might have taken him for a public official or a political personage, if not for his cast-off clothes. At intervals he would come running in, all breathless with exciting news of some market development he had received from the "highest authorities." He spoke like a man of some education and considerable financial experience. The younger element in our board room would receive him with shouts of disbelief and ridicule; they would pull his nose, throw his battered hat across the room, and make sport of him as if he were an old circus clown. And yet at the end of a good day they would also take up a little collection and turn over to him a few dollars, before sending him off to other board rooms with some farcical "tips" of their devising. "The Jimmys are important in a way," one of the old traders said. "The market is made up of gossip—even false gossip tells us something."

I sometimes encountered Jimmy out in the street, enjoyed talking with him, and bought him a sandwich and coffee. He had seen over seventy summers and was steeped in the lore of Wall Street in the eighteen eighties and eighteen nineties. Standing by Trinity Church, he pointed to the doorway of the ancient brick building across the street, at the corner of Broadway and Wall, which then housed the First National Bank of New York. There was a large old man, with a severe countenance, wearing sideburns of Civil War style, coming out of the bank's doorway. "There's George F. Baker, Senior," Jimmy said. This ninety-year-old, the long-time ally of the elder Morgan, owned what was called the richest bank in the world, founded by him in 1865. Only a hundred or so millionaires and their corporations were permitted to be his depositors. With his pool of money he controlled a large group of Eastern railroads, and was the dominant figure in the directorate of the vast American Telephone and Telegraph monopoly. He looked like a caricature of the nineteenth-century capitalists, who (like Rockefeller senior) had survived through the nineteen twenties long after the others were gone.

Jimmy walked down Broadway with me, talking of the

old order in Wall Street at the turn of the century, when he had been manager of one of the leading brokerage firms. Pointing to one of the lower office buildings, he said reverently, "Twenty-six Broadway." These were the headquarters of the Standard Oil clan. For Jimmy the decisive power of America's financial capital lay in the hands of the Rockefeller grouping and the Morgan-Baker banks. They were the great heavers and shakers, and the history of the Street was filled with the drama of their massive competitions. (Later, inspired to read the old annals, I found that John Moody in his book published in 1904, *The Truth About the Trusts*, had charted the dominant financial powers in exactly the same terms.) Jimmy recalled the "Northern Pacific panic" of 1901 caused by the battle between Morgan and Harriman for financial control of the Western railways. Harriman, head of the Union Pacific, had been supported at the time by the Standard Oil's banks and by Kuhn, Loeb. The competitive bidding for the key Northern Pacific stock —which drove the price to $1000 a share and nearly bankrupted half the Stock Exchange members—had been directed for Morgan by a famous master of market maneuver, James R. Keene, called the Silver Fox of Wall Street. His associate in the wild day's floor trading of that "cornered" stock had been Harry Content, another old-time manipulator of stocks, who still survived and had his office in the building where I worked.[2]

Jimmy remembered H. H. Rogers, a notorious partner of Rockefeller in the Standard Oil directorate, and leader of their forays in the market, as the most picturesque character of the group. Of Rogers it was said that he frankly hung out the black flag of piracy at 26 Broadway, to the alarm of John D. Rockefeller himself. The Standard Oil group then worked together with the National City Bank (headed by James Stillman), moving its pools in and out of important corporations, running up their price for a time, then unloading them upon the public. Behind the wars of the copper barons of Montana in 1907—which brought tumult and panic to Wall Street—there was the power of the Standard Oil ring that ruled or ruined the industrial concerns or banks it had singled out for exploitation.

Thomas W. Lawson, the "crusading" Boston stock speculator—who sometimes pretended to be a "financier for the people" and wrote the exposé *Frenzied Finance* in 1908—was sometimes employed by Rogers as a pool manager. In Wall Street Lawson actually pioneered in using publicity methods that were to become familiar fifty years later when used by Robert R. Young in his struggle for control of the New York Central Railroad. Inserting large advertisements in the metropolitan newspapers, he would assail the management of a certain corporation, announce his own plan of action—to buy in its stock at advancing prices—and so win a large following of small-fry speculators. Thus Lawson became a force in the marketplace, but when he moved his operations to New York he fell afoul of the mighty H. H. Rogers. The stocks Lawson and his followers bought all collapsed suddenly, and he was quickly made to walk the plank. Thereupon this verbalizing financier insisted on publishing in newspapers and popular magazines the story of how he and his followers had been betrayed by the "anaconda" of the market, the Standard Oil ring. Loudly he called for state or Federal government investigations of the Rogers-Stillman ring's machinations, and once more exhorted the public to follow his lead and take advantage of the "inside information" he furnished freely to small investors. Later Lawson fell into disrepute; charges were made that he sold his own followers short, and he himself went bankrupt in the market panic of 1907. For several years, however, Lawson had stirred things up in sensational fashion, and again I found he had used Mr. Harry Content as his marketmaker. What was more, he had depicted Content as the hero of his topical novel *Friday the Thirteenth,* naming him, with scant invention, "Barry Conant."

In his rococo prose Lawson, as a novelist, described Conant as the acknowledged

> Prince of Brokers . . . a handsome miniature man with a fascinating face lighted up by a pair of sparkling black eyes . . . and with a black moustache parted over white teeth which, when he was talking, looked like those of a wolf.

Conant, according to Lawson, would walk onto the floor of the Exchange coolly, then would turn into "a compact mass of human springs bursting from its clamps" as he went into action. The wars of Wall Street ended always at three o'clock in the afternoon, and at the close of trading a few more stock gamblers who had contended with Conant were "switched into eternity." After business hours the Prince of Brokers was a gay blade, given to convivial company and womanizing. Sometimes after a big day he might be seen attending record-breaking diamond sales at Tiffany's, then located on Union Square; meanwhile, according to Lawson, "unclaimed corpses appeared at the Morgue," and sadly enough "a few innocent girls, whose father's fortunes had gone to swell the System's gold, would that night be turned into street walkers. . . ."

I was much intrigued by this romantic literature of finance, and a while later arranged through a friend to meet Harry Content in his office. By then he had reached the scriptured age of seventy, a small thin man with a shy smile, bald and wrinkled. After having survived more than fifty years of the market turmoil, he seemed like an extinct volcano. He had come to work in the Street as long ago as 1877, when he was fifteen, taking a job as a "runner" or errand boy for brokers. In the eighteen nineties the metropolitan newspapers regularly reported his activities. American Sugar was then one of the most important media of speculation, and Content was often found acting on the Exchange floor for its corporate sponsors. In March of 1893 the *World*'s financial reporter described Content and another floor broker selling huge blocks of American Sugar, which had recently been quoted at more than $100 a share; the stock underwent a great collapse, falling as much as 27 points in a single day's session. On May 5, 1893, American Sugar sold at low as 62. At that point Content was seen to have turned to the buying side; a powerful rally carried the stock upward until it reached 90 again. Bernard Baruch, a younger market operative who was often associated with Content, related afterward in his memoirs that when Sugar touched the lower sixties, he had joined Content in buying the stock and thus, when its big recovery followed, he had been able to make his first "killing" in the market.

In 1900 and 1901 Content conducted himself like a soldier of fortune, now serving under J. P. Morgan, or now executing orders for Morgan's famous adversary, E. H. Harriman. When Morgan bought out Carnegie Steel and proceeded to merge it with other companies to form U.S. Steel, the new shares of the amalgamated corporation had to be introduced to the stock market public. Morgan thereupon called in James R. Keene to "stabilize" the early trading in the new stock of what came to be called "Big Steel"; and Keene engaged Harry Content to help him. Content's expertise consisted in his trick of concealing trades of large blocks of shares so that the existing market level was not seriously disturbed. Usually he worked quietly with "middlemen," or "two-dollar brokers," as they were called on the floor of the Exchange. Sometimes his orders came through large brokerage firms having many branches in different cities. Although many thousands of shares of Big Steel were distributed by him, the stock changed very little in price. "I sold a hundred and twenty thousand shares of Steel for Morgan on that first day and only had to buy back twenty thousand," he said to me when describing the event. It was uncanny.

A curious story was told about him years later by Baruch. In managing one of his pool operations, buying large amounts of copper stocks for the Guggenheims, Content worked as usual to conceal his movements, but had the "feel," as he said, that someone unknown to him was following him up, buying competitively when he bought, selling when he sold, and apparently divining his secret purpose. Content reported his suspicions to his syndicate associates and then resolved to counter with evasive measures. He feinted at retreating from the market by selling several blocks of shares, whereupon the "mysterious unknown" also sold; Content then swiftly reversed himself and made a sudden grand charge upon the market, bidding up the price boldly, buying all that was offered, and completing the accumulation required for full control of the stock.

In reflecting afterward on the black arts of such men as Keene or Content, I was easily led to understand why aspiring novices like myself were regularly at a loss to gauge the short swings of the market. Those men proceeded with full intelligence, whereas we were in the dark. Indeed Bernard Baruch used to boast that he could find out more about the exact condition of some corporation than its own directors. Later I came upon some oral testimony by a millionaire financier who made his profits by lending money to the market manipulators. He described Wall Street of the nineteen twenties as "strictly a gambling casino with loaded dice— the few sharks taking advantage of the multitude of suckers." [3]

Harry Content retained the most vivid recollections of the old-time Wall Street when everything, including the buildings, was on a smaller scale, while the dramatis personae seemed larger, more individualistic, and more romantic. He remembered as a runner going on errands to Morgan's bank, then a small building with a wrought-iron facade and wide round-arched windows, within which Morgan himself could be seen sitting at his desk. Morgan would arrive every morning at the appointed time and leave in the afternoon in his coupé drawn by the same gray cob. In his early twenties Content was already a floor broker executing orders on the Exchange for leading financiers, including Morgan, whom he described as habitually gruff and arrogant. Many who had felt Morgan's whip hated him. It was said of him that if he had only one share of stock in some corporation, he would take the head of the directors' table and cow the others.

Among the famous plungers who were Content's clients were former Governor Roswell P. Flower, an upstate New York farmer and grain trader, who at the turn of the century became the biggest bull of the era and a market leader; John "Bet-a-Million" Gates, whose wild market operations made legend; and "Diamond Jim" Brady, inveterate gambler and sybarite. With such as these Content would go off in a carriage after the market's close to Madison Square, then the center of fashionable life, and stop at Delmonico's Restaurant, which boasted a pretty terraced flower garden, where the men ate and drank well and talked over the day's events.

Content, in short, provided a living link with the gaslight age, and in talking with him (it was in 1932), I conceived the idea of writing about the past of Wall Street and its "robber barons," as the Populists used to call the big moneymen of those days. But already in 1928 I had begun to meet some of the later money lords—no longer as a poor subaltern in Wall Street's army whom they would disregard, but as a writer for the magazines whose notice they craved. (Even the repute of a John D. Rockefeller had been salvaged by the public relations man Ivy Lee.)

On returning to the United States, after a year in Europe,

I was strongly impressed by the changes that had taken place in this country: the skyscrapers were going higher, the motorcars were more numerous and larger; and industry and commerce were rapidly expanding. The mounting prosperity and free-spending tempo of our business society were highly visible. In Europe some importance was now attached to the gradual recovery of Russia in the aftermath of war and civil conflict, and to the start of her first Five-Year Plan. But the progress of United States industry was far more impressive. *Who Will Be Master—America or Russia?* was the title of a current work of prophecy by Lucien Romier, a French writer on finance, who observed our excesses and foresaw reverses to come, but fully appreciated the enormous American potential and left no doubt of his choice.[4]

In the autumn of 1928 I went on a tour of the large Midwestern cities to observe for myself the so-called "New Era Capitalism" in the industrial heartland and to give a report of its leaders in articles for a popular magazine. I proceeded to Chicago by train—the luxurious "Twentieth Century"—and within a fortnight visited Detroit, Cleveland, and Pittsburgh, where I interviewed a number of business leaders. In Chicago I met Louis Swift, one of the nobility of beef and pork, and Julius Rosenwald, the biggest of our merchant princes and long the guiding genius of Sears, Roebuck and Company. In Detroit I met Charles F. Kettering, one of the key men in the General Motors directorate (famed for his invention of the self-starter), and in Cleveland I saw one of the two Van Sweringen brothers, kings in the railway field, who commanded the Chesapeake and Ohio and other roads. But the one who impressed me most and whose comments I long remembered was Melvin Traylor, president of the First National Bank of Chicago, a Kentucky farm boy, who had worked his way through law school and become in early middle age the head of one of the nation's largest banks. Men of large affairs are seldom candid in talking to a representative of the press, but Traylor was outgoing, gracious, and uncommonly public-spirited. For a while his Midwestern admirers boomed him as "presidential timber." (At the 1932 Democratic Convention the Illinois delegates, at any rate, voted for his nomination as vice president.)

We were then at one of the peaks of the securities market boom; stocks had been bid up again in November and December to what appeared to be dangerously high levels. Traylor was concerned about the bad farm situation in the Midwest; he was also worried about the money squeeze just being felt. The Federal Reserve system, after long tolerating a rule of easy money (3½ percent in 1927), had finally raised the rediscount rate to 5 percent. Traylor looked out of the window of his office into the winter fog over Chicago. He said: "I'm trying to see the way ahead, but I am in a fog, such as we have now. I see there are dangers before us, but I cannot see the road ahead clearly."

At the time the nation's public leaders, Coolidge and Mellon, were telling us that our road led only to more prosperity. With few exceptions, such as Traylor and Paul M. Warburg of New York, most of our financial experts gave utterance to an unmitigated optimism. Even John M. Keynes, who played the New York market from London by cable, declared that the great bull movement was unstoppable, and the present Wall Street system for getting-rich-quick was not only working well but was *infallible*.

Presently we will be examining the system and its practitioners.

THE PYRAMIDS OF POWER

A traveler in the Middle West visiting the great cities of the plain, such as Cleveland and Chicago, could see with his own eyes how the new breed of money lords had begun to change the very landscape. In December, 1928, the brothers Mantis and Oris Van Sweringen had almost completed Cleveland's new downtown business center, which had been under construction for several years, with its high office buildings, department stores, and banks grouped around the plaza of the Union Terminal Building surmounted by a forty-story tower. On one of the topmost floors of that tower, the new masters of railroads made their headquarters; and from their high perch the brothers could look down over the rich level midland country crisscrossed by the steel tracks of their five big railroads, which made up the nation's largest railway combination. And from below, the Clevelanders could look up to the Van Sweringens in their high tower as successful and respected magnates who had helped rebuild Cleveland. Once poor boys out of the lower middle class with no more than a grammar-school education, they now, as both realtors and railroad barons, commanded a fortune reckoned in nine figures.

In booming Chicago, Samuel Insull, master of an almost endless network of gas, electric, and traction companies, reigned as the city's most powerful magnate; he too was changing the landscape by building a palatial edifice to his own glory. In the closing days of 1928 it was still a wide excavation at Wacker Drive in the heart of downtown Chicago. The lower floors were to house the Chicago Civic Opera, while the rest of the forty-two-story structure would contain the new headquarters of the Insull light and power combine. The form of this broad-based building, with its forty-two-story tower set well back and two broad wings twenty-two stories high on either side, suggested a huge arm-chair, which Chicagoans aptly named "Insull's throne."

Both Insull and the Van Sweringens in their different fields headed great holding companies, which were rapidly expanding their assets by buying and merging smaller companies; this they accomplished by using "other people's money," in part bank credit, but more and more often money derived from the sale of securities to many small investors attracted by the prospect of capital gains offered by those holding companies.

At about the same period that saw the rise of the Van Sweringens and Insull to financial fame, Amadeo P. Giannini, a native of San Francisco and a former produce merchant, built up a large chain of branch banks in California, first called the Bank of Italy. Like Insull and the Van Sweringens, he managed the expansion of his branch bank system through the device of a holding company, Bancitaly Corporation (later known as Transamerica). The holding company, by exchange of shares, bought up small banks in different cities in California—and even in neighboring states—whereupon the value of these acquisitions apparently increased substantially by their merger into the large bank chain. Consequently the market value of both the bank stock and its affiliated holding company rose in such spectacular fashion that a numerous following of small investors, excited by the growing profits of the Giannini organization, steadily bought the stock of his corporations. There were others in the nineteen twenties who sold securities on a grand scale to the American investing public through holding companies, investment trusts, and bank "affiliates." Notable among them were Charles E. Mitchell, head of the National City Bank of New York, and Ivar Kreuger, the Swedish match king. These two, together with Insull, Giannini, and the Van Sweringens, were to be known to fame, albeit a dubious fame, as the Pied Pipers of the bull market era of the nineteen twenties.

Insull, Giannini, the Van Sweringens, and Mitchell, were essentially finance capitalists who constructed great corporate pyramids with funds drawn from the public's savings. The finance capitalists, rather than industrialists modeled after Carnegie or Ford, were the miracle makers of the age. The methods they pursued were later judged unsound, but they were not unlawful at the time; they were favored by the exuberant economic optimism that all America seemed to embrace.

A crude prototype of the later Pied Pipers had appeared in Boston earlier, in the summer of 1919. He was an ex-convict named Charles Ponzi, who had formerly been a peddler and a waiter, and one day decided to become a wizard of finance. He had a plan that seemed simple and foolproof; armed with $150 in cash, he advertised his willingness to borrow money from the public at 50 percent interest for forty-five days, and 100 percent for ninety days. By taking advantage of differences in official and actual rates of exchange, he planned to use the money to buy international postal coupons in one country where the rate was low and sell them in another for a higher price. It was not a bad idea, but it became complicated in operation and could not work on a large scale. Ponzi paid interest promptly on the money he received, but soon was reduced to paying it with fresh capital that came in floods. The more investors he attracted, the deeper he went into debt. After he had taken in nearly $10 million and issued notes for more than $14 million in eight months, his operation was exposed as a fraud, shut down by the authorities of Massachusetts, and Ponzi was soon back in jail.

The great money lords, the Van Sweringens, Insulls, and Gianninis were not swindlers like Ponzi; yet their method in financial operations also smacked of magic. They were like alchemists who could turn paper into gold at will, and like Ponzi, they too excited the appetite of the public for easy money.

The Midas touch came to Samuel Insull rather late in life, when he was already in his sixth decade. A native of London, son of a lay preacher, Insull served as a stenographer in the London office of Thomas A. Edison's British telephone company. The "little cockney," as his American employers called him, showed so much zeal and brains that in 1881, at the age of twenty-one, he was invited to come to the United States and work under Edison himself as his private secretary and financial factotum. Over some twelve years Insull served faithfully as the inventor's principal aide in all business dealings and became the executive vice president of the Edison General Electric Company, which manufactured equipment for the early power stations. When Edison, who had sometimes been financed by J. P. Morgan, lost control of his electrical manufacturing company in 1892 (it was merged by Morgan together with the rival firm of Thomson-Houston into the General Electric Company), Insull was out of a job. Insull himself had dared to oppose the Morgan policies on one occasion. There had been some criticism of Insull's management; it was said he tended to overborrow. In any case the new controlling interests did not want him, and he moved on to become the $12,000 a year president of the Commonwealth Edison Company of Chicago, a pioneering lighting company which the Edison interests had recently helped to establish. The inventor, who was not consistently a good businessman, suggested that Chicago, with its dense and growing population, might be a good place for the new light and power industry.

The operation of the early electric utilities did not make for easy riches; much capital and heavy equipment was needed to produce current, and usage was at first light under competition with gas. Insull's company, in which he owned but a small share at the beginning, grew slowly. He was a bachelor until almost forty, with a habit of gambling on the schemes of hare-brained inventors that lost him money he had saved or borrowed. He also had since his youth a taste for the company of pretty actresses, and at length, after his remove to Chicago, married a very attractive one.

Commonwealth Edison was well managed by Insull, who knew this business; it began to expand in the nineteen hundreds when the advancing technology of electric currents brought high voltage transmission over longer distances. With several financial associates Insull bought up some small town and suburban light companies. The first group of five small utilities, acquired in the early nineteen hundreds, he amalgamated into a new company, the Public Service Company of Northern Illinois. This required capital, of which he did not have much then. Up to age fifty Insull had not seen any big money, though later, by 1921, he would be drawing in salaries a total of $250,000 from Commonwealth Edison and three other utilities. He borrowed from banks and had backers put up more for Northern Illinois, whose revenues began to grow rapidly, and whose powerlines were interconnected with

Commonwealth. But his credit was under strain, and he looked for ways to ease his situation.

Up to now he had not desired to go beyond Chicago's suburbs, but as his authorized biographer relates, "he, like other men, had to face his moment of corruption." [1] A friendly broker who was a director of Commonwealth suggested that the best way to finance his new undertakings was to form a holding company and turn over the new properties in exchange for its securities. The new holding company would not rate as highly as Insull's operating utility, Commonwealth Edison, but it could probably finance its expansion in the future by selling its own securities at a discount. And so Insull formed his first holding company, the Middle West Utilities Company, in 1912. He had been worth a million dollars or so (above extensive loans), but now things started to move for him, and he began to stake out a huge utility holding-company empire.

As one authority on the electric power industry has testified, a holding company grouping such as the Middle West Utilities was so organized that "the owners of about one-third of the stock, representing a book value of $28 million, not only control an investment of $353 million in operating companies but are the beneficiaries of any increase in the earning power of that vast capital." [2]

In forming his first holding company toward 1912, he learned the secret of how to make big paper profits overnight by the financial legerdemain of inter-company exchanges. He would gather in several small power companies with assets amounting to about $4 million, then turn them over to Middle West Utilities and receive from his own holding company some $12 million (face value) of preferred and common stock. In a good market he might realize two or three times as much as those subsidiaries cost him. As his sympathetic biographer, Forrest McDonald, relates, he became highly excited by these first quick gains and was tempted to add more and more small power companies to his main holding company. Then he went on to set up new holding companies, even piling one upon the other in the form of a pyramid of holding and operating companies. It should be noted that the powerful General Electric interests, through their securities affiliate, Electric Bond and Share, had been carrying on similar maneuvers for many years. Morgan's also had its United Corporation as a giant holding company in the same field. In the nineteen twenties, in competition with these and other strong contenders, Insull sometimes had to pay very high prices for the equity shares of central stations in Illinois, Indiana, Wisconsin, and other states. To cover these purchases he would cause his holding companies, Middle West, and Insull Utilities, to issue masses of paper securities—notes and preferred and common stock. Large management and "engineering" fees were also charged against the subsidiary companies; and big paper profits were recorded when the holding companies sold each other properties at rising prices. For example, he turned over to Middle West a block of securities of Northern Illinois Public Service, which had cost him $383,000 and received in return $4 million in preferred stock of Middle West and some 70,000 shares of its common. He then sold the preferred shares for cash to investors, and returned a minor part of the cash realized to Middle West, but kept the remainder, especially the controlling or voting shares. At all events he had the power to buy with one hand and sell with the other, and mark it up as "profit." It was a somewhat new way of using old tricks, issuing watered stock in quantity and obtaining cash for it from the investing public.

But how could one be sure of maintaining market support, that is public interest, in such amounts of new, undigested, holding company paper? Insull's growing organization attended to that too. During World War I, as a patriotic service, and because of his devotion to his native England,

Insull had directed a campaign in which a billion dollars of United States war bonds were sold to the plain citizens of Chicago. He had thereby earned much public applause; but he had also noticed how the public liked the convenience of the income-bearing securities, and he promised himself that he would one day turn to selling the public masses of securities in his own corporations and thus raise capital on an undreamed of scale.

In several Western states there was a strong political movement to have public utilities as local monopolies, owned and operated by town governments. Insull was at the head of the private power companies' trade association, which reacted with a powerful lobbying campaign against the municipal ownership movement. Insull himself became a force in the politics of Chicago and Illinois by virtue of the funds from his companies' treasuries that he distributed to friendly legislators for their election contests. As a public relations ploy he also initiated a "customers' ownership" drive, declaring that "the best way to win friends for the utilities was to get the people to invest their money in them." [3]

As early as 1914, at the beginning of the war in Europe, when the nation experienced a temporary panic, one of the Insull power companies had urgently needed some $400,000 for generating equipment, but found bank credit cut off. A young district manager had thereupon undertaken to sell 6 percent preferred stock of that local company to customers in his district and had promptly raised the sum required. Insull remembered that experiment. In 1920 bank money was tight again; now he established within his main subsidiaries a security-selling department in which a "force of trained salesmen—transformed hordes of employees (who might be department heads or meter-readers) into stock jobbers. . . ." [4] As the Insull holding companies, in their expansive action, issued ever more paper securities, Insull's sales force moved from door to door to find investors who would buy them.

Whereas only a few thousand held such securities in 1919, ten years later there were 250,000 owners of Middle West's 6 percent preferred shares and many more owners of the common and preferred stock of Insull Utilities Investments and Commonwealth Edison.

After thirty years Insull had never forgotten that Morgan had thrown him out of the General Electric Company, and so he tended to avoid the great money center of New York like the plague. Instead, two of Chicago's leading banks, the old First National and the Illinois Trust, financed his companies and shared in underwriting their bond issues. An independent Chicago investment firm, Halsey, Stuart and Company, which became an aggressive competitor of the big New York investment houses, handled the distribution of Insull holding company and Commonwealth Edison bonds and shares to small banks and investors throughout the Middle West. Thus Insull carried on with his plan of "customer ownership," involving many passive investors as so-called "partners." Meanwhile his expanded combine of utilities, gas, and traction companies, as it stood in 1928, was "owned by everybody and therefore owned by nobody," as his biographer relates, and very few, apart from a few insiders, knew what the old man with the pince-nez was really doing.

Like other public utilities, Insull's were regional monopolies and came under the regulation of the Illinois Power Commission, whose chairman for many years was Frank L. Smith, an ambitious downstate politican. In 1911 Commonwealth Edison advanced loans of $6 million to Chicago's elevated railways company, then undergoing reorganization, and the Edison Company's leading customer for power. These transactions led to control by Insull of Chicago's entire elevated railway system. In 1913 he also became chairman and directing head of the People's Gas Light and Coke Company, founded by the notorious "robber baron" Stephen Yerkes, which had previously been a strong rival in the illuminating field; People's Gas suffered from both financial and political troubles at the period, and Insull took it over. In fact wherever Insull turned, he faced regulation and negotiations with politicians; thus, throughout his career he had both feet in politics—local and national.

At heart the utilities had an adversary relationship to the public, which called for better service and lower rates, while the utilities looked for increased profits. In between these interests stood the politicans—governors, legislators, city-councillors, and the state regulatory commission—as more or less honest brokers; but in Chicago and Springfield they were often less than honest. Insull's lobbying was generally managed through the nationwide Association of Edison Electric Illuminating Companies, in which he was a leading figure. He expended much of his companies' money to support the friendly Governor Frank Lowden's bid for the presidential nomination by the Republicans in 1920; and he did the same for Mayor "Big Bill" Thompson of Chicago, as well as other politicans who might befriend his company. When a Public Utility Commission was established in Illinois, Insull and his lawyers helped write its enabling act! The Commission chairman, Frank L. Smith, was long thought to be in Insull's pocket. When Smith later campaigned for the U.S. Senate, Insull's and other power companies raised $500,000 for his electioneering expense, but did this in such scandalous fashion that after being elected in 1926, Smith was actually unseated by the Senate.

In the late nineteen twenties Samuel Insull was regarded by Chicagoans with awe, but not with affection. To improve his public image he gave much effort to sponsoring the Chicago Civic Opera and its diva and director, Mary Garden. Later Miss Garden said that Insull had no taste for music and plagued her to produce only those familiar Italian operas that would appeal to the untutored public. Chicago's reform element, led by Professor Charles E. Merriam and

Harold Ickes, stigmatized him as a "brazen" and "arrogant" monopolist. So he appeared when testifying in 1926 before a Committee of the U.S. Senate about admitted money payments of as much as $272,000 made by his companies for the campaign expenses of Frank L. Smith. "God only knows," exclaimed Senator George Norris, "how many Senatorial campaigns Mr. Insull has financed!" And the crusading Chicago lawyer Donald R. Richberg, who later served as one of President Franklin Roosevelt's principal aides, called Insull Chicago's "gold-plated anarchist."

Little did he care what the reformers said. At the end of 1928 he formed a super holding company named Insull Utilities Investments, which would embrace all the properties he controlled—Middle West Utilities, Commonwealth Edison, and many other corporations. From Insull Utilities he received in exchange a large block of preferred shares as well as three quarters of a million common shares with stated value of $7.54 each and warrants for as much more of the same. When the stock was listed on the Chicago Stock Exchange in January, 1929, it opened at $30 a share. During the summer of frantic speculation that followed, it rose as high as 149! The other "Insull stocks" were correspondingly elevated. On paper, Insull's fortune mounted suddenly to more than $150 million. "My God," the old man was heard to exclaim at the time, "I'm going to buy me an ocean liner."

The American people had long feared and agitated against monopolistic railroads. Now in the nineteen twenties the Van Sweringens of Cleveland were creating a combination of railroad systems, controlled by a pyramidal holding company of their own device, and setting at nought the plans drawn up after the war by the Interstate Commerce Commission and Congress. The Van Sweringen operation paralleled that of Insull in electric power and of A. P. Giannini in the banking field.

Who were the Van Sweringens? Mantis J. and his older brother Oris P. Van Sweringen were of Dutch-American stock. They had grown up in Cleveland, where in 1905 while in their twenties, they worked as office clerks and in their spare time carried on a small business in real estate options. From the start these quiet-mannered, personable young men showed a knack for working out large propositions with a small amount of their own capital, that is, by the liberal use of credit. Their first big operation was in the Shaker Heights suburban development, whose growth had been somewhat slowed by lack of good transportation to downtown Cleveland. Forming a first holding company (a common device in the real estate business), they sold some land but retained control of their company, through which they raised more capital funds. After several years they began to buy acreage in downtown Cleveland on the Public Square—long intended for a civic center—which they planned to use for a rapid transit terminal. Then with the help of associates and banks, they acquired a small railway, the Cleveland and Youngstown, which could be used for their suburban line to Shaker Heights. Toward 1912, however, they cast their nets further when they learned that the New York, Chicago and St. Louis Railroad, known as the "Nickel Plate," which owned land they needed for their proposed terminal in Cleveland, was expected to be sold off by its owner, the New York Central. The Nickel Plate was a sizable Midwestern trunkline plying between Buffalo and Cleveland; it had been built parallel to the Central's tracks in 1881 by a group of financial pirates in order to blackmail that railroad. William H. Vanderbilt, who ran the Central, had been forced to succumb to the blackmail and buy control of the Nickel Plate. For several years the ICC had been pressing the Central to divest itself of its small "rival." At length, in 1913, the Central's president, Alfred H. Smith, offered to sell controlling stock in the

523-mile-long Nickel Plate to the Van Sweringen brothers for $8,500,000. Smith, a Cleveland man, had done business with them and liked their style. Although the brothers had been prospering of late, they were only able to put up $2 million in cash (most of which they borrowed from banks) and offer notes payable over fifteen years for the rest, terms which the Central generously accepted.

The young Van Sweringens knew nothing about railroads when they took over the Nickel Plate, whose bonded debt totalled $58 million; they used only $500,000 cash of their own. In order to carry the large personal liability of $8 million they had assumed, they formed a new holding company, the Nickel Plate Securities Corporation, which took over their debt. It issued 25,000 shares of $6 preferred stock as well as 250,000 shares of common stock with voting power, most of which the Van Sweringens retained for themselves.

The Central was pleased to leave the Nickel Plate in friendly hands and treated the Van Sweringens as secret allies, even extending the time for their note payments. The brothers were also favored by having J. J. Bernet, one of the Central's ablest executives, transferred to the Nickel Plate as its managing president. During World War I the road's traffic increased sharply; in seven years its dividends alone were enough to pay the purchase price for its control. The Van Sweringens were then able to complete the construction of the Cleveland Union Terminal, which was also profitable.

They had put the perpetual money-making machine of the holding company to full use, bringing in other people's money, borrowing on the extended-repayment plan, and buying up other railroads, whose controlling stock they used as collateral for more loans. By forming still another holding company, they were able to take over two more Midwestern roads and round out the Nickel Plate in 1922 as a 1700-mile system. For this they issued 150,000 shares of Nickel Plate preferred stock, underwritten by Guaranty Trust and Lee, Higginson, and wound up with voting control of Nickel Plate, their personal debts paid off, and $3 million cash to boot!

Wall Street now buzzed with the exploits of the Van Sweringen brothers. When the important Chesapeake and Ohio Railroad's stock began rising mysteriously in the market, rumor rightly attributed this to the "Vans' " secret buying. Behind the scenes there was quite a comedy going on as the Cleveland agent pursued Collis P. Huntington's heirs, an aged daughter and her husband, who had controlling stock to the extent of 73,000 shares of Chesapeake and Ohio. The hereditary owners knew nothing of the business but were justifiably afraid their stock would be worth much more later; at length, however, they accepted an improved offer of the Van Sweringens of some $7 million at about $95 each, for 73,000 shares of the railroad. To raise the needed funds the brothers simply caused the Nickel Plate to issue to the public second mortgage bonds for $7,200,000, and thus were able to cover the purchase price for working control of the great coal-carrying road at no cost to themselves. Later the Chesapeake and Ohio rose to more than 300 and was split up. The Van Sweringens capitalized on these big gains and launched new undertakings.

They were wonder-workers who had brought a new excitement into the relatively stagnant pond of railway finance. Many now sought to anticipate their moves in the market or to imitate them profitably. The brothers enjoyed the favor of the Morgans (bankers to the New York Central) and of George F. Baker too; they had entered the highest financial society. Baker's First National Bank next advanced them credit to buy control of the Erie; exploiting their credit, they bought up still other railways: the Pere Marquette, an important connection to Detroit and automobile shipments, and the rambling Missouri-Pacific, created by Jay Gould. With these purchases the Van Sweringers extended their domain from the Atlantic to the Rocky Mountains! The Van Sweringen combination by the late nineteen twenties embraced a broad diversity of properties: real estate developments, railway terminals, hotels, a department store, coal mines, trucking companies, armored cars, dairy farms, and finally, five big railway trunklines, which together ranked with the Pennsylvania's and New York Central's among America's five leading transport combinations. Their total trackage exceeded that of whole nations like England.

The two brothers were quiet of manner and "average" in appearance. But Oris, older by two years, was fiendishly clever at working out corporate devices to do the tricks he wanted done, sometimes making them so elaborate that he himself could not fathom them! He and his brother lived together in a very retiring way at their gentleman's farm "Daisy Hill"; they were confirmed bachelors, who ate together, slept in the same room, and generally avoided society. When Mantis finally married at the age of fifty, his elder brother was evidently much troubled at finding himself alone for the first time in his life.

They appeared to have a capable staff of assistants, including the well-known Cleveland financial forecaster and bank executive, Leonard P. Ayres, and skilled railway operators such as J. J. Bernet, who had moved up to head the Chesapeake and Ohio. Railroading, formerly America's greatest industry, was considered a "sick" industry after World War I. Roads that had been well maintained, such as the Chesapeake, were profitable, but big trunklines like the Erie and Missouri-Pacific looked unhealthy, even following receivership and reorganization. The "financiering" of the Van Sweringens did not contribute to their improvement.

But still they went on buying with other people's money.

As the banker Otto Kahn of Kuhn, Loeb and Company later testified before a Senate Committee, there was

> . . . a perfect mania of everybody trying to buy everybody else's property, and the railroads were not excluded from that. New organizations sprang up. Money was so easy to get. The public was so eager to buy equities and pieces of paper, that money was . . . pressed upon domestic corporations as upon foreign governments.[5]

In order to improve the railroads' service and also strengthen their finances, a plan for the consolidation of the major trunklines into regional systems had been drawn up for the ICC by Professor William Z. Ripley of Harvard, an expert on transport affairs. But the Van Sweringens ignored these directives. They were as if enthralled by the combination of holding companies they were constructing, whose component railway properties they selected according to their own fancy in the Middle West, the South, and even away Down East in Maine. The market for railroad stocks fairly boiled as they bid for the shares of roads like the Erie and the Missouri-Pacific—for which they were to pay dearly.

By the end of 1928 the brothers had borrowed from bankers and leading brokers the sum of $35 million on their own personal notes; however, they reckoned their equity at current bull market values at three times that figure. When I encountered the brothers in Cleveland, they were dreaming up a still greater holding company, in fact, a super holding company by means of which they would transfer their indebtedness to the investing public, while retaining full control of their "empire." But that was still a secret which the coming year, 1929, would unfold.

Amadeo P. Giannini, the California banker, was another man who came to wield vast money power during the twenties. He too had his "day of genius" when in 1917 he formed a holding company in order to do legally what his banking organization could not do under existing state law. At the time he commanded a medium-sized branch-banking business, the Bank of Italy, that catered to small depositors drawn from the numerous foreign language groups of San Francisco. The bank had ten branches mostly in or near San Francisco with about $20 million in deposits; but Giannini was resolved to develop a statewide chain. California law, however, forbade the purchase of the stock of one bank by another, although it permitted the purchase of a bank's "assets," including its capital, surplus, and premises. For a time Giannini and his partners, as a group of individuals, bought up various small banks by using their own personal credit and obligating themselves for large loans.

It was the State Superintendent of Banks who one day suggested that it would be permissible for Giannini and his associates to use a holding company as a corporate instrument for purchasing other banks. An earlier model had been the securities affiliate of the National City Bank of New York, the National City Company. Giannini had his lawyer draft the by-laws for what he called a "syndicate for the purpose of facilitating the purchase of banks." It would be a company attached as a twin to the Bank of Italy, in which the bank's stockholders would participate in proportion to their holdings of Bank of Italy stock. Giannini's first holding company was named the Stockholders' Auxiliary Corporation, and it acted as the alter ego of his growing bank.

The establishment of the affiliated holding company marked a big turning point in Giannini's career; he was able to borrow against its collateral and "purchase deposits" by buying other banks on a grand scale. Within two years his chain of banks expanded by leaps and bounds, creating branches in eighteen California cities and increasing its deposits fourfold.

Giannini, though a man of little education, was something of an original who contributed a good deal that was novel to the banking art. He believed fervently that a widespread banking organization with hundreds of branches in varied regions and commercial centers—like the branch banks of England and Canada—would be safer and more stable than the locally centered banks; the whole system would strengthen the parts against loss or panic.

The Bank of Italy, which had begun with small savings accounts of Italian-speaking depositors, grew into a giant institution that embraced a huge clientele representing all of California. Its success and its spectacular profits made Giannini known to the entire country. He then ventured to penetrate the great money center of New York and launched a campaign to build up an interstate, in fact, a worldwide banking institution. To this end he formed a new and bigger holding company, the Bancitaly Corporation, which was to facilitate the larger plans that obsessed him. Bancitaly became the favorite medium of a horde of speculators in the markets of the late nineteen twenties; its rise in value was phenomenal, as was the appreciation of its affiliated banks. During a period of some years Giannini too was credited with possessing the Midas touch; he was a giant who threatened the power of the Morgans, Bakers, Stillmans, and Rockefellers even in the huge money center they had long controlled.

2

THE WIZARD BANKER FROM CALIFORNIA

In the spring of 1928 a correspondent of the Boston *Transcript* wrote from San Francisco of the tremendous "bubble" that had floated up there (and elsewhere) in the securities of the Giannini enterprises:

> If anyone doubts whether Giannini is a name to conjure with, he need only journey to California and he will hear the most astounding tales of quickly garnered wealth by those who are staking their all on this Second California Gold Rush engineered by the picturesque Italian-American banker. The Bank of Italy and its affiliated Bancitaly Corporation have made fortunes for many of the "common" people of the Golden State, particularly the Italian-Americans.
>
> So large and so persistent have been the profits . . . in Bancitaly shares that the creator of the enterprise is idolized. He is regarded as a veritable wizard of finance, a magician whose every move . . . produces a golden stream of profits for his followers.[1]

Nothing like this frenzy of speculation had been seen since the discovery of the Comstock Lode, wrote another financial reporter, B. C. Forbes. He had been talking with Italian waiters and barbers, some of whom had bought Banc-italy stock several years earlier in 1922 at $200 a share and now found its actual market value had risen, after having been split up, to the equivalent of $1050 a share. Several of the North Beach residents, having sold a few shares, had traveled to Italy, their pockets bulging with cash; thus even in Europe excitement mounted over the easy money created by Mr. Giannini of San Francisco.

It should be remarked that at the same period in Chicago there was a speculative bubble in the Insull utility holding company securities; as in Cleveland in the "Van Sweringen railroads," and in New York's huge financial marketplace in the new investment trusts that were being sold to the public en masse by leading investment bankers such as Dillon, Read; Lehman Brothers; Goldman, Sachs; and finally even J. P. Morgan.

Holding companies and investment trusts reflected old ideas of finance capitalism in use since the early nineteenth century in England. But by 1929 they had become so popular as a means of "sharing in America's endless industrial growth" that they absorbed about a third, or $3 billion, of all America's annual savings.

Some doubts had arisen earlier about the propriety of listing these holding companies, or investment trusts, for trading on the New York Stock Exchange. In 1926 its Board of Governors had employed a certain J. B. M. Hoxsey, veteran vice president of the Bell Telephone System at Atlanta who was an expert in calculating depreciation in utilities, to study and report on this question. Hoxsey wrote that holding companies such as Insull's in utilities and the Van Sweringens' in railroads were . . .

necessarily bad . . . a mere exploitation of what may be termed the surplus earnings of the operating companies during periods of prosperity, and [held] a temptation to rape the subsidiaries for the benefit of the holding company.[2]

The investment public, however, had developed a "mania" for buying pieces of paper, as Otto Kahn later termed it, including all the holding companies that were composed in great part of watered stock. There had been one of those recurrent financial bubbles around the turn of the century when the "robber barons" Whitney and Ryan, and "Bet-a-Million" Gates had combined tobacco and traction companies and steel manufacturers into industrial trusts and issued enormously inflated new stock to a gullible public. Even Morgan's steel trust was about one-third water. A season of expiation followed.

In a time of easy money, from 1927 to 1929, once again the investing public, it was observed, were happy to surrender their rights of ownership and all voice in the nation's enterprises as long as dividends came to them regularly, and with them capital gains. Above all they did what so-called authorities insistently advised them to do; they entrusted their savings to the direction of the reputed experts in their different fields, such as Insull in utilities, the Van Sweringens in railroads, and Giannini in banking.

In the nineteen twenties the bankers and finance capitalists, using the most ingenious corporate and banking devices in their expansive drives, appeared to dominate the American economic scene; the masters of industry, heading long-established monopolistic concerns, seemed more like what we later came to call "organization men," at least by comparison with such predecessors as a Carnegie of 1880, or the inventive Ford of 1905 to 1913. Charles E. Mitchell was a Yankee from Boston's suburbs who became a driving security salesman and rose to be head of the giant National City Bank of New York, after forming its securities business into its most profitable department. The Dutch-American Van Sweringens were low-keyed in approach, but insatiable in their appetite for combinations of railways; the English-born Insull showed a singular greed for money and power and stood in constant terror of adversaries who threatened his "empire."

Giannini was different; stemming from a minority ethnic group, Italian and Catholic, that had not formerly provided leadership in finance, he was more outgoing and high-spirited than his WASP contemporaries. On the other hand, as a native son of the Golden State, he was a Westerner to the core— ebullient, optimistic, a true Babbitt with his booming style of salesmanship. Though he had little formal schooling, he was naturally quick of thought, fast-talking, and had a keen memory; in manner he was very approachable and could be gracious as well—though also quick to anger. When he impulsively interrupted or shouted down people, his suave university-bred son (and partner), Mario, would sometime chide him. "Well, I'm just a roughneck," he would exclaim on such occasions. "I grew up along the docks of San Francisco—I don't know any better, I suppose." Withal, he was, even in old age, a handsome and commanding figure of a man, six feet two inches in height, broad-framed, and with the imposing head of a Roman emperor. For long years he could be seen sitting at his desk in the open counting room of his big bank on Montgomery Street, San Francisco—"the people's bank" he called it—greeting hundreds of persons of high and low degree by name, dispatching his business interviews at top speed, a decidedly visible personage in the commerce of the West Coast, and a good deal of a politician as well.

Giannini's parents were of thrifty North Italian peasant stock, hailing from the province of Genoa. His father, Luigi Giannini, had had a little schooling; at age twenty-one he was able to marry a neighbor's daughter, Virginia de Martini, then only fourteen. A year later, in 1869, he set off with his bride on the long journey to California, which they reached by one of the first Union Pacific trains to cross the continent. He settled in San Jose, fifty miles south of San Francisco, at the head of the bay, bordering on the Santa Clara Valley. There was already a colony of Italian settlers and farm laborers in the area, including a school friend of Luigi Giannini, who had urged him to come to this rich land. The young Gianninis had some capital and were able to buy very cheaply a small hotel in San Jose. The profits of this enterprise enabled Luigi to purchase a forty-acre fruit ranch a year later. At the same time, 1870, his first son was born and named Amadeo Peter. The Gianninis lived at the ranch, having disposed of the hotel, and the boy grew up in a favored environment—a world of blossoming apricots and plum trees and fields of strawberry plants. Two more sons were born to the Gianninis; then a tragedy befell them. When Amadeo was only seven, his father was shot and killed by a crazed farmhand. The young mother continued to run the fruit ranch for several years, until she remarried. Her second husband was a teamster named Lorenzo Scatena who hauled produce from the Santa Clara Valley to the produce market in San Francisco. Soon after their marriage the Scatenas moved on to San Francisco, where Lorenzo worked for a commission house dealing in produce at the market by the docks.

Amadeo attended school in San Francisco and made an excellent record. "I can still spell almost any damn word," he used to boast long afterward. His handwriting was so neat and correct that at the age of twelve he wrote letters for his stepfather, an amiable man to whom he was greatly attached. His later career showed that he was also well trained in arithmetic, particularly in multiplication. Scatena by then had branched out as a commission merchant and had to go off at midnight to begin his work of provisioning the city before morning. The boy Giannini, after having once gone with his stepfather to see the fantastic nightly bazaar at the harborside with its mountains of fruit and vegetables under flaring gaslights, its ships and carts, and its traders shouting in every language conceivable, was fascinated by the business. He used to steal off Saturday nights to work with Scatena; and at fourteen he resolved to quit school and "get ahead," despite his mother's wish that he continue with his education. This she managed in the case of her second son, Attilio, who eventually won the degree of Doctor of Medicine at the University of California—thanks to the help of his brother Amadeo.

They were a close-knit, affectionate family, which now included three Scatena children. The oldest boy had the drive of the typical widow's son; devoted to his mother, he evidently wanted to replace his lost father and become her protector. All his life his manner was paternal and protective toward those who stood close to him. (Later on he used to call his hundreds of bank employees his "boys and girls.") After attending a little business college for several months and learning double-entry bookkeeping, he was given a full-time job at L. Scatena and Company. He was only fifteen, but he was almost full-grown and weighed 170 pounds. At the waterfront's produce market he easily held his own not only with rough-handed folk, but with sharp trading Yankees, Portuguese, Syrians and Jews. Soon he was authorized to drive out with horse and buggy on buying trips in the rural areas outside San Francisco. He came to know the countryside from the Sacramento Valley down to the Santa Clara, and its ranchers and truck farmers found him a good mixer and a square shooter. Amadeo hustled and laughed or brawled his way along, signing contracts for whole carloads of apricots, lemons, cantaloupes, grapes, or cherries. While other prodigies might write dissertations on physical science at sixteen, A. P. Giannini was a prodigy of commerce in perishable green goods, who enlarged the profits of L. Scatena and Company. When he was nineteen, A. P. was awarded one-third interest as partner in his stepfather's business, which then earned $18,000 a year in profits. Ten years later he was head of the firm and made it the biggest commission house in San Francisco. This accomplishment had been the ruling idea of this fiercely competitive youth; once it was achieved he lost interest in produce and stepped out of the business. He kept a little office downtown where he attended to his real estate investments—now worth about $100,000—and began to show some interest in the politics of the North Beach section, the locale of the Italian-American community.

San Francisco, the city of pleasure, seldom saw young Giannini at its many balls and dinner parties until some time in 1892. He was a large and personable young man with wavy black hair and long moustache. On Sundays you could see him going to mass in a cutaway and silk hat, sporting a cane. It was at church that he met Clorinda Cuneo and became a suitor for her hand. She was the daughter of a leading man of business—"lace curtain" Italian-American, one might say—as the Gianninis now were. A. P. soon overran his competitors and led Clorinda to the altar. She was to be, in his waterfront lingo, his "best bargain"; their marriage endured forty-nine years to the date of her death in 1941. The newlyweds moved out of the city to a roomy gabled house in suburban San Mateo, and in time three children were born to them.

It was by chance that A. P. got into the banking business. In 1903 his father-in-law died leaving an estate of about $500,000 to a dozen heirs, one of them Giannini's wife. It was A. P., by now a leading figure in the city's Italian community, who was entrusted with the management of the Cuneo properties, mostly real estate but including a minority interest in a small bank, the Columbus Savings Association. After looking into its affairs, A. P. had himself and his stepfather Scatena elected to the bank's directorate. It had only $5 million in deposits, and A. P. discerned that its loan department was used mainly to support the real estate operations of its officers and directors. He tried to wake up the bank and bring in more depositors, but the controlling group spurned his proposals for improvements and ousted him from the board. Giannini departed in a great huff, roaring at his opponents, "I'll start a bank of my own and run it in my own way."

In October, 1909, he and Scatena (who had also resigned) put up $20,000 and persuaded business friends and relatives to contribute the rest of the capital of $150,000 with which Giannini planned to start a new bank to be run "solely for the benefit of stockholders and depositors, without entangling alliances or rake-offs." The new bank was located just across the street from Columbus Savings, at Columbus and Washington Streets, and its name, "The Bank of Italy," was nicely calculated to win away the clientele of the rival institution. Shrewdly, Giannini had also taken over the popular teller of Columbus Savings by paying him five dollars a week more. There were the accents of a reformer in the young Giannini, as well as those of a driving ego. But he had some ideas of his own about bringing in small depositors, "the sort of people who never used a bank," and also of making numerous small loans that were likely to increase deposits. A valued business friend, James J. Fagan, vice president of the Crocker National Bank, undertook to advise him. Admittedly Giannini knew little about the intricacies of the business, but he seldom listened to any counsels but his own. Years later he said, "Because we were new to the game we had to do unusual things."

As a great seaport San Francisco boasted some strong old banks doing an international business, such as Wells, Fargo, and Crocker National; it had also some smaller institutions specializing in French, Swiss, German, and Italian depositors. Like lawyers and doctors, the established professionals in banking considered it unethical to advertise for business. But the impetuous, hustling Giannini sent three of his clerks fanning out through the North Beach district and the water-front market soliciting the deposits of Italian immigrants. He himself went pounding along Mission Street and out in the country to look up farmers, who kept their gold coins in chimneys, and preached the gospel of 4 percent for savings. Indeed he not only advertised for new accounts in the foreign-language newspapers but for *borrowers* as well—an unprecedented act. "Well, we want business, we got to let people know about our bank," he used to say. He was, in short, a compound of Italian bravura and American brass. His little Bank of Italy was entirely different from the marble-walled and marble-hearted affairs on Montgomery Street. After a year and a half it had nearly $2 million in deposits. California was forever growing, and Giannini's loans, in great part for mort-gages and building construction, brought in a much higher interest rate than the average short-term business loan at 6 or 7 percent. Unlike Columbus Savings, the new Bank of Italy serviced checking as well as savings accounts. Instead of confining himself to the Italian sector, A. P. soon was bring-ing in accounts of people of old American stock, with whom he had done business. As president of his bank, he also made it his consistent policy to distribute as widely as possible its 3000 capital shares (of $100 par value) in lots of 100 shares at the maximum.

On April 18, 1906, at 5:00 A.M. the earth beneath the San Francisco peninsula began to heave and shake, and soon most of the city's downtown buildings began to burn. With considerable difficulty A. P. made his way from the suburbs into a city given over to chaos, arriving at his bank at 8:00 A.M. to find that the staff had sensibly drawn reserves of $160,000 in gold and currency, as well as notes for more than a million dollars from the Crocker National Bank's vaults, and were ready to move to a place of safety. By then the advancing flames were three blocks away. "We had only an hour to get out," A. P. recalled. The bigger banks at Montgomery Street and along Market Street were to find their vaults inaccessible for many days thereafter, whereas the little Bank of Italy was able to load its cash and paper into a couple of wagons and transport them in a zigzag course along the water's edge to San Mateo, where Giannini buried the gold in his garden.

In San Francisco various legends have been woven around the exploits of the young Italian-American banker who made of catastrophe his big opportunity. While others gave way to despair, Giannini appeared at a meeting of the city's leading businessmen to argue that San Francisco would be rebuilt quickly and be bigger than ever. Many of the banks were closed down temporarily. But Giannini vowed he would stay open, and he set up a tent and desk on a pier in the commission-house district and put up a placard reading: BANK OF ITALY—OPEN FOR BUSINESS. There a clerk accepted deposits and honored checks, while Giannini told everyone that the reconstruction of the city would be a golden opportunity for business and advertised that the Bank of Italy would lend money liberally to home builders.

Though the city was half-destroyed, with 25,000 buildings in ruins, it rebuilt itself with surprising speed as Giannini had predicted, and business increased for the Bank of Italy. For a while its operations were centered in a private house at Van Ness Avenue that had been spared from the fire; a year later, after increasing its capital to $500,000 the bank moved to larger premises in a nine-story building at Clay and Montgomery, the "Wall Street" quarter of San Francisco. The bank by then had two branches in the city. The year 1907 had been one of panic and bank runs, but the Bank of Italy had weathered the storm. Because there was no Federal Reserve System at the time, a great many small country banks closed down, for as A. P. observed, "every bank stood alone." But in Canada, he noted, where big units operated numerous branches, there had been no runs and no failures.

After the 1907 panic, the California Bank Act of 1909 introduced a more strict supervision of banks; it also permitted the establishment of branch banks throughout the state, subject to the approval of the state banking superintendent as to their public convenience. While the new law was being debated, Giannini visited Canada and made a study of their branch system. On his return he informed his board of directors that he planned to develop the Bank of Italy as an institution with branches all over the state of California. The separate branches, he contended, would strengthen and get business for each other. "We could diversify our risks," he pointed out, "through units based on different geographical sections and trades."

His first jump out of town was to San Jose, his birthplace, then a city of 30,000 people with a strong Italian minority. But the majority of the San Jose bank's depositors were non-Italian; its owner, Prentis C. Hale, a leading merchant, agreed to become a director and vice president of the Bank of Italy and remained in charge at San Jose. Then Giannini took over a small bank in suburban San Mateo, and James J. Fagan of Crocker National, who owned shares in this latest acquisition, joined the Bank of Italy as a director (later becoming a vice president). The Bank of Italy was now beginning to become less Italianate and more American. Two more small Market Street banks in the mercantile center of San Francisco were added in 1910. Wherever possible Giannini kept the old staff on the job; he also brought in several experienced Canadian bank officers to help run the growing branch system. In an open Packard car he rode about spying out future locations for branches, but mainly purchasing deposits by merging with smaller banks. In the five years after the earthquake his bank had grown fivefold in resources (some $11 million) and consisted of six branches.

"It was easy to merge banks," A. P. explained afterward. "As soon as you have bought a bank you have assets and cash; and as soon as you take over you get your money back." He hustled and pushed, as he had learned to do in the fruit-and-produce trade, hauling in depositors and advertising for borrowers. The Nob Hill financiers scoffed at his "boomer" style of action, hinting that his undigested branches and small loans would be profitless. The rich old banks preferred a "wholesale" business with big depositors and estates in trust, leaving the small businessman to A. P.'s "people's bank." He used to bristle at such criticism, saying roundly: "It was no secret that we wanted to make money and make the bank grow. And I cannot for the life of me see how going after business as any mercantile firm would do is undignified."

Defying precedent he made a great leap south four hundred miles to Los Angeles, the hastily growing rival of the "Queen City," adding three more banks, one of them centrally located at Fifth and Hill Streets. Hitherto the two cities had kept their banking houses apart from each other. But now the motion picture boom was on; land values were rising swiftly as Los Angeles increased its population to 300,000. A. P., moreover, was a perpetual "bull" on California and its land and its farms. He even bought in several shaky rural banks with bad paper, preventing local failure, a socially useful action.

A severe reform governor, Hiram Johnson, now held office in Sacramento; his Superintendent of Banks, W. R. Williams, found Giannini sometimes "careless of forms," as in his takeover of a small Los Angeles bank without first obtaining the formal approval of the state authorities. In 1913 Williams fined the Bank of Italy $1000, which Giannini for a while refused to pay. In the end they patched things up; Williams was won over by the enthusiastic Giannini and agreed that the branch system could become a great public convenience, especially in rural districts. When several years later, in 1917, Governor Johnson went to Washington as a U.S. Senator, Williams resigned and accepted a higher-salaried post as cashier of the Bank of Italy chain. Williams had freely given approval to the dozens of new branches the bank had established in recent years. San Franciscans raised their eyebrows at this unexpected appointment of Giannini's former critic and remarked that he had large perquisites to give those state officials who examined and regulated his affairs. A. P. simply shrugged off such innuendoes; his business rivals acted in much the same way.

In the busy and prosperous war years A. P. swept up and down the Central and San Joaquin Valleys, gathering in a string of banks in important towns that were destined to become sizable cities: Fresno, Stockton, Bakersfield, and Modesto. He had always known how to delegate much of his work to assistants—and indeed preferred to free himself of detail and routine. By now he had a team of skilled men; his chief aide was an accomplished San Francisco-born lawyer, James A. Bacigalupi (later made president of the Bank of Italy); his vice presidents, James Fagan and A. J. Mount, were veterans of banking. A. P. also discovered talent in men such as his young Italian-American chauffeur, who went up the ladder rapidly and became a vice president. These and other sharp-eyed agents scoured California, spotting banks that were to be absorbed, examining their assets, weeding out their "bad" or slow notes. Then having received their report, A. P. himself would surface to negotiate the deal, sometimes on a gruff take-it or leave-it basis, and at low cost; sometimes, if he badly wanted the location, at a surprisingly high bid that was too tempting to refuse. There were some complaints that Bank of Italy crushed out small operatives by threatening to establish a competing branch in the same town. After a purchase the sign painters would come during the night, and the next morning the citizens of Gilroy or Redwood City would see the shingle of the Bank of Italy replacing that of their old "First National." Giannini's organization often acted in the preliminary arrangements with speed and secrecy to prevent the shifting of deposits. By 1919 the Bank of Italy consisted of more than a hundred branches and held assets of over $127 million, making it one of the three largest banks on the West Coast.

Governor Friend Richardson and his banking superintendent, C. F. Stern, however, proved to be no friends to the Bank of Italy's expansionary program; the American Bankers' Association and the recently established Federal Reserve System were also hostile. They contended that a weak branch of such a system, like the weak link in a chain, would imperil the other branches; and that the old "family doctor" relationship of the country banker would be lost in Giannini's "chain-grocery" system as it penetrated rural areas. The bank was also criticized for having absorbed considerable amounts of bad paper; as a consequence charters for new units were delayed, while the Governor called for restrictive legislation.

Giannini was angered when he learned that two rival banks in Los Angeles were being favored with charters for new branches that were denied him. Strong opposition only goaded him to further demonstrations of his cunning and fighting power. "If you can't do a thing one way, you do it in another way," he said.

The "other way" was the legal instrument of a syndicate, the Stockholders' Auxiliary, a sort of holding company actually, with which he, with Scatena, Fagan, Hale, and others, after 1917, purchased stocks of banks they wished to merge with their own. The syndicate, which had its own capital and could borrow money, did what the Bank of Italy could not legally do.

Denied new acquisitions by a hostile state government, he formed two new bank chains under another corporate identity. One of them, the Liberty Bank, had its San Francisco office across the street from the Bank of Italy's headquarters in a desirable location that A. P. feared might fall to some rival operator; it developed a number of its own branches in the city and out of town. In Los Angeles the Bank of America was founded in 1921, ostensibly by a banker named Ora Nonette, and grew to be quite a large branch system in time. After a while it became known that both the Liberty Bank in San Francisco and the Bank of America downstate were owned by a holding company called "Bankitaly," whose shareholders were identical with those of the original Bank of Italy. A. P. liked the name of that added bank in Los Angeles and intended to use it for the nationwide branch system he was now resolved to establish.

The sheer size of Giannini's operation caused fear among his fellow bankers and inspired growing opposition, especially among country town bankers, who formed the California League of Independent Bankers and pledged never to sell out to the Bank of Italy or any other branch system. These opponents assailed Giannini in newspaper advertisements as a "monopolist" who crushed out competitors. The state superintendent of banks also continued to seek ways to curb the great banking juggernaut, until one day it was reported that the Bank of Visalia, situated in an important agricultural center, was about to close its doors and that only the Bank of Italy stood ready to help it. Superintendent Stern was now unable to hold Giannini off, except at the risk of a local panic, and he yielded. Having reversed himself he went further and granted charters for other pending mergers with the Bank of Italy; then he resigned to take an executive position with one of Giannini's rivals in Los Angeles.

In the political field the rising banker followed the pattern of most leading businessmen. A. P. pretended to be neutral, giving donations to both major parties, but he was deep in state and national politics all his life. He had lobbyists looking after his interests in Sacramento, and Bank of Italy's corporation lawyer, Senator William G. McAdoo, in Washington, D.C., taking an active part in national legislative matters touching banks. In 1926 A. P. determined to use his power to elect the man of his choice as governor of California.

Dissension had recently broken out between Governor Richardson and his ambitious Lieutenant Governor, C. C. Young, both Republicans. The public issue between them was supposed to be the question of an increased appropriation for schools, which the conservative Richardson opposed, while the insurgent Young favored it. But the secret issue that lay between them was A. P. Giannini. Young challenged Richardson for the gubernatorial nomination.

The Republican primary contest was expected to name the next Governor, as their party then was favored to win the state election. On the eve of the primaries, President Bacigalupi of the Bank of Italy sent telegrams to its branch offices all over California calling on its personnel of 4000 managers and clerks to go out and ring the doorbells of 100,000 enrolled Republicans and urge them to vote in the primaries for Young. This sudden thrust by the powerful bank was enough to carry Young into office. A. P. never used such blunt methods again, for at the time there was much unpleasant talk about Young as "Giannini's Governor." On being sworn into office the new chief executive appointed a former school teacher as his superintendent of banks. One of A. P.'s aides afterward allowed that while this official "may not have known much about banking, he was a mighty good superintendent for the Bank of Italy."

In February, 1927, thanks to the new superintendent's favorable rulings, Giannini was able to toss his several different branch bank groupings—the Liberty Bank, the Bank of America of Los Angeles, and some others—into the one big basket of the Bank of Italy. This now became a great chain of some 300 branch offices in 185 California towns, with resources in deposits and capital funds of $750 million, constituting the largest institution of its kind west of the Hudson River and ranking third in size in the nation.

At this same period a new national banking act was passed by Congress, Senator McAdoo being one of the drafters of the law. It sought to encourage state banks such as Giannini's to enter the national bank system, but also, in response to majority opinion among United States bankers, restricted branch banks, that is, "froze" them in their present status. Several years earlier the Bank of Italy had joined the Federal Reserve System as a member. Now in 1927, to everyone's surprise it also became a national bank, which added to its prestige. A. P. had hurried under the wire with his flock of new banks to accept more severe regulation under the new law, which also froze his big rivals in California to the existing number of their branches. He thus held a commanding position in the race for banking power and meanwhile was not really restricted by the new law, since his various "dummies," or holding companies, were rapidly gathering in other banks in California and other states.

In its enormous growth during its first twenty years, the Bank of Italy had more than kept pace with California's mushrooming population. But fresh drafts of capital were constantly needed; and this was raised by having the banks sell new stock in small lots to the original stockholders, to its several thousand employees, and also to thousands of its depositors. From its original par value of $100, with a dividend of $5, the stock had gradually risen by the time of World War I to more than $200; in the nineteen twenties, following steep increases of dividends and split-ups of shares, the market value of the Bank of Italy shares rose above $1500. For the long-term investors the Bank of Italy shares proved to be a veritable Comstock Lode. The shares were very widely distributed, according to Giannini's plan, to have many small stockholders owning from ten to fifty shares scattered all about, while control rested in himself and his inner circle through the bank's affiliated holding company.

Beginning in 1924 (when Giannini was contemplating moving in on New York itself) he sent a team of salesmen through the Middle West contacting Italian-American communities and selling small lots of stock of his new holding company, Bancitaly Corporation, which proposed to invest its funds in a variety of bank stocks. His agents wired him on May 24, 1926, that they had succeeded in selling nine thousand shares to eight hundred individual investors, adding, "Enthusiasm growing . . . You will have wonderful army for future expansion." Bancitaly had been a small affair prior to 1924; but with several boiler-room operatives selling its stock throughout the country, it accumulated much capital, invested $43 million in eighty-one banks, and by 1927 showed annual earnings of $11 million, a tenfold increase in three years. Giannini's stock-selling agency was the exact counterpart of Samuel Insull's in Chicago, which sold utility holding company stock. The ability to sell securities through his own agency to masses of small investors all over the country gave A. P. Giannini a feeling of enormous power. Curiously enough he himself accumulated only a modest amount of shares of either his bank or Bancitaly.

"I don't want to be rich," he used to say. "To avoid being rich was one of the hardest things I tried to do!"; and he used to add, "You know I'm a comparatively poor man." At age thirty he had won a good competence to live on, and had half a million dollars in real estate. He had simple tastes, lived very modestly and told everyone it was ridiculous to want more money than he had. Compared with Insull, or the Van Sweringens, Giannini does not seem to have been overcome by the greed for money itself. He may also have had some enduring suspicion of paper wealth.

To be sure he had $50,000 in salary and perquisites. As in managing his father-in-law's estate, he had arranged to draw a 5 percent fee from the holding company as his share in promoting its capital gains. Against this account, on one occasion in 1928, he drew $2 million in cash, turning over two-thirds of it to the Giannini Foundation for Agricultural Economics he established at the University of California at Berkeley. (In 1930 he claimed that some $2 million more was owing to him as fees.) Like him, his son and relatives held no large amounts of Bank of Italy shares directly. The affiliated holding company, Bancitaly, however, concentrated more than 22 percent of the giant bank's capital shares in its hands, and A. P. was in control of that.

What this great monopolizer wanted was power, wielded through his organization; moreover he always wanted to make the organization *bigger*—"the biggest bank in the world." He was a very proud man, like many self-made men, proud of the power that came to him through the faith of associates and of the hordes of stockholders he commanded, whose numbers swelled by 1929 to more than 200,000! Although he had an able and intelligent son in Lawrence Mario Giannini, his chief lieutenant, and other valued associates, he was always the whole show in his organization. He had "power without ownership" as Berle and Means defined it in 1933 in *The Corporation and Private Property,* but it was none the less valid and dominant.

Like Alexander, sighing for new worlds to conquer, Giannini looked beyond California in the late nineteen twenties. Napoleon, also a brainy Italian, had turned east to invade Russia; A. P. now turned his gaze eastward toward the larger stage of New York. Nearing sixty, he might have rested content with being the overlord of banking in the Golden State. But as he himself said, "I'm a man that can't stop going." He must buy more and bigger banks; he must lay siege to the financial capital of the world, so that, entrenched upon the Eastern as well as the Western shore of the continent, he might realize his dream of a transcontinental banking empire.

In 1927 and 1928 New York saw a good deal of A. P. Giannini, the 220-pound giant of California banking, and the press was much intrigued by him. He stayed in a suite at the Ritz Carlton Hotel at Madison Avenue and Forty-sixth Street, where he kept his door open to all comers—there was neither servant nor secretary. Evenings he liked to dine in a spaghetti house in Greenwich Village with friends. To the press he was a knockout for personality, and as one reporter wrote, he had ". . . a titanic head, a face like a rock, and a voice like a howitzer." New York was intensely curious about his new ventures, and some elements in Wall Street were uneasy.

"I would make branch-banking nationwide and worldwide," he declared in 1929 before a Senate committee. "It is coming, gentlemen, and you cannot stop it." As in California, so in New York, he began his movement of penetration by establishing a landing base in some small banks, then spreading out. In 1919 the Italian-American Chamber of Commerce had invited A. P. to set up a bank catering to the estimated 400,000 Italian-Americans in the metropolitan area. He had sent on his brother Attilio and Bacigalupi as his envoys, and through the newly chartered Bancitaly Corporation of New York, purchased two neighborhood savings banks; in 1924 a small commercial bank was added to the others. His brother Dr. Giannini gave up medical practice and headed the New York operation for several years.

Then A. P.'s agents learned that a long-established Wall Street trust company, the Bank of America, was for sale. There had been a struggle for its control between the Morgan-sponsored president, E. M. Delafield, and the well-known Ralph Jonas of Brooklyn, the ambitious head of the Manufacturers Trust Company, who had bought a large block of the Bank of America of New York shares. Giannini was also on hand with one of his own generous bids, and while Morgan and Company did not own a share of that bank's capital, they were influential enough to have Giannini, the California Italian, chosen over Jonas, the Jewish Brooklynite. According to A. P.'s son Mario, the Morgans thought they could more easily control Giannini. "We took over in March, 1928," he related afterward, "only after I had the approval of the House of Morgan."

The key importance of this old-fashioned bank was that it did a trust business with large estates and corporations in the Wall Street money center. The big New York banks such as Chase, City, Guaranty, Bankers, Morgan, and First National were immensely powerful in strategic industries and railroads through the masses of securities they held in trust, which furnished a very lucrative business beside that done with depositors. Giannini's banking combination, up to now, had small depositors for the most part, and many savings accounts, but very little trust business. Combining this bank with his three other units in New York, A. P. now had an important $400 million trust company, and a foothold in Wall Street.

But soon after this purchase he was called down to see F. D. Bartow, one of the partners at Morgans, and told that the ownership of banks by holding companies such as Bancitaly was regarded with disfavor. Bancitaly was told to divest itself of all but 20 percent of Bank of America of New York.

The Federal Reserve authorities feared that a bank might make "sweetheart" loans to its affiliated holding company. Then if the company were caught in a stock market crash, its decline might trigger a decline in the affiliated bank's stock, and even cause bank runs.

A. P. was angered; he told Jackson Reynolds, president of the First National Bank of New York, that he was a boy from the great West and not accustomed to taking orders from people. Reynolds gave him sage council: "Mr. Giannini, you have made a great success. I do not presume to advise you. But if the Morgans tell you to lie down and let them walk over you, if I were you I would do it."

At first A. P. complied with the orders from Morgan's and began to reduce his holdings in the Bank of America of New York. Then he changed his mind and bought it all back. The devil, he thought, with Morgan and the Federal Reserve, which also frowned on his holding company controls. The result of these operations was that the Bank of America stock, for which he had paid $510 per share, underwent tremendous gyrations on the unlisted market in New York, and wound up selling at $1520.

A financial columnist noted at the time that "Giannini seems to put the Midas touch on any enterprise he . . . takes over." Bancitaly Corporation, which owned Bank of America of New York stock, reflected recent extraordinary gains in its portfolio by rising from around $200 to $688, at the period of Giannini's big push in the Eastern money capital. The holding company stock was then split up four to one and began to rise again. In 1928 A. P. created more branches for his Bank of America of New York and to finance them began selling large quantities of Bancitaly Corporation stock, which soon had $130 million in paid-in capital and controlled banks on both coasts with more than a billion dollars of resources. And at both ends of the continent hundreds of branch managers were cajoling their customers to buy stock in the holding company. "By the way, Mr. Brown, how about buying some shares of Bancitaly?" The Eldorado quality of Giannini's enterprises was such that few could resist these suggestions.

A. P. Giannini gave no more thought to the Morgans. He himself could create wealth beyond the dreams of avarice as long as his ventures flourished and their securities kept rising. As Insull learned and as the Van Sweringens also discovered, Giannini saw that the allure of the finance capitalist's operations, in the realm of paper magic, surpassed everything else.

As one banking authority observed at this stage: "A. P. Giannini was ahead of us. He saw that there is not enough profit in commercial banking. The big money is in the other end of the business—in financing, in distributing securities, in handling investments." For example, there were enticing possibilities for intercompany transactions that permitted the almost infinite pyramiding of paper wealth. A year earlier in California the Bank of Italy had sold a new issue of 50,000 shares of its capital stock of $100 par value to the Bancitaly Corporation at $550 per share. Now watch that block of 50,000 shares.

Twelve days later the Bank of Italy split up all its capital shares five to one, for it was easier to distribute them at lower prices. The shares were so popular that they quickly climbed from about $120 to $300, or the equivalent of $1500. The Bancitaly Corporation now had 250,000 shares of the mother bank that showed, at one stroke of Giannini's fountain pen, a paper profit of $47.5 million. It was natural that the holding company stock should show a continual rising trend in the spring of 1928, when its split-up shares, amid frenzied buying, rose from about $120 to $223.

Giannini was well pleased with his feats in the market. However, he made some public statements to the newspapers in California aimed to discourage excessive speculation in the stocks of his several companies, which had gone "far beyond their present value." But a great bubble had been blown up over the wizard's shares—Bank of Italy of California and Bank of America of New York, which were sold over-the-counter, and Bancitaly Corporation, listed on the New York Curb and the San Francisco Stock Exchange. Giannini's warning words—too little, and perhaps for the record—were not widely reported, and were generally ignored. His speculative followers used their savings, their dividends, and even borrowed money from loan sharks at 12 to 15 percent in order to buy more Bancitaly. Some banks and reputable brokers refused to grant such loans, but the loan sharks were protected by agreements giving them authority to sell out the collateral if its market value fell below a certain level. It was reported that they had very large holdings of Bancitaly stock against loans.

Giannini went to Europe at that point, while rumors had it that he would soon establish important bases in London and Paris as well as Chicago. He already had control of the small Banca d'America e d'Italia of Milan. Before leaving New York his associates had suggested that the several holding companies should form a committee to review all future investments, but he responded angrily, "I don't want any committee. As long as I'm around here I'm keeping everything in my vest pocket."

In Italy his was a triumphal progress: the King made him a Knight of Malta; the Pope received him graciously; and Mussolini also showed him marked consideration. A. P., like many Italian-Americans, and not a few Anglo-Saxon Americans as well, was believed at that time to be "soft" on Fascism, because, as it was said, Mussolini made the trains run on time and curbed labor. Those were A. P.'s years of glory, which he later remembered with pride, saying, "In 1928 I made eighty millions profit for the company in one year, and ninety millions the next year!"

The bull market underwent a test in the late spring of 1928, when the Federal Reserve raised interest rates. Bancitaly stock had begun to decline toward the end of May and continued to decline for several weeks, though efforts were made to support the stock by young Mario Giannini and Bacigalupi with funds drawn from Bancitaly's own treasury. On Saturday, June 9, however, the stock sagged very badly, and Mario cabled his father in Rome saying he feared a bad fall in their stock would injure their prestige. A. P. ordered Mario to hold the fort. Suddenly that weekend rumors spread by wire from New York to San Francisco that A. P. Giannini had fallen ill of a "heart attack" in Rome. On the following Monday morning a mob of sellers appeared at the Bancitaly trading post in the Curb Exchange, offering the stock at any price it might bring. At this point Bank of Italy President Baciga-lupi withdrew all supporting bids that had been placed in the market "on a scale down," which had the effect of taking the plug out of the bathtub. In a single session Bancitaly fell from approximately $200 per share to $109 before it was sta-bilized by short sellers and renewed support came in. The incident was described later as a "baby crash" especially affect-ing various bank stocks that had been subjected to volumi-nous speculative buying. The Giannini holding company stock, however, was down some 40 percent overnight; the higher-priced Bank of Italy and Bank of America of New York had correspondingly steep declines; there was at the same time a sharp fall, though less extensive, in Chase and National City Bank of New York. Nothing, however, equaled the collapse of Bancitaly Corporation. It had a mob of weak holders with their margin accounts held at the loansharks, who dumped their collateral on the market as prices fell. Astute operators in Wall Street usually have intelligence of these weak places, sometimes through informed bankers. The bears must have calculated also that Bancitaly was using up its cash reserve in trying to support its own stock, a maneuver that makes for reverse leverage.

During the two-day panic that struck the Giannini com-panies—accompanied by nerve-wracking newspaper head-lines—the banking officers in charge feared bank runs might follow. That was why the Morgans and the Federal Reserve authorities had urged Giannini to separate his holding com-pany from the banking organization. In any case a number of depositors as well as stockholders were frightened into closing out their accounts by the newspaper reports about the "thou-sands of speculators shaken out by the bursting of the 'Gian-nini bubble.' "

A. P. was in a sanatorium suffering from a painful attack of polyneuritis—not heart trouble as the gossipers had it. He suffered even more severely in his pride. It was his suspicion that an important banking competitor in San Francisco had inspired the bear raids. At the thought of his detested rival, he was roused to great wrath; he pulled himself together, jumped out of bed, and took the first boat to New York.

In the Street there were now rumors that his holding company had used up masses of cash and had been obliged to borrow money in the struggle to defend itself; some estimates of the decline in value in Giannini securities came to as much as half a billion dollars! It was true that Bancitaly Corporation had had to increase its loans from banks it controlled to some $60 million, and now indeed held masses of its own stock that had cost far more than it had paid for them.

As soon as he disembarked from his boat, A. P. received a summons from Morgan's to come over to the "Corner" at once. He went. Bartow and Thomas W. Lamont now spoke to him sternly about the business of "supporting the market"; [3] disaster for his holding company might have engulfed the affiliated banks in unacceptable losses, as they and the Federal Reserve authorities had pointed out repeatedly.

Giannini, the eternal boomer, had received a rude lesson; his prestige was blemished. Yet he seems not to have been concerned about financial losses he and his son had sustained, for their holdings in securities were of moderate amount. What he most feared as he rode back to California was that another such market crisis might bring about loss of control of the banking empire for the House of Giannini.

At the railroad terminal in Oakland he was met by a little band of his associates who had for him only wan smiles. The optimist in him revived. He laughed off the "raids" of speculators, and proffered hopeful forecasts in interviews with reporters, saying, "Well, it's good to know that so many loyal friends can lose a pocketful of cash and still welcome me home."

One cause of the deep troubles of the House of Giannini in the crises of June 13, 1928, was that it had to support the stocks of so many different companies in the securities markets of New York and the Pacific Coast; there were 5 million shares of the Bank of Italy, almost 10 million shares of Bancitaly Corporation, as well as those of Bank of America of New York, and of several unconsolidated branch banks in California. Now A. P. and his son conceived of a scheme to take all these different institutions and place them in one big basket, that of a mammoth holding company for which they dreamed up a new name, the Transamerica Corporation, a title reflecting Giannini's long-cherished vision of a continental chain.

In early autumn things were going much better and the markets were booming again. To help revive confidence, A. P., on his return from abroad, had caused Bancitaly Corporation to raise its annual dividend rate from $2.50 per share to $4—an action that may have been less than wise in view of some secret troubles with which the big chain was now afflicted. In Los Angeles, where one of the largest recent acquisitions had been the Merchant's National Bank, a sizable amount of "bad" real estate paper had turned up, which would one day have to be written off as loss. Nevertheless his stocks were rising again, and Giannini proceeded to circularize the stockholders of the Bank of Italy and of Bancitaly Corporation, inviting them to exchange their shares for new Transamerica stock. He used the argument that their investments would be less vulnerable to manipulation by stock market sharpshooters if they were embraced in one enormous concern.

In the case of the Bank of America of New York, which his holding company Bancitaly controlled with a 51 percent majority, it proved impossible to consolidate, as the Federal Reserve System and the Delafield-Morgan minority opposed control by a holding company. Giannini decided to bide his time and fight the Federal Reserve and Morgan later on; but they feared Giannini's grandiose schemes and resolved to drive him out of New York. Statements he made in an interview in 1929 with B. C. Forbes, the financial journalist, may have alarmed the New York bankers even more. He declared that he proposed to go into investment banking and underwriting in a big way, commercial banking alone was too routine for him. "The bank of tomorrow," he said, "is going to be a sort of department store handling every service the people may want in the way of banking, investment, and trust management."

In November, 1928, the super holding company, Transamerica, rose majestically into view, a gargantuan corporation capitalized with ten million shares. The Bancitaly stock was absorbed in it share for share in even exchange; and 99.6 percent of the profitable Bank of Italy of California's stock was exchanged at the rate of one share for one and three-quarter shares of Transamerica. Early in 1929 a split-up of Transamerica stock put it at $10 par value, with 24 million shares outstanding. The billion dollar holding company was now so large and so widely distributed among so many small stockholders that it seemed impossible for any of Wall Street's manipulators to "corner" it. Giannini evidently did not try to enrich himself by securing a great many of these shares, but he was highly resolved to maintain his strategic control and management. The new company was listed on the New York Stock Exchange's big board early in 1929 under the symbol of TA. Giannini promised it would be as a "Federal Reserve" to its investors.

Meanwhile he took certain further measures of defense that were to have important consequences. He had a huge financial institution on the West Coast and now had another planted in the East in the heart of Wall Street, but he felt that he did not know the ways of the Street well enough. He had been taken by surprise in June, 1928; as he explained afterward, "I was green there and looked for financial talent."

On a visit to New York in September, he had met Elisha Walker, head of Blair and Company and a director of several large corporations, some of which he had successfully promoted. Forty-nine years of age then, the keen-eyed Walker was considered a rising figure in the Street, ranking high in the second echelon of investment bankers, after Morgan and Kuhn, Loeb. His principal associate was the French financier and economic consultant Jean Monnet, formerly associated with the Rothschild bank in France. Almost overnight A. P. decided to make a bargain with Walker, and he paid a generous price in an exchange of Transamerica stock to take over Blair and Company and its reputedly efficient securities distributing organization as a needed auxiliary for his banking group. Walker was the first representative of Eastern finance taken into the Giannini family business.

In May, 1929, at a banquet in San Francisco, A. P. presented Walker to his California associates as one of the nation's outstanding financiers, and one who could be trusted to direct the far-flung affairs of Transamerica. A. P. was almost sixty, and it was now reported that he planned to resign his chairmanship of the giant holding company in 1930 and have Walker replace him, with Jean Monnet as vice chairman.

With the association of Walker in his grand patriotically named enterprise, California's titan of banking, who had begun business a generation earlier with small colonies of Italian depositors, had finally succeeded in "naturalizing" the pyramidal organization he had constructed. In the year that followed, the Bank of Italy in California was also to be renamed the Bank of America, National Trust and Savings Association.

3

CRASH!

In Wall Street the bull market's golden rout was in full progress and "joy was unconfined," as Byron wrote of Europe's capitals on the eve of Waterloo. The great market romances of pool manipulators and their followers with "glamor" stocks or "blue chips" continued with unfailing ardor. This movement was accompanied by a great deal of discussion in the press of the "New Era" of American capitalism, fostered by modern mass production systems and an advancing technology that was creating new materials, new articles of commerce, and endless wealth. University economists, with few exceptions, argued seriously that the astonishingly high levels of equity prices were but a reflection of the tremendous changes that were in store for our free enterprise economy.

Estimates of the number of Americans who were holders of common stocks in 1929 have differed widely. The number of day-to-day marginal accounts at Stock Exchange firms stood in the neighborhood of a million; but the total of those who held and borrowed against unlisted stocks of banks and utilities has been estimated in recent years at some three million. Some estimates, counting all who were possibly involved in common stocks through the "drives" of the Gianninis, the Insulls, and the "employee incentive plans" of corporations, as well as buying of investment trusts shares, have gone as high as fifteen million persons, embracing most of the middle-class families and many of the skilled workers.

In the two years following 1927, investment trusts had increased their sales to the public, distributing an estimated $3 billion in new investment trust shares during 1929. Some of these trusts were vehicles by which artful financiers passed on to the public the bulk of their much mortgaged and pyramided holdings, while keeping voting control in their own hands. Such was the U.S. and Foreign Securities Corporation promoted by Dillon, Read. Harrison Williams, the utilities magnate, in partnership with the firm of Goldman, Sachs, distributed some $200 million in shares of Blue Ridge and Shenandoah Corporation, leaving himself working control of a huge combination through an inner-circle corporation, Central States Electric.

In the *Ladies Home Journal* for August, 1929, John J. Raskob, vice chairman of General Motors, published an article entitled "Everybody Ought to Be Rich," in which he explained how by setting aside a small sum of $15 a month to be invested in good common stocks, and by reinvesting the dividends, everyone could accumulate a fortune approximating $80,000 within twenty years. Raskob's plans involved the selection of stocks that would appreciate steadily with the help of reputed financial experts (such as himself) managing an investment company, to whom the public's savings would be entrusted.

The investment trusts and holding companies not only

incurred the risk of choosing mainly equity shares, but also brought in the factor of leverage by issuing debt and pre-ferred securities, having a fixed income, against their collat-eral, thus magnifying the velocity of gain (or loss) for the common shares of such companies. As Otto Kahn testified in 1933, money was so easy to get, and the public was so eager to buy, that a trust promoted by Lehman Brothers at a price of $100 per share rose to $135 on its opening day, before its man-agers had had a chance to make a single investment. Indeed certain of these investment bankers (but not the Lehmans), after successfully launching one trust, would then promote a second, which would proceed to bid up the shares of the first; in this environment of intoxicated expectations, both holding companies would rise without halt.

Friends of the British economist John Maynard Keynes recall that he came to New York in 1929 with the express pur-pose of speculating in the stock market. He declared that this bull market had a sort of built-in profit-making machine and was a "sure thing." (Keynes was said to have been wiped out completely in the autumn bear market of 1929; an inveterate speculator, he recouped his losses in later years.)

One of the most impressive underwritings of 1929 was that of the pyramided Van Sweringen holdings of railway and other properties vested in their new super holding company, Alleghany Corporation. This was distributed by none other than Morgan and Company through an initial offering of some $180 million in debentures and preferred shares and 4.5 million of common shares of $5 par value. The famous brothers had arranged their pyramid in most ingenious form. They personally owned 80 percent of the Vaness Company, which in turn owned 50 percent of General Securities Corpo-ration, which turned over the Van Sweringens' blocks of equity shares in five big railroads to the new Alleghany Cor-poration in exchange for its capital of some $180 million and also 41 percent (about two million shares) of its common stock. The common stock, though pure water, held voting control in the whole railroad empire, embracing more than three billion in assets at current prices. The Van Sweringens, who always owed large sums to a consortium of banks, and especially Morgan and Guaranty Trust, used their new funds to buy more railroads. In 1929 their choice fell on the Missouri-Pacific in the Southwest, a sprawling network of 13,000 miles of track that had been jerry-built by Jay Gould. Only recently it had been released from receivership, yet control of its preferred and its worthless common stock cost $100 million. Spreading from the Middle West to California, the Missouri-Pacific gave the Van Sweringens virtually a transcontinental system—but one which contravened the ICC's plans for railway consolidations.

The private correspondence of the Morgan partners showed their awareness of Alleghany's speculative character. They admitted that they usually avoided dealing in such securities, but they had received as part of their underwriting fee 250,000 shares of Alleghany common stock at $20 a share, part of which they profited from, part of which they decided to distribute at cost to their "preferred list" of clients and friends, such as Owen D. Young, John J. Raskob, William Woodin, Calvin Coolidge, Senator W. G. McAdoo, General John J. Pershing, and Charles Lindbergh. The shares opened in the market at $37 and rose as high as $56. It was all decidedly risky, to be sure, but the Van Sweringens were the greatest railroad kings since the days of Harriman and Hill. The Morgans, together with affiliated banks, had long financed their hitherto successful undertakings.

Everyone who could manage it, apparently, was borrowing money to buy shares of stock that was expected to rise 100 percent within a few days or weeks! Other Morgan-sponsored corporations were in the forefront of the bull parade. The twice-split General Electric stock, for example, rose to a value of more than $1500 a share. This corporation over the years had the practice of accepting from the various utilities it supplied with power equipment, payment in their bonds and shares in lieu of cash; these securities were held in the portfolio of General Electric's subsidiary holding company, Electric Bond and Share, which wound up with control of utilities all around the country. After having been prodded by the Justice Department to divest itself of such holdings, General Electric spun off Electric Bond and Share to its own stockholders. On being listed for public trading in 1928, this holding company stock promptly rose 100 percent. Thereafter it seemed that, whenever there were reports of Bond and Share buying another utility holding company, the stock of the company to be acquired also rose 100 percent overnight.

The continuing advance of high voltage transmission allowing for the hook-up of local power stations in far-spreading interstate grids, inspired an ever greater competition to buy the operating companies. The tall pylons bearing high-tension conductors now began to crisscross the entire country. In the Middle West Insull kept bidding for local power companies against Harrison Williams, head of the North American Company group, or Howard Hopson, organizer of the overblown Associated Gas and Electric, and also Cyrus Eaton, the rising Cleveland financier who headed Continental Shares. And there was also stern competition from J. P. Morgan's company, which launched the United Corporation in 1929 as a super holding company for utilities; and added to this was the Commonwealth and Southern, which grouped together power companies of the Southeastern states.

Another Morgan-sponsored giant was General Motors, in which their clients, the Du Ponts, had invested war profits from chemicals and explosives. The rise of General Motors in the period of annual restyling of automobiles had been fabulous; from 1925 to 1929 its split-up shares had risen from an average of $75 to $750. Not only were the Du Ponts and John

J. Raskob, their former aide—who kept touting General Motors shares in public interviews—vastly enriched, but likewise Alfred P. Sloan and Charles F. Kettering, whose smaller companies had been merged into General Motors. The seven Fisher brothers, whose old coach works made the bodies of GM cars, retired toward 1928 and arrived in Wall Street loaded with about $500 million, it was rumored, with which they played the market.

The Rockefeller family, which had profited enormously in the recent war years, scarcely lagged behind any other group. Their international holdings had become more diversified than in the past and included control of the huge Chase National Bank, then the largest in America. An old New York money clan held the National City Bank, managed by Charles E. Mitchell; its stock also rose to fantastic levels (above 700 dollars), and it profited as well by the mass sales of new securities through its affiliate, National City Company. One notable operation of that season brought about the balloon ascent of Anaconda Copper; its market price rose from $60 in 1928 to the level of $125, at which price the National City Company distributed a large amount of the speculative mining stock to thousands of small investors, representing it as a "sound investment in America's future growth."

A "new money" group also operated in the New York stock market with an audacity that caught the eye of the public, especially because of their promotion of Radio Corporation of America. The stock was new, having been spun off by the big electrical equipment manufacturers General Electric, Westinghouse, and Western Electric. The broker Michael J. Meehan, acting as its floor specialist, managed the pool trading in this stock (which was considered unethical conduct even in those woolly days). Associated with him were a lively Irish band including John J. Kenny, Tammany Hall's favored building contractor; Bernard E. Smith, a well-known "sharpshooter"; and Joseph P. Kennedy, a professional speculator who hailed from Boston. The bull-like roars of Mike Meehan were heard above all the tumult of the Exchange floor as Radio rose week by week, from 85 to as high as 549, while thousands of fascinated speculators were drawn to trading in this famous stock.

The agents of the new giants, Insull and Giannini, actively sponsored their holding company shares in the market. Some of the old celebrities of the Street also served as leaders of the bull faction, among them W. C. Durant, the founder of General Motors; Arthur Cutten, the former Chicago grain broker; Jesse Livermore, cool and secretive as ever; and Harry Sinclair, the notorious oil-well driller, who had done a brief term in Federal prison after his fraudulent business with the Navy's Teapot Dome reserves.

In March, 1929, the average trading volume per day rose to three million shares, threefold that of the early nineteen twenties. The Federal Reserve, thoroughly alarmed, raised the rediscount rate to member banks to the high level of 6 percent, so that call money for brokers' loans became suddenly scarce and rates jumped to 12 percent, and on one day, as high as 20 percent. The Reserve Banks also put pressure on banks to reduce loans on stocks "selectively." As in the spring of 1928, a "baby crash" again jarred the cheerful market; blue chip stocks swiftly declined as much as ten to twenty points in single trading sessions. Mitchell of the National City, though he was also a director of the New York Reserve Bank, now defied the Federal Reserve authorities and placed large sums of cash in the call-loan market, declaring that his bank "was under obligations . . . to avert any dangerous crisis." The leading stocks steadied after a few days as call money rates eased again to 10 percent.

The cautionary moves by the Federal Reserve Banks were not taken without cause. After having pumped easy money into the market throughout the late nineteen twenties, their officers had become frightened in the autumn of 1928 at the 50 percent increase in the call-money total, which then reached four and a half billion. In the course of the following year the amount of money on loan in Wall Street virtually doubled, reaching more than eight billion. More than one-third of this was in the hands of lenders, other than banks, such as private corporations and European lenders who were taking advantage of the high rates, but who would pull out at the first sign of danger.

It was at this point that the old banker Paul Warburg, one of the founders of the Federal Reserve System, gave his warning of an impending decline in the stock market. A number of skeptics among the professional operation, those who liked to play the "bear" side, tried to sell stocks short in March, 1929, holding that they had risen far higher than any expectation of future profit or growth might warrant. Among these was one of the new-rich financiers, Bernard E. Smith, a practiced manager of syndicates and pools. But as he related afterward, as soon as he sold leading stocks short they seemed to rebound with greater force; he and his associates suffered very heavy losses in buying back stocks for delivery. Arthur Cutten, W. C. Durant, and the Fisher brothers resumed heavy buying of their favorite stocks; Anaconda and Montgomery Ward rose again under a flood of orders; and Meehan and his team of floor brokers carried on all sorts of high jinks on the Stock Exchange as Radio Corporation of America jumped some sixty points in four days.

That summer a lone financial consultant, Roger Babson, prophesied a disastrous fall in the stock market, but even he later qualified his predictions. Afterward Bernard Baruch related that he liquidated most of his stocks at the beginning of the year, and Joseph P. Kennedy made the same boast. Both men had tended to work as insiders, mainly in special situations, where a company was being reorganized. (Both also tended to embroider things.) John J. Raskob then had as his aide a young analyst named Robert R. Young, who had been a minor official at Du Pont and later at General Motors. Young advised against Raskob's plan for a new investment trust in a letter of August, 1929, describing the stock market as having "flimsy underpinnings." "Equishares," Raskob's project for making everybody rich, had to be abandoned not long afterward.

One is led to believe that nobody, or almost nobody, saw what was coming. The summer of 1929 was a season of euphoria in the financial world, although reports of declining factory output, automobile sales, and railway freight traffic were coming in as warning signals. The high Reserve Bank money rate was also a traditional signal for retreat.

In September the market leaders reached their peak; many blue chips, undergoing corrective reaction, looked "ragged," and, with few exceptions, tended to decline gently during the first half of October. On Friday, October 18, the whole market began to go down swiftly, and declined even more sharply in the next day's half session. The same steep downward trend continued on Monday, with high-grade stocks such as General Electric and American Telephone losing five to ten points. Leading economists such as Professor Irving Fisher of Yale, and the magnates Mitchell and Raskob, made cheerful pronouncements to the press; but an attempt to rally the market failed, and panicky selling came in strong on Wednesday, October 23. The high-priced favorites fell through veritable air pockets, with Westinghouse dropping 35, General Electric 20, and Commercial Solvents all of 70 in a single session that saw an unprecedented trading volume of six million shares. Now there were reports of many margin calls being sent by brokers to their clients.

The next day—Black Thursday—panic convulsed the whole public of investors and speculators. The same mob that without reason had bid up all stocks to unreal values, now, as unreasoning as before, was selling everything down, at any price. Moreover a great many of them converged upon the Wall Street community and its board rooms, thousands upon thousands of them, in order to see the continuing disaster with their own eyes. The whole world was selling America's stocks.

Eyewitnesses recall the crowds of Thursday, October 24, filling the streets outside the Stock Exchange and standing on the steps of the old sub-Treasury Building, silent, expressionless, as if turned to stone. I was no passive onlooker, for I had my own small stake in that demented market. In the past year my portfolio of securities, purchased with the proceeds of a modest inheritance, had doubled in value, though I managed my account entirely on a cash basis. I had hoped to work up a little competence to allow me at least partial economic security, so that I could write as I pleased. The wished-for competence had now gone up the chimney—"where the woodbine twineth"—as the old traders used to say. I had shared for a while the hopes, even the illusions of America's middle class and now suffered their common fate.

What had triggered the "greatest stock market catastrophe of the ages," as the sober *Commercial and Financial Chronicle* described it? The gradual erosion of values in September and early October had undermined margin accounts; when brokers began to call for cash, or to "dump" pledged securities in under-margined accounts, the downward movement became an avalanche. The numerous investment trusts that had been relied on to bolster the market were then driven to make forced sales of large blocks; their blue chips fell. Some of them from 300 or 400 per share by 77 to 96 points in an afternoon, as on October 23. The next morning *there were simply no bids at all* for the equities of America's largest corporations.

I remember on one of those days, October 23, taking the subway downtown to visit my broker's board room. It was a minute or two before 10:00 A.M. as I reached the Wall Street station. I heard—and I can still hear it—the sound of running feet, the sound of fear, as people hastened to reach posts of observation before the gong rang for the opening of trading. Hypnotized by their panic, the crowds in the board rooms stared in horror at the stockboards or the tape recording their progressive ruin. Brokers and their clerks, who had been up all night at their paper work, calling for margin hour-by-hour, looked drawn and haggard. Owing to the record-breaking volume of trades, which swamped all communication facilities, the tape fell two hours behind, then by noon four hours behind! You could see your General Electric on the tape at $180, but the floor broker's telephoned message from Broad Street said that it was really selling for $40 or $50 less! Even the clocks seemed to have gone wrong. The crowds of customers in the board rooms all reacted in different ways. Some cried out their astonishment at the unfamiliar prices they saw, or at the sweeping changes in their fortunes recorded in a few hours, or even minutes; others laughed in disbelief, or made little self-deprecating jests, such as, "It's only money," or "easy-come easy-go." But it was too stunning an affair to be laughed off; a whole great class, between two and three million American families, were being stripped of their wealth.

"They'll all come back," a broker said cheerily. I wanted to believe it, but doubts assailed me. Things seemed to have gone too wildly wrong to be righted easily. Few living men had ever seen such a panic.

As always, the bell rang at 3:00 P.M. for the close of trading, but everyone stood riveted there for two, three, or more hours longer watching the retarded tape tap out the unthinkable losses of that day. During the fortnight that followed October 24, about $34 billion in market value disappeared! The whole Wall Street citadel of wealth and power, with all its paper symbols, had collapsed in ruin.

The newspapers covering the day's events made quite a legend of how the "Morgan bankers' consortium" on Black Thursday had contained the panic by sending Richard Whitney to the Exchange to bid up leading stocks. (They did not stop the decline then.) Actually, when the market began its great downward plunge, the leading men in finance were caught off guard. J. P. Morgan was in England, Charles E. Mitchell had sailed to Germany, and E. H. H. Simmons, veteran president of the Stock Exchange, who had lately remarried in his old age, was honeymooning in Honolulu.

The big bankers in New York kept in touch with one another by telephone. At noon on October 24, Albert H. Wiggin of the Chase Bank, sitting before his ticker, was heard to exclaim, "This is no bear market, it's a panic—we have got to do something." He put on his hat and headed for the Corner, out of habit, and because Thomas W. Lamont had called him to a lunchtime meeting. At Broad and Wall he almost collided with Mitchell, who had hurried back from Europe on receiving the dire news from home. George F. Baker, Jr., chairman of the First National Bank, was on hand, as was W. C. Potter of the Guaranty Trust, and other bigwigs; Lamont presided. An important personage among those present was George L. Harrison, the new Governor of the Federal Reserve Bank of New York, who had succeeded the late Benjamin Strong. He was a bureaucrat but he commanded the funds of the largest Reserve Bank. At this first hasty conference the bankers agreed to supply credits of up to $240 million for a syndicate that would buy leading stocks and thus try to stabilize the market. The bankers' "pool" was the same scheme that the elder Morgan had used to stem panics in past times. The press was waiting for word.

Someone urged that the Stock Exchange be closed down, as at the opening of World War I, but he was overruled. Their syndicate must begin to buy. But would it work to stop the raging panic? No one really knew if there would be enough money available to the banks to take over the tremendous amount of brokers' loans that was expected to be called (by non-bankers) the next day. But one thing they agreed upon was that they must work together to restore confidence—for confidence, that precious, elusive thing, had flown. Meanwhile the bankers preserved an icy calm; and the vivacious Lamont tried to reassure the public in a low-keyed press statement admitting that "there had been a little distress selling."

In the course of their meeting they had drawn up a list of stocks to be bought and handed it to Richard Whitney, well known to be "Morgan's broker." As vice president of the Stock Exchange, Whitney was now, in the absence of Mr. Simmons, its acting president. At 1:30 P.M. his large, well-groomed figure was seen striding swiftly across the floor of the Exchange toward Post 2. Fevered newspaper accounts described him as "running" or "charging like a bull" into the crowd trading in U.S. Steel; but running on that floor has always been forbidden. Whitney called out to the specialist broker at the "Steel" post: "I bid two hundred and five for twenty-five thousand Steel." This was quite an order, amounting to $5 million, at a price above the last sale. The market rallied, Steel steadied at 206¼. Whitney then went on to the trading posts where specialists kept book on other blue chip stocks, offering to buy large amounts in blocks of 10,000 to 25,000 shares at prices somewhat above the market. A modest rally had already begun at noon when it was reported that several leading New York bankers had been seen going into Morgan's. J. P. Morgan and Company were formerly thought to control the banking and investment world of New York and even, some believed, the machinery of the New York Stock Exchange, whose powerful governing committees were usually led by persons like Richard Whitney, wearing the "Morgan collar." The Morgans were the great insiders and their prestige was at its height. The advent of Whitney, society man and fox hunter, regularly used as the great bank's floor broker for routine buying of gilt-edged bonds, had its psychological impact; his bids lent strength to the momentary rally, so that prices for that session showed a partial recovery. Over land and sea went the word: *"Richard Whitney halts stock panic*—Morgan broker buys 25,000 Steel at 205—Heroic action rallies market." National fame touched Whitney from that moment on. Everywhere he was known as "the man who halted the market panic of 1929" and as a gentleman of sublime "courage." Actually, he had bought much less than was supposed—only two hundred shares of Steel, for example. He had done a bit of stage acting, reducing his buying as prices rose a little. The bankers were not throwing their cash away like drunken sailors, but they were anxious to conserve a war chest for future use in worse emergencies that some of them had good reason to expect.

Meanwhile there was the roar of cheers, as on a battlefield after a successful charge. Dick Whitney had become the hero of the day, and all that he did henceforth was to be as if touched with deeper meaning—the way he smiled narrowly and his merest wisecracks were noted and reported everywhere. A few months later the grateful members of the Stock Exchange elected him president in place of Simmons. At forty-two he was the youngest man ever honored with that office. Whitney embodied the grand old myth of the Morgan bank's power and leadership dating from the golden years of "Jack" Morgan's father, J. Pierpont Morgan, who acted as *the* central bank of New York before there was a Federal Reserve System, and towered over other financiers by sheer force of character and will. But that myth was soon dissolved amid scenes of universal selling, renewed after the weekend and continued in great waves for days on end.

The "hero of the day" looked his part, as if he had been selected with care out of an army of Hollywood extras. He was impeccably and formally dressed; a big man physically, over six feet tall, he carried his two hundred and ten pounds lightly, with the tread of a former Harvard athlete. His features were large, regular, and handsome in a heavy way; his hair was jet black, a little flecked with gray, and his eyes deep set under prominent downward slanting brows. If one had been able to catch up with him during those turbulent days, he might himself have explained that he was, in fact, no hero at all. What he did was only in the line of business: it was not his money but that of the bankers' syndicate he was employing, and no "courage" on his part was involved. Moreover his grandstand play of October 24, 1929, worked for only a short time, only two days.

Whitney had served in fairly routine fashion as a Morgan functionary on the Exchange for seventeen years. He himself was a model of the old nepotistic Yankee plutocracy in the Street, where rich families, after having their sons polished at Groton School and Harvard, put them to work in stocks and bonds. Through his family, Whitney had close ties to Morgan's—his elder brother George was a partner there. He had married an heiress, lived in a Fifth Avenue town house, and as a country squire, in an estate in the fashionable suburb of Far Hills, New Jersey. Richard Whitney carried himself with the aplomb and pride befitting a representative of the old Wall Street elite. But this did not endear him to the new breed that operated without the favor of the Morgans, such as "Joe" Kennedy and Bernard E. Smith.

There had been a lull in the storm and Whitney was able to take an early train to New Jersey on Saturday and preside over a meeting of the Essex Fox Hounds—"something I really like," he said. But on Monday torrential selling engulfed the market again; trading volume rose to sixteen million on one of the worst days that followed, when, as Whitney related, the Exchange's counting machine broke down. His own informed guess for that record-breaking volume of trade was "over twenty-three million shares, counting odd lots."

Something like insanity possesses our "free and liquid market" for securities in such seasons of high excitement: on one day men seem wildly eager to exchange their hard cash for the paper of "Radio" at 500, or "Alleghany" at 50, be-

cause they spell high profits; on another day the same speculators stampede to sell their shares at no matter what price so
that they may realize their cash again.

A clearer idea of the ravages of the 1929 catastrophe may
be obtained by observing its impact on the fortunes of several
of the bigger money lords, whose careers we have been following: Insull, the Van Sweringen brothers, and Giannini.

At first they appeared outwardly undisturbed by the
seismic shock of October, 1929. Alleghany Corporation and
Giannini's Transamerica underwent a grand collapse, to be
sure, but Insull's public utility shares showed more resistance
to the 1929 break than in the later stages of the depression
market. Once things had stabilized somewhat, Insull began to
borrow more money through the issuance of bonds by his
holding companies, Middle West Utilities and Insull Utilities,
and again expanded his purchases of power stations in New
England or gas pipe lines in the Southwest. Moreover he
seemed obsessed by the fear that rivals might seize control of
his companies, a control he now sought to make perpetual for
his own family, his son Samuel, Junior, and his younger
brother Martin J. Insull, who occupied top executive offices in
his organization. Cyrus Eaton, the powerful Cleveland financier in iron and coal and public utilities, was found to have
bought up large amounts of the-Insull-controlled utilities,
such as Commonwealth Edison and People's Gas, for his own
investment trust. After the Crash, being supremely confident
that it constituted only a temporary setback, Insull decided to
buy in Eaton's holdings of 160,000 shares of Commonwealth
Edison, People's Gas, and Public Service of Northern Illinois. To pay for all this he increased the floating debt of his
companies (and his own personal debt) by some $48 million
in June, 1931, borrowing most of it from the Continental
Bank of Chicago, but a good part of it, $20 million, from New
York banks.

By the summer of 1931, however, public utility stocks, which had hitherto held up strongly, began to go down like everything else. Insull ordered his agents to "peg" the market for his principal stocks, Commonwealth Edison and Middle West Utilities, while his teams of salesmen struggled to sell off to small investors the added shares that were being accumulated. As Insull's great strength had consisted in his credit with masses of small investors, he struggled with might and main to shore up his falling securities. But in the renewed panic it was impossible to play this game. Pegging, that is, defending his stocks in the market, drained away all cash and credit; the total depreciation of his top-of-the-pyramid holding companies ran to $330 million by 1932, with Middle West falling from $57 to 25 cents, and Commonwealth Edison, though an operating company, falling from $450 to $50. The Insull organization's treasury was left only with a mass of wasted paper.[1] Early in 1932 the discovery of some of his irregular transactions in the form of intercompany loans and unsecured loans to a stockbroker who failed caused the banks in New York and Chicago to move in (secretly, at first) and take over his affairs.*

The Van Sweringens, in the emergency, perpetrated the same blunders as Insull, with the same predestined results. As the market crashed, Mantis J. Van Sweringen, the elder brother, was busy trying to buy another railroad, the Boston and Maine. He also marketed a new issue of $30 million of debenture bonds of Alleghany Corporation, which

---

* Forrest McDonald, in his official biography of Samuel Insull (pages 290–299) deduces a "plot" by the Morgan-controlled New York banks to foreclose on Insull's empire, and win over the financial business of his Chicago investment bankers, Halsey, Stuart and Company. The principal New York creditors, however, were the Chase and the National City Bank. While they and Morgan's carried some of their "preferred" clients through the panic, the collapse of the Insull holding company structure was up to that day the largest in world history, causing losses of more than a billion dollars to over 100,000 small investors, according to the Chicago *Tribune*, June 9, 1932.

not long afterward was unable to pay its interest charges. In the autumn crash, railroad shares fell faster than anything else. Even the strongest of the roads, Chesapeake and Ohio, lost 30 percent of its value overnight, while others declined much more; so that Alleghany common, thanks to its leveraged position, multiplied these losses several times, and fell from about $50 to less than $10. The Van Sweringen brothers held two million shares of Alleghany common, on which they had borrowed up to the hilt. Like Insull they used much of their credit to "peg" or defend their stocks, so that more and more of the depreciated shares accumulated in their hands, multiplying their losses rapidly—a sure recipe for bankruptcy. The Van Sweringens' volume of trading in their own railroad stocks and holding company shares at the brokerage firm of Shields and Company reached the amazing total of 125 million shares, as reported in 1936 by the U.S. Senate's Subcommittee on Railroads. Evidence was also given that at one point the Morgan bank had called in the Van Sweringens and asked them politely to stop buying more railroads as they were already insolvent! When they wound up the disastrous action of pegging Alleghany and other shares, they owed their broker, Shields and Company, approximately $40 million (in excess of collateral) as personal debt, and had no assets of any value left to them.

Morgan and Company and Guaranty Trust, their principal bankers, were aware that if the railroad kings were allowed to go bankrupt, Shields, one of America's largest brokerage firms, would also be forced to close down, bringing with them many houses in the Street. This time the bankers' syndicate, with Morgan and Guaranty Trust bearing half the load, resolved that the best way out was to carry the Van Sweringen brothers—in the hope that their affairs would improve after several years—and cover their losses with a "rescue loan" of $39,500,000. Alleghany stock had had another great fall in the autumn of 1930; eventually it sank to thirty-seven and a half cents per share. Nevertheless the bankers took over the wasted Van Sweringen collateral and put it in one of their skeleton closets, of which, by then, there were many in Wall Street. The insolvency of the famous railroad magnates was carefully concealed, while they were left ostensibly in charge of their combination of roads, continuing to manage them as if nothing had happened. After a short while they were unable even to pay interest on the "rescue loan," yet their bankers awarded the ruined men $100,000 a year in order to keep them in the style they were accustomed to and prevent the public from learning of their real condition. The Morgan group had not only financed the Van Sweringen roads for many years by underwriting their many bond issues, but they had also promoted the sale of $20 million of their holding company's debenture bonds and stocks. Therefore the Van Sweringens' disaster was treated with more consideration than was shown to Insull, several months later in the spring of 1932. The Van Sweringens' personal insolvency during five years was one of the best kept secrets in Wall Street.

Amadeo P. Giannini had barely recovered from the "baby crash" of March, 1928, when the debacle of October, 1929, was upon him. He had made some defensive moves earlier, concentrating the shares of the Giannini-controlled banks in California in the hands of the Transamerica Corporation, though he was not permitted by the Federal Reserve to do this with the shares of the Bank of America of New York.

In late September Transamerica's shares, recently split in two, were quoted at $65, equal to the high levels of the preceding year. On Black Thursday, October 24, traders were amazed by the extraordinary spectacle of Transamerica riding out the storm, holding at between 62½ and 65, while some of the blue chip industrials were down more than 50 to 75 points! Transamerica's stock was being defended by strong hands.

A. P. was at his San Francisco headquarters conferring with his new generalissimo, Elisha Walker, on the day that panic set in. Their express determination to support Transamerica stock in the market and protect their investors was now made public. (Later, Walker held that he had questioned the wisdom of such action, but was overruled.)

For four terrible days Transamerica held its ground against world-wide selling. Like Insull and the Van Sweringens, A. P. was determined to maintain the faith of his 200,000 stockholders—his main source for venture capital used in expansion—and stubbornly ordered that all shares offered were to be bought. It was the certain way to compound disaster, for the Transamerica coffers were soon loaded with a million additional shares of its own stock sold by more and more panicky investors as well as by "bears," who knew what they were doing. To make a "scientific retreat" in such circumstances, so that one may return alive to fight again later, is the wise strategy of the market; but to stand and buy everything is to compound losses in geometric progression. Reserves of credit were swiftly exhausted.

A. P. was at length persuaded to withdraw all support after October 28, when Transamerica had closed at 62½. On the day of madness that followed it had a delayed opening; there were no bids whatsoever at any price, then it appeared on the tape at the New York Stock Exchange at 20½, showing an overnight loss of about 70 percent! Support buying came in again and part of that terrible loss was recouped.

Two years later Walker, then chairman of Transamerica, having replaced Giannini, revealed to the public that during the 1929 panic "at Mr. Giannini's direction, Transamerica stock was maintained at a high and artificial level, from which it fell rapidly when support was removed." During the four weeks preceding October 28, 1929, over $68 million had been expended for 1,090,000 shares of Transamerica at an average cost of $62.50. This policy of pegging the price, when everything else was falling, Walker declared, left the corporation at the end of 1929 with few liquid assets and a large indebtedness—mainly to its own bank. This affair was known in the trade as "Giannini's $68 million blunder." Moreover, unlike the Van Sweringens, Giannini could expect no help whatsoever from the Eastern money-center banks, who wanted to drive him out of New York. That Giannini could survive such fearful losses says much for his fighting power.

It was not the Morgan consortium, or Whitney, who "saved Wall Street"; it was the Federal Reserve System. In the days that followed Black Thursday the commercial bankers soon realized that their $240 million credit would not be enough; their abiding fear was that *several hundred Stock Exchange firms might close their doors,* creating utter chaos. Some of the brokers were already diving out of the windows of skyscrapers. The bankers met again in the evening of October 24 at Lamont's apartment and debated closing the Exchange for a while. They also feared that $4 billion in loans held by "others than banks," including foreign concerns and lenders like Standard Oil and Electric Bond and Share, might be called for immediate payment, and they would have to take the load.

Distress selling grew worse in late October, and the bankers met again, this time at Morgan's library as "Young Morgan" had come back from Europe. Now George L. Harrison, who had succeeded Strong as Governor of the Federal Reserve Bank of New York, spoke up and promised help. Though it was not supposed to rescue unfortunate speculators, the "Fed" would intervene. The Reserve Banks' role in the crisis has not hitherto been reported adequately, but is described in Harrison's diary of the time.

"The Stock Exchange should stay open at all costs," he urged, and added: "Gentlemen, I am ready to provide all the reserve funds that may be needed to permit the New York banks to take over the call items of out-of-town banks and 'others' [lenders] if my directors agree."

The bankers took heart. Harrison struck a bargain by which the main New York Clearing House Association banks were to take up the "outsiders" call loans, while the Reserve Banks at once started "open market" operations to purchase masses of U.S. Government bonds and bills of acceptance that would permit an expansion of bank credits several times larger again than the sum of those purchases. And so Governor Harrison was the boy who put his finger in the dike. There was some friction between the big New York unit of the Federal Reserve System (which held 60 percent of its assets and much gold) and the politically appointed Federal Reserve Board at Washington, which was supposed to authorize such action—perhaps after long delay. Harrison obtained the support of his own bank's directors late that night and went into action the next morning; but when he reported to Washington what he had been doing, Chairman Roy A. Young told him that his procedure had been highly irregular. There had never been such an emergency, Harrison countered, the world was "on fire." He added, "But it's done and can't be undone," for he had begun buying Government bonds from the New York banks in great chunks of $100 million a day. As he had foreseen, this put those banks "in money," that is, it increased their credits at the Reserve so that some four billion dollars of credit could be pumped into the depleted money market.

As Harrison related afterward: "The day after the market crash of October 24, I knew there was going to be a huge calling in of brokers' loans and a complete breakdown. Actually loans were called in on the part of 'others than banks' to the extent of $2,200,000,000. No money market could stand that." Harrison had to move at once. Thus the New York commercial banks were enabled to carry their unprecedented load; and the Stock Exchange stayed open in the face of the world's selling, while America's corporate securities were losing in value a sum about equal to the cost of World War I.

In the money panics of 1893 and 1907, J. P. Morgan alone had acted as the central bank at New York. Passage of the Federal Reserve Act in 1913 had changed this; a $50,000-a-year functionary, Governor Harrison, took charge during the crisis. He was a polished sort of bureaucrat. The son of an Army officer, he had studied at Yale and Harvard Law School with distinction, clerked under Supreme Court Justice Holmes, then joined the legal staff of the new Federal Reserve System and risen to be Governor Strong's deputy at New York. (Strong, formerly a J. P. Morgan lieutenant, had named Harrison as his successor.) A. P. Giannini, an "outsider," always had the conviction that Morgan's together with the great clearing house banks of New York, continued to dominate the policy of the semi-public Reserve System through its most powerful unit at Liberty Street, New York. (Incidentally, when Harrison retired from the bank in 1939, he was named chairman of the New York Life Insurance Company, long a part of the Morgan domain.)

In the three weeks that followed Black Thursday, during which panic conditions continued, confusion and fatigue plagued the brokers of the Street, who kept the office buildings downtown ablaze with light until three in the morning, as they tried to catch up with mountains of paper work.

Whitney remembered those days as having the atmosphere of a war calamity. The members of the Governing Committee of the Exchange and several bankers including Lamont met secretly at lunchtime down in the basement under the trading floor of the Exchange. The place was blue with the smoke of cigarettes which they nervously lit and threw away. At these "cellar meetings" there was renewed debate on the question of closing the Exchange, which Whitney always stoutly opposed. Their gloom grew as the news of the latest quotations would be brought to them. Out of rumors of these cellar meetings came the Street legend that Thomas Lamont and Whitney sat in a hole under the trading floor of the Exchange, watching the course of the Morgan stocks through a "periscope." Whitney had lived for years in a routine way doing business on orders from Morgan; but now he rose to the occasion, and, holding his head high, assumed the role of a leader. The press reported his every move.

> Richard Whitney, acting president of the Exchange, hat tilted on his head at a jaunty angle, sauntered nonchalantly across the floor half an hour before closing time, and left the room with a debonair smile. . . .

The frightened financiers listened to him, leaned upon him. It is hard to judge who was more terrified, the stampeding public or the group of insiders who struggled to avert disaster. On one of those days of panic, Whitney and his colleagues were issuing from a secret conference in the Exchange cellar. As they neared the door, Whitney said to the others in his crisp Boston accent: "Now get your smiles on, boys!" With their hearts dead within them and their simpers frozen on their faces, the financiers marched docilely behind their chosen captain out of the Exchange and across crowded Broad Street.

The Exchange was forced to declare special half-holidays and rest periods for the relief of clerical personnel. On such occasions, as always when important decisions by the Governing Board were proclaimed (to suspend a member-broker, or delist some stock), the acting president would mount the rostrum of the Exchange, ring a little bell for silence on the floor, and make his announcement with an air of authority that became habitual after a while.

In mid-November the market finally turned upward; again Whitney and other brokers for the Morgans and the Rockefellers were seen buying large blocks of shares, and cheer upon cheer rose from the crowd on the floor. The New

York Stock Exchange claimed credit for staying open and for conducting business as usual in the face of the greatest market panic recorded in history. Its machinery had "bent, but not broken." Whitney was covered with glory; he had shown the qualities of a true leader of finance, coolness in action, discretion in speech, the ability to talk freely without saying anything of significance, and to handle the biggest deals with a poker face, save when the situation was so bad that it called for a broad smile.

He wore the mask of a leader, and he was more of an actor than anyone then realized. He had lost all he had in the Crash, some two million of his own and his wife's money. When the aging Mr. Simmons came back and announced that he planned to retire as president of the Exchange, the members, in April, 1930, as with a single accord, voted Richard Whitney their president. By then he was known as "Mr. Wall Street"—and he played the part everywhere in bold style.

The investing public awoke to find that it had been thoroughly bled. Now ugly rumors were being circulated about skullduggery in high financial places. Members of Congress, reflecting the change in public opinion, proposed bills to investigate the securities exchanges and to regulate them. Whitney, along with his other duties, now took the stump and delivered speeches before businessmen's associations, in which he stood forth as the uncompromising champion of the old free-market system, controlled only by the law of "supply and demand" and ruled only by the Board of Governors and Business Conduct Committee of the New York Stock Exchange, a private club which had never tolerated any governmental interference. He also appeared frequently in Washington as an active lobbyist in the interests of the Exchange.

It was only two years after the high drama of October and November, 1929, when, upon assignment, I came to interview Whitney and wrote about him. He was enthroned in the regal presidential suite on an upper floor of the Exchange, dressed in a black cutaway, and carried himself with reserve as he spoke. I found his smile an affair of facial muscles and his eyes cold; he was tense underneath. In speech he was articulate and forceful, but in effect he uttered nothing but platitudes. He said that the great New York Stock Exchange had always, with wisdom, rejected controls of any kind, except that of its own organization. Whitney was sworn to defend its autonomy as a "free and open market," which would "dry up" if there were interference by politicans. As to the claims of politicians who proposed to investigate the workings of the Exchange, he only said darkly, "The public is looking for a goat."

We had been through a great deal in those dark years; business activity had shrunk, unemployment was rife—but Richard Whitney had changed not a whit. At this time even in Wall Street there were new men who had begun to criticize Whitney's unyielding stance which, in their view, generated hostility in the public and in Congress. I ventured to remark that the decline in the economy, as in the security markets, had been going on for a good two years, and asked him whether this did not signify some decided change in our whole position. With an air of confident authority he replied "Oh, the market will come back; it always does." In my article I represented the New York Stock Exchange as an imperious sort of private club that resisted change from old traditions and old procedures, and pictured the Morgans' broker Whitney, who ruled over it, as a kind of stuffed shirt —the article was entitled: "Groton-Harvard-Wall Street."

4

THE BEAR RAIDERS

During the winter and spring of 1930, the securities markets made quite a handsome recovery, with leading stocks regaining from a third to a half of their losses. The investing public cheered up a great deal—until the stock market broke down again in May and June, and declined by gradual steps thereafter. By then the bad news about the depression in business and the spread of unemployment was more generally understood than before.

When the market underwent its first great slide in October, 1929, it was noticeable that large blocks of shares were offered at any price they might bring, but there were few takers. Much of this was distress selling for weakened margin accounts; but the *Wall Street Journal* on October 24, 1929, reported that "a lot of short selling was going on . . . and a lot of selling to make the market look bad." When the bulls were in despair and the bears fell upon them with sudden heavy offerings, it certainly tended to put things down faster. Rumor had it that the "dapper white-haired boy," Jesse L. Livermore, had been leading the bear raids, but the truth was that he had not played a large part in the decline; like many gamblers he had fallen on evil times and his affairs grew worse and worse. There were others who worked to depress values, some in the highest places.

President Hoover felt called upon to restore confidence by assuring the public that there was really no depression; yet he was deeply concerned about the debacle in Wall Street. At the end of November, after things had calmed down somewhat, he invited Whitney to dinner at the White House and in his scolding way asked him about the plungers and bear operators. Whitney told him in his most authoritative tones that it would be improper to try to stop such transactions; he promised however to investigate the records of member brokers through the machinery of the Exchange. A few weeks later he reported that there was "very little short selling."

At the same period the President called a conference at the White House of leading industrialists and railroad magnates and urged them to maintain capital expenditures for plant and machinery so that business volume and employment could be sustained at high levels. Present were men like W. C. Teagle of Standard Oil, Alfred P. Sloan of General Motors, Owen D. Young of General Electric, Walter Gifford of AT&T, and Robert S. Lovett of the Santa Fe Railroad. They all promised in so many words to do what they could to keep business going at high levels. In succeeding months the President and his Cabinet secretaries began to issue the unguarded expressions of optimism for which they were reproached later, such as those that we had experienced only a "slight financial setback" that would be forgotten in ninety days, and that employment was on the increase while agricultural conditions were also favorable. Some voices were raised to challenge such statements; in New York, Governor Roosevelt's Industrial Commissioner, Frances Perkins, reported that 1929 had seen "the sharpest decline in employment" in ten years. In Wall Street's board rooms there were also certain astute operatives, who noticed the Hoover Administration's habit of ignoring the unpleasant facts of life, and who began to take advantage of this weakness.

Revival of the business boom had been prophesied from Pennsylvania Avenue for the autumn; but instead there was a very steep rise of unemployment and a renewal of the declining movement in the stock market. On October 15, 1930, a conservative Republican politican, Senator Simeon Fess of Ohio, was quoted in the press as having declared that

> Persons high in Republican circles are beginning to believe that there is some concerted effort on foot to utilize the stock market as a method of discrediting the Administration. Every time an Administration official gives out an optimistic statement about business conditions the market immediately drops.

Most American presidents had never done anything about depressions or unemployment. At first Hoover, too, thought everything should be left to nature's cure, that is, the passage of time. But the picture continued to darken: in November, 1930, the Democrats gained effective control of both houses of Congress; in the summer of 1931 business and employment were down further; and there was an international crisis over the devaluation of the British pound, which caused gold to be drained from the United States. In view of all this the President went to work on some ambitious plans to have the Federal Government interfere actively in the economic situation in order to bring about recovery.

It had become habitual in high circles to attribute blame for at least part of our troubles to a group of destructive bear operators in Wall Street. In the autumn of 1931 Senator Wolcott of Connecticut, a friend of Mr. Hoover's, moved to have the Senate conduct an investigation into the workings of Wall Street and its Stock Exchange and the alleged intrigues of short-selling bears who seemed to be wrecking everything. Bernard E. "Sell-Em Ben" Smith was reported to be one of the leaders of this band of financial pirates; the general public had come to know his name and repute when the New York *World* printed a front-page story under the headline:

SELL-EM BEN MADE TEN MILLION
IN LAST MONTH—WALL STREET HEARS

What a wonderful country, one reflected, reading this, where one of our extremely rugged individualists would thrive in the midst of a great depression. As I had formed the habit of seeking out and writing about men in the power centers of the business system, I set out to see this very curious Smith—at the time when he had come under investigation by the Senate—which was not easy.

Most intriguing was the current Wall Street rumor that Smith, the new wizard, used a secret weapon, which consisted of timing short-selling raids with Hoover's public predictions of early recovery. The man now enjoyed the fame of the Street's old-time privateers, such as James R. Keene, John "Bet-A-Million" Gates, and the Jesse Livermore of earlier days. He was not only characterized as a "pirate," but actually wore a black patch over one eye. At the mere mention in high quarters of prosperity returning, or being "around the corner," he would charge into battle. On the floor of the Exchange, or in board rooms, whenever the market began to fall, Smith's war cry would be heard: *"Sell 'em!—They're not worth anything!"* It was all both comic and painful, while the President lulled the public to sleep, Smith and his merry band went through their pockets. Though there was gossip printed about him, no journalist had been able to interview him and no tabloid camera man had been allowed to photograph him, for like the greatest operatives in the Street he shunned publicity. His place of business and telephone were kept secret, and he figured as a "mystery man."

Bernard E. Smith, then, belonged to the breed of money men who throve on hard times. We had come down from the Plateau of Prosperity to the Valley of Depression, but there we had found financial leaders of a new sort. They were the bears, so-called, who profited from the losses of innocent, average people, and who left their offices humming a cheerful tune at the end of each business day. Everywhere the big pieces were being broken up into little ones, and the soft-headed finance capitalists who had constructed their high pyramids of paper (now in ruins) were giving way to steel-nerved men, who appraised everything in a mood of cold realism, and sorted out the broken pieces of those crumbled structures. They were the bears, the jolly bears!—and they appealed to the mood of black humor that pervaded us in those lean years.

Did we need the bears? The European exchanges had limited or banned short selling. The short-selling operation was like the selling of futures in the commodity markets, where you sold a contract for ten thousand bushels of wheat in April for September delivery, though you did not yet have the wheat at the time of sale. So it was with the short selling of stocks, where first you sold the stock, and in order to deliver it, you borrowed the specified number of shares temporarily from brokers' holdings of those securities. You then bought the same shares back on some later occasion, hopefully at a profit, and returned them to the lender. It was exactly like the bull's first buying cheap and selling dear, but in reverse order. The public however felt bitterly toward all the market makers, and especially the bears who spread gloom and doom for their own gain. And yet I found I liked the idea

of the man Smith; he, at least, was not one of the crowd of
fools led by the Pied Pipers, or by the political soothsayers in
Washington, who may have caused losses to the public with
their poor advice. Smith had a mind of his own, as well as a
superior means of intelligence, and one respected him for
that.

With some effort I learned where I might reach him by
telephone, but was informed by his secretary that he positively
refused to see me and wished nothing published about himself. I then wrote him a letter stating that I had collected
information about him that was interesting to me, and that I
would write about him in any case, but preferred to seek his
help to make sure that what I would publish was fair and
correct. There came a reply by telephone, a certain Mr. Emil
Hurja (later well known as a lobbyist in Washington for
divers special interests) called me and said that he worked at
public relations and Mr. Smith occasionally used him as a
consultant. He would be glad to meet me, and made an appointment for the next afternoon at a speakeasy. He looked
me over and listened while I argued that no harm, but some
good, would come out of my proposed articles. A few days
later I was told that Mr. Smith would see me after all in his
office, and I came down just after the closing bell had ended
market trading for the day for my first encounter with the
great man.

I found Smith on the fifteenth floor of an office building
at 52 Wall Street, in a private suite of two small rooms attached to the main office of W. E. Hutton and Company,
long established as one of the leading firms on the Exchange.
Here he had been operating for many years, clearing a part
of his business through Hutton's office, but a great deal
through other channels as well. The notorious leader of the
bear party, who was regarded as a self-made "genius" of the
market, had simple quarters: an old rolltop desk with two
telephones, a stock ticker, some filing cabinets, heaps of the

large volumes of Poor's *Manual of Corporations* overflowing the shelves and surfaces of furniture, and no other decorations. A middle-aged woman secretary sat nearby, feeding him telephone calls; messengers came running in with notes, telegrams, or papers for him to sign.

Smith was then in his middle forties, a stocky man of medium height, with a thick neck, a ruddy moon-face, and a wide jaw. His thinning hair was light brown, his one eye was blue, the other, the right, was covered—the consequence of an accident in boyhood. In appearance Smith was not only plain, but without distinction; he was comfortably dressed in a sack suit and soft-collared shirt. In manner of speech, however, he was very forthright and confident, even brusque, though not without geniality; his voice carried the accent of the old Irish community of Hell's Kitchen in Manhattan. You might have passed him in the street without noticing him, or taken him, perhaps, for a fireman in mufti. Like the other famous New Yorker of his name—the ex-Governor and presidential candidate—he had come up from the "sidewalks of New York." He had little schooling, but was none the less sharp for all that. His talk ran to a sort of shrewd kidding, but it could be provocative too. It was said that persons of high estate such as Lord Rothermere were among his international clientele. Another of his wealthy clients, Stuyvesant Fish, one of the older ornaments of Wall Street, said of him: "Ben Smith is a rough diamond; he has the charm of the perfectly natural."

He began by asking me very bluntly how much I would receive for writing such as article as I proposed to do. I told him. He said, "I'll give you double that if you agree not to do the article." There were three other persons present: Thomas Bragg, his partner, a sharp-featured gray-looking man; Hurja; and the secretary, all of them grinning at Smith's remark. I got up from my chair and made as if to take off my coat and fight, meanwhile voicing high indignation at his proposal. He laughed like a mischievous small boy and cried, "Now, now, sit down, don't get angry, I was only foolin'." He then unbent, asked what was wanted of him, and proceeded to answer me freely.

He was a native New Yorker, born in 1888, the son of Irish Catholic immigrants of the working class, and had grown up in the tenements of the West Fifties. Before he was twelve he had had to leave school to help his parents, selling newspapers at first, later taking a job at $3 a week as an errand boy in Wall Street. Within three years he was holding a responsible clerical position at a broker's office and speculating on his own. As a boy he had been a member of street gangs and had become proficient at shooting craps beside the railroad tracks on the West Side. The gambling spirit was strong in him, as in other denizens of Wall Street; when he was only sixteen he made a quick fortune of some $30,000, as he related, and enjoyed spending part of it. "But they took nearly all the rest of that first pile in the panic of 1904," he added. After that he never forgot that "stocks went down much faster than they went up."

With his money suddenly gone, he became a rolling stone, wandering about the United States as an itinerant laborer, or signing on as a sailor. He then came back to New York to enter business with friends: selling rubber tires and exporting used cars to South America. He once took charge of a ship's cargo of secondhand cars, which he tried to sell to the natives of Peru. When the expedition wound up as a total loss, he decided to explore the country, and, as he phrased it, "I went fishing in a big lake on top of the Andes." Every now and then he would return to work at some brokerage office in New York for a period and try his hand again at the market with indifferent success.

With his love of excitement and travel, Smith would have enjoyed soldiering even before the United States was involved in World War I. He was disqualified, however, by his eye injury; but in 1916 he volunteered for service as an ambulance driver in the American unit of the Red Cross and went to France, where he stayed for several years. It was there he met a young American relief worker, Miss Gertrude Davis, daughter of a well-to-do California businessman. After the war's end, having found winning ways in the market again, Smith journeyed out to California and was married to Miss Davis.

The roaming about the world and the thrill-hunting stopped. Smith now became office manager of the Wall Street firm of Prentiss, Slepack and Co., for whom he had clerked as a boy. Many years earlier the firm had been founded by John D. Rockefeller's brother William, an inveterate stock gambler, and was patronized by men like James Stillman; it had been a training school for Ben Smith. Over the years he had retained the friendship of some of the Wall Street grandees he had met at Prentiss's, such as Percy Rockefeller, the younger Stillman, and Stuyvesant Fish. People with money found it both amusing and profitable to do business with Ben, blunt of speech and a square shooter.

Wall Street had its wags, people whose antics helped to relieve the nerves of men made edgy by the ever present dangers of the market. Ben was one of the most irrepressible of the jokers. On one occasion he was seen selling a leading stock at the specialist's post on the floor of the Exchange, while against him stood another broker who kept buying everything Sell-Em Ben offered. Finally the other man took Ben aside and whispered to him, "Hush, Ben, don't sell that stock. Do you know whom I'm buying it for? Sun Life." Sun Life Insurance Company of Canada was famous for its huge reserves of cash and its bargain hunting. But Ben, unfazed, quickly offered one inside tip for another, "Secret?" he whispered. "You better stop buying. Do you know whom I'm selling it for? Sun Life!"

Coming into the office of his old friend Thomas Bragg, Ben suddenly remembered he had a telephone call to make and picked up the instrument on Bragg's desk.

"Wait a minute," cried Bragg: "I'm short of Telephone. Drop that thing—don't give them any more business now."

"Ah, you don't know me, Tom," Smith rejoined. "I'm shorting Telephone myself. After I get done using that phone, I just pick it up and drag it after me, wires and all, see?" And this he did with a sweeping gesture of his arm.

Smith had often tried the short side of the market with success. One of his confreres said: "It was Ben's chronic disposition to be a bear. When the public buys heavily they are more usually wrong than right, he believes; then after a while those overbought stocks go down in a grand smash. There's fast movement and more thrill on that side." But he worked both sides of the market for pools.

"In 1926," Smith related, "I found I was making too much money for other people and would do better working for myself." With funds of his own and some loans from rich clients he bought a seat on the New York Stock Exchange for $150,000 and began trading on his own account. Since his boyhood days in the Street he had known Bragg, a small, thin, sharp-faced man, who had also risen to membership in the Exchange. Working together, the two men acquired options on blocks of stock from corporation directors who sought additional capital, and by pool manipulation they disposed of the stock in the market at prices above the option.

Smith participated in some of the important bull market pools of 1929, notably in the stock of Radio Corporation of America, directed by M. J. Meehan, and of Commercial Solvents, in which Harry F. Sinclair played a principal part—while the stock ran up from 150 to 400 in a few weeks. He also placed half a million dollars of his own in the Anaconda pool, in partnership with Percy Rockefeller, Fred J. Fisher,

John J. Raskob, and others; the dominant member of this large syndicate, however, was the National City Company and the banker, C. E. Mitchell.

When the tidal wave of selling struck Wall Street in October, Smith related, he was in the north of Canada looking over some mining prospects. By telegram he learned belatedly that stocks he held were all declining at high speed. After some difficulty he got a long-distance connection through to New York and clung to the telephone all day while he not only sold everything he owned (at great loss), but also, in most cases, doubled his orders to sell; that is, he was selling twice as much as he had held, and going short. Hiring a private plane, he flew back to New York to find the market in pandemonium during the last week in October, and in a sort of rage at himself for ever having believed in that overdone bull market, continued his selling. "I was right in the first place and all along!" he exclaimed at the time, and continued his selling, especially of Anaconda Copper. He was particularly embittered because corporate insiders and executives of the National City Bank had surreptitiously unloaded large quantities of Anaconda's shares without informing Smith and Bragg, members of the syndicate, about what they were going to do. Anaconda's price underwent an overnight collapse, falling from $110 to $75 in suspicious-looking circumstances. Smith, a square shooter with regard to business associates, was outraged not only by the loss of half a million dollars, but by the deception practiced upon him and Bragg. He went roaring about the Exchange floor like the Bull of Bashan, vowing he would have the blood of the Anaconda's directors. "Sell 'em," he cried. "You'll see that lousy stock go begging at $5 a share!" In 1932 it sank as low as $4.

Hard-headed and skeptical, Smith was also a very clear-eyed analyst who made it his business to obtain exact information about the nation's economy. After 1928 he had noticed the unevenness of the country's prosperity, especially in the area of agriculture. He became certain that the farmers' troubles would effect the important farm implement industry and prepared to act upon his conviction. Following the Crash of October, 1929, he made up his mind to ignore the statements of officials of the national government and depend entirely upon his own means of intelligence.

Like other "wizards" of the Street before him, he was an artist at "hiding a trade." But whereas the great politician may immortalize himself in his public addresses, and a great artist in his enduring canvases, an artist of speculation graves his designs only on the ticker tape. Only a few watchers of the eternally moving tape, who have a true understanding of its meanings, can appreciate thoroughly the effects it achieves, and can interpret the fleeting ciphers that bespeak so much drama, so many hand-to-hand encounters, so much struggle for glory and loot. Each night the miles of paper ribbon are duly gathered up by hundreds of charwomen downtown, and all the stories it tells are swept out as so much waste. If we could recover a few strands of this tangle and read of the activities of a certain week in May, 1930, we would have almost intact one of Ben Smith's chef-d'oeuvres.

One of the history-making stocks in those days was known as Case Threshing Machine Company, and Ben was much involved in it. This concern has been long established in the manufacture of farm machinery for domestic and export trade. To the Street, however, the high-priced Case meant only one of the fast "action" stocks on the Big Board, the medium of true gamblers. With a small capitalization of 195,000 shares, the floating supply in brokers' hands was narrow; orders for a few hundred shares would set Case doing hops, skips, and whirls. Case would gyrate up or down at the slightest pressure, for ten, twenty, or even as many as thirty points in a day's session.

From 1925 on, a bold-handed pool had carried Case from a price of approximately $40 to $500 a share as of September, 1929, though the company paid only six dollars in annual dividends. In the debacle of October and November, the value of Case shares lost all of 300 points. During the recovery movement of early 1930, however, this mercurial stock regained more than half its loss and ran up to about 350. This strong upturn was accompanied by Street rumors that an important bear crowd, headed by Ben Smith, had been trapped by a "corner" in Case. Supply of the stock was so tight that it was difficult for the shorts to borrow the certificates for temporary delivery, even by paying special charges to brokers. And to buy back would be ruinous; if the bears tried to buy their way out, their buying might quickly drive the stock to 500, or even higher, and they would have to pay the piper.

Smith *was* short of Case, and at this dangerous crisis in April, 1930, he hired an airplane, flew out to the Middle West, and studied the ground himself. He assured himself that the farmers were getting into very poor shape—crop prices were falling, farms were being foreclosed, and sales of farm tractors were declining. There seemed to be no economic reason for Case to be selling at artificially high levels. Smith flew back to New York, held his ground, and sold more Case, as his admirers recalled.

Still for a while it did not give, and the crowd in the "bear trap" was reported to be somewhat desperate, though Ben always wore his broad smile. At this stage of things, in May, 1930, there came the second crash, represented on market charts as the "Hoover Decline." There had been more statements from Washington about conditions being "sound" and "no cause for alarm," followed by a selling wave that broke over the whole list. Leading stocks lost 10 to 60 points. At the Case post, the hand of Ben Smith was strongly felt; this inflated stock, allegedly "cornered" by the bulls, sank out of sight within a few short days, falling from 350 to 156½. By 1932 there was plenty of Case available at 30. "It looked as if I was wrong," Ben Smith said, "but I hung on and won out."

Wall Street's old hands, such as Harry Content, were outspoken in their admiration of Smith's courage. It was then that the newspapers reported the rumors of his big profits and represented him as one of the great "market makers" of the time, a leader of the bear movement.

"I'm not a bear raider!" he exclaimed in response to my queries about how he operated on the short side. "We just try to make our living around here, like anybody else, is all." "It's still lawful in this country," he went on, "for a man to speculate in the hope of making an honest dollar."

A speculator, he argued, was one who tried "to sell things at a higher price than he paid for them." The bull and the bear had the same purpose. But when a man had sold a stock short, he had to go into the market eventually and cover his short position by buying that stock back, which often tended to send the market up. With a hard laugh Smith added: "There are times when you don't even have to buy in what you've sold. Sometimes the stock goes so low that—well—it's thrown out the window."

"Who has been causing all the worst trouble around here," he went on. "The bears? Maybe it was the *bulls*." It was the leaders of the bull movement, the respectable men, who had led the public down the garden path and tempted them to buy the watered stock they were promoting. It was not the bears who had aroused the greed of the public, or deceived crowds of "suckers." It was the conservative bankers who had fostered the overextended condition of the market in 1929, when the public were encouraged to buy stocks at four or five times what they were worth. When overextended conditions developed, then the bears helped to let the water out of an inflated market.

"Stocks don't go up by themselves," he pointed out. "Each stock has its daddy." It was the bullish "daddies"—

promoting their pools—who ran prices up. The bear, in any case, did not himself bring about bad economic conditions or bamboozle trusting people into buying over-priced securities.

Smith could have told more to the Senate Committee than he did about men like Mitchell, and Albert Wiggin in particular, who, in 1933, was exposed by the Senate Banking Committee as having secretly sold short for his own profit the stock of his own bank, which he was employed to manage faithfully and defend. Wiggin's private corporations were also shown to have participated in bear syndicates in which Ben Smith and Tom Bragg participated. Wiggin was an aging, dignified, and complacent banker, who was certain he had done no wrong—certainly nothing unlawful at that time. But the Rockefeller interests, after a while, brought about his retirement as chairman of the Chase Bank.

In private talk Ben Smith would vent his disgust at the stuffed shirts of the political as well as the financial establishment. Were not the optimistic statements made by the President and Mr. Mellon, "the greatest Secretary of the Treasury," calculated to mislead the public? Mr. Hoover's Secretary of Commerce had even issued a report in 1930 declaring that agricultural prospects were *improving*. Smith had investigated the report with the aid of his own specialists and found it entirely false. "We must face the facts," Sell-Em Ben said. "For too many years we have been living on bunk."

How did he operate his own intelligence system? Where did he find the little true facts? "I watch the market, the tape, sure. I see which stocks go down faster than they go up, yes. But that," pointing to one of the two telephones on his desk, "helps me more than anything else I've got." Smith would open up his telephone line to Toronto, or Chicago, or London, or Amsterdam, keeping tuned in to the vibrations of world events. Over the wires, from all parts of this and other continents, reports would come to him; they would come from his agents and investigators, from great capitalists, from other brokers, and even from secret informers within the great banks themselves.

The man was a paradox. Feared and hated for what he did by many persons in high places, he was one of the most honest of men, one who lived by the truth. "It's not the bears who have been selling the public the high-priced stuff," he protested. His candor and independence of mind were admirable. There were some disadvantages to his kind of public fame as a destroyer of bullish myths, but some advantages as well. He was a superior soul who lived in a world of clear realities. Most people lived really in a papier-mâché world, furnished with much American buncombe that could suddenly fall apart, as it did in 1929. We got our misinformation from the press, City Hall, the Capitol at Washington, the White House, and the mouthpieces and flunkies of the supposedly great. We bought what we were told to buy, believed what we were told to believe, or lost everything and starved when we had to, docilely, unromantically. Smith felt under no compulsion to believe what he called hooey. He had his own mind and used his own media of information, trusting neither Mr. Herbert Hoover nor Mr. William Randolph Hearst.

The procedures of the Wall Street market were under the closest scrutiny of the authorities in Washington in 1931. In September the British pound sterling suddenly was devalued, and there was again a crash in the markets of the United States, for it was believed that the sterling devaluation would tend to diminish whatever was left of our export business. Now the dollar came under pressure in the foreign exchange market, amid rumors that it too would be devalued, and the Federal Reserve went into action to "defend" the dollar by raising the rediscount rate sharply (after having tried low interest rates to help recovery).

The new crisis was weathered in some fashion; but

President Hoover was at length roused to attempt positive action and bring the Federal Government to intervene in the declining economy. This he had previously refused to do. He had spoken for the way of "rugged individualism," had urged reducing the Federal budget and tightening our belts, while we waited for the hard times to pass. Finally he considered remedial measures, even inflationary ones, that might stimulate recovery. Governor Harrison of the New York Reserve Bank now came forward with a scheme for expanding bank credit that he had formulated with the help of several of the nation's leading bankers.

The Federal Reserve System was America's adaptation of the European central banking institution in regional form; half was public, half directed by representatives of the commercial bank members. Though it had twelve branches in the "Reserve cities" around the country, the New York unit, holding most of the System's money and bullion, was the tail that wagged the dog. In 1929 Harrison presided over a board that included Charles E. Mitchell, Albert H. Wiggin, W. C. Teagle (head of Standard Oil of New Jersey), and Owen D. Young (chairman of General Electric). Russell C. Leffingwell of Morgan's once described Harrison as "the perfect type of public servant devoted to a quasi-public career." Besides fulfilling its duty of regulating things monetary in the United States, the Reserve Bank of New York had pursued a policy of cooperating with the government banks of Europe's great powers to stabilize world currency and money markets. Hence Harrison spent much of his time abroad at hush-hush international conferences with Europe's central bankers, such as Sir Montagu Norman of the Bank of England, Hjalmar Schacht of the Reichsbank, and Clément Moret of the Banque de France, upon whose decisions the fate of the world was supposed to hang. The polished Harrison tried to act both as a diplomat of the international financial world and an *éminence grise* in politics; he was well spoken, a congenial poker-player, humorous, but not without a touch of malice.

Out of Harrison's discussions in September, 1931, with a group of leading financiers a tentative plan was drawn up for the strongest banks to raise up a credit of $500 million to be administered by a projected "National Credit Corporation." This organization would make large loans, thus creating new money and stimulating business activity, while the Reserve Banks would cooperate in expanding the money supply. Hoover at first approved of the plan, though by now he desired more liberal provisions of credit than the private bankers would allow.

One warm Sunday in October Harrison shepherded a flock of about twenty New York and Chicago bankers to Washington to meet with the President. They found Mr. Hoover in a mood of unrelieved gloom. Though the New York people in the contingent had pledged about a third of the capital for the big credit pool, he scolded them for not going far enough. Some of the bankers were dubious about the whole idea, and one of them said, "Well, we might as well go and play golf—it's a fine day." Another, referring to the President's querulousness, said, "Well, these things take time, Mr. President. You remind me of the impatient bride who woke up the morning after the wedding and asked, 'Where's the baby?' " The plan of the new Credit Corporation was announced to the press with some fanfare, then dropped completely.

Hoover, meanwhile, had been offered an alternative plan, which struck him as more feasible: a Government credit bank which would lend the United States Treasury's money on liberal terms to shaky banks, insurance companies, railroads, real estate corporations, and farmers. Out of this grew the Reconstruction Finance Corporation, established by an act of Congress in December, 1931, which undertook to put much new money into circulation; at the same time the Federal Reserve was allowed to relax its rules so that currency could be issued against long-term United States bonds, thus releasing more of its gold for circulation.

The purpose of the RFC was to have credit percolate downward through the economic coffee pot to help business and increase jobs. In its first year, 1932, it worked to bail out banks that had become illiquid with bad or slow paper, such as General Dawes's bank in Chicago and A. P. Giannini's Bank of America in California; it also administered large loans to railroads, like the Van Sweringens', whose funds had been wasted in ill-conceived speculations. Such financing as it performed at the beginning was on so modest a scale that it created no new business and added few jobs. The RFC did begin to advance money in 1932 to city welfare bureaus for doles to the unemployed, but its operations did not have a large effect until the free-spending President Roosevelt came into office.

The Federal Reserve Bank's experts, meanwhile, attempted their own cure by monetary controls aimed at expanding the supply of money. The strategy of "open market" purchasing of bonds by the Federal Reserve Banks had been used earlier; but now it was employed on a gigantic scale by Harrison, who headed the Open Market Committee for the country's twelve Reserve Banks. Under the new banking rules, he had one billion dollars more in gold available. With these funds he began to buy $100 million in U.S. Government bonds every week during ten successive weeks up to May, 1932, by which date a hoard of $1.1 billion in bonds was accumulated. These transactions, of a size unequaled in the history of any central bank, put cash in the hands of the Reserve's member banks and were expected to form the basis for the expansion of loans or investment in the ratio of 10 to 1. It was believed that such a grandiose "reflation" of the banking system, totaling some ten billions of dollars, would surely revive business and employment and perhaps even assure the reelection of Hoover in November, 1932.

The experts watched the operation with the same excitement that experts in 1970 watched the deflationary experiment with a 9 percent prime bank rate under President Nixon, and found that it failed in a big way. There were various reasons given at the time; the trouble with managing money is that in the real world, as opposed to some theoretical world, "perfect laboratory conditions" can never be assured. Fear spread again in international money markets; in 1932 gold began to drain out of the country to France and Switzerland in ever larger amounts, and the total of bank deposits in America was reduced. Renewed bank runs and more bank failures all around the country sponged up the added money supply. Currency and gold were being hoarded. The central bank experts had tried every trick they knew under the existing rules, and all had failed.

To compound confusion, President Hoover, regarded generally as the champion of conservative finance, had a serious falling-out with the big bankers of New York, largely over the activities of the bear raiders in Wall Street. In January, 1932, he again called Richard Whitney to the White House and told him he had better have the New York Stock Exchange "clean house." Whitney evidently tried to reassure the President, but without avail. As Hoover's memoirs report the meeting, he warned Whitney that, if nothing were done, he would ask Congress to investigate the Stock Exchange with a view to Federal legislation. Early in March the Senate formally authorized an investigation of securities markets, particularly the New York Exchange and the procedure of short selling, by the Senate Committee on Banking and Currency. Hearings were to begin in April.

At this same time a committee of New York bankers, with a view to bolstering the prospects of the Republicans in the approaching electoral campaign, were organizing a large pool to support the demoralized bond market (for non-government securities)—and thus rally the stock market as well.

This new consortium had been formed thanks to the efforts of Secretary of the Treasury Ogden Mills. But soon Mills heard that "certain important interests," who were discontented with the Government's policies, were refusing to help the bond market pool. Thomas W. Lamont of Morgan's, one of the disgruntled group, wrote President Hoover a long letter-memorandum protesting against the Senate's proposed investigation of the New York Stock Exchange. Several other bankers also wrote in the same vein, urging Hoover to have the investigation abandoned. It was as if the President were begin threatened with an ultimatum. Very properly President Hoover rejected these requests.

In early April, 1932, the nation's press and radio stations were filled with reports of financial scandals and rumors of worse things to come. The stock market experienced still another sinking spell, with the Dow-Jones index of thirty prime industrial stocks falling to a figure that amounted to only one tenth of the composite of September, 1929. It was in these parlous days that the Senate Committee on Banking and Currency opened its investigation of stock exchange practices and subpoenaed Richard Whitney to appear as the first witness.

"Mr. Wall Street" was poised as always, spoke with polite condescension to Senators who were ignorant of Stock Exchange usages, and in short admitted nothing and denied everything. Once more he sang his song about this country having grown great "through speculation" and about its market in securities that must be kept forever free of government control, lest it "dry up." The suggestion that brokers used their own customers' securities to depress or even "demoralize" the market in those stocks was flatly refuted; the club rules officially forbade bear raids for such purposes. The amount of short selling was insignificant, Whitney contended, and he handed over a list he had been asked for naming the

350 leading short sellers, nearly all of them bearing names that nobody recognized. Who had ever heard of such names as Shermar or Lurlyn Corporation? They were obviously "dummies"—in this case names of concealed accounts "owned" by the wife or daughter of Albert H. Wiggin of the Chase Bank. Whitney laid stress upon the honesty of Stock Exchange members. His unyielding manner in dialogue with the Senators gave them the impression that he was "arrogant" and "uncooperative." He even lectured them about the urgent need to cut Government expenses and the wages of its employees, though Senators were then earning but $10,000 a year, only one-tenth of the sum Whitney lived on.

A minority faction in Wall Street that was independent of the Morgan influence now began to oppose Whitney's policies as self-defeating. But no one dreamed that the "hero of 1929" was having his own secret troubles over unthinkable losses and was driven to borrow, on the sly, more than he could every repay—even from charity and trust funds in his care.

In the list of short sellers, meanwhile, the name of Bernard E. Smith had figured prominently; he was therefore one of the first to be subpoenaed by the Committee. Sell-Em Ben came rolling into the Senate Committee's Hearing Room laughing and bantering with the reporters. He allowed that he was not only happy to tell the Senators all about his business, but he would even "give them an earful." In his testimony he gave quite a vivid picture of how the big operators worked, for he unblushingly described what was considered the seamy side of Wall Street's business—the pools in Anaconda Copper, Radio Corporation, and other stocks.

The committee's legal counsel raised an interesting question: was not Michael J. Meehan, the floor specialist in Radio stock, also a participant in the Radio pool, and had he not therefore broken the rules of the Exchange? (Specialists kept book for both buyers and sellers and were supposed to stand, so to speak, above the battle.) Smith replied quickly "No I don't think Mr. Meehan has ever been a member of any pool. It is in his wife's name." There was prolonged laughter.

Smith's frank testimony, and Thomas Bragg's as well, were useful because they revealed that rules of ethical conduct were seldom enforced on the New York Stock Exchange. As Smith said off the record, "You could get away with murder." He described himself as no "bear raider," but one who earned his living like any other man of business by trying to make a profit on the "long" side as well as the short side. In explaining his pool operations, he pointed out that these were based on syndicate agreements with the directors of corporations, who wished to distribute issues of their stock at prices above an option they granted to Smith and his associates, thus providing those corporations with added capital funds. There was nothing in the law that forbade a man to make an honest profit, he argued, whether by long or short operations; and the Senators could not gainsay him.

"I would just as lief play bull, if they'd let us," he declared. But the boomers in foregoing years had raised prices of stocks until they stood far above any reasonable ratio of earnings to market prices. It was the bull leaders, not the bears, he insisted, who had precipitated the Crash. Smith's testimony was marked by frank contempt, not only for the Old Guard of Wall Street, but also, by implication, for Government leaders—Coolidge, Mellon, Hoover—who had, knowingly or not, misled the public. The depression, he contended, was made worse "by the kind of government we've been having for nearly four years." The reformers among the Senators continued to hold such pool manipulations as Smith's a shady business; but his forthright testimony came as a breath of fresh air after the long speeches of Richard Whitney.

In that spring of 1932 the declining movement reached its nadir; the country's gold was being drained away, and this, many foresaw, would lead to the devaluation of the dollar. Ben Smith invested his bear-market profits in gold-mining shares of companies operating in Canada and Alaska. He said: "Tell 'em I'm a bull now—a bull on gold." As he had foreseen, the dollar became depreciated in 1933, and in 1934 the price of gold was increased by approximately 70 percent, from $20 to $35.30 an ounce. The appreciation of established gold mining shares, however, was far greater in proportion.

The scarlet woman, after she has had her career and known some pecuniary success, turns for future security to invest in diamonds and emeralds; the bear operator, for his part, turns to gold.

5

THE MONEY MEN ON TRIAL

The late winter and spring of 1932 saw the lowest ebb of the economic cycle. Unemployment reached an estimated total of fourteen million before stabilizing at about that level. Farmers rioted in "strikes" against foreclosures and the low prices of corn, milk, and potatoes; and thousands of country banks closed their doors. In the large cities the soup lines extended themselves interminably, while private and public welfare bureaus distributed food and meager doles. In metropolitan New York, not only the central thorougfares but even the downtown financial district looked downright shabby, for paint was peeling off many building fronts. At the corner of Wall and Broad Streets, army veterans had set up apple stands, which the Morgan partners passed as they arrived and departed on each business day.

The financial world, too, was afflicted by fearful scandals.

On March 12, Ivar Kreuger committed suicide in his luxurious apartment in Paris, just as agents of his American bankers finally moved to investigate his highly secret business records. This singular financier had floated $250 million in bonds and stocks of Kreuger and Toll, his international match monopoly, mainly in the United States through the firm of Lee, Higginson and Company, which ranked as one of America's three leading investment bankers. Though one of their partners was on the board of directors of Kreuger and Toll, neither he nor the other directors had ever managed to see Kreuger's records. When his vault was opened after his death, it was found to contain only the notations of a bankrupt; the cupboard was bare. The huge sums turned over to the holding company were gone. He had spent and gambled it all away long ago, while maintaining the impressive facade of a financial genius, who practiced the utmost reticence about his affairs even with his closest colleagues, presumably because they were given to understand that his secret dealings turned upon winning governmental monopolies from kings and ministers. In the various biographies of Kreuger that have appeared since his death, no one has made it clear whether his associates guessed that these negotiations were furthered by continued bribes, which they chose not to question. At any rate the Mystery Man Kreuger was discovered as the most artful and, quantitatively, the greatest swindler in all history.

After the Kreuger scandal came the downfall of Samuel Insull. Two holding companies at the top of his public utilities pyramid had become insolvent, and, by 1932, he had finally exhausted the credit of the third holding company, Middle West Utilities, for he had used up all its cash to support Insull stocks in panic-ridden markets. He had also loaned $10 million raised on his own unsecured note to the Insull-affiliated brokerage firm that handled his transactions, but this firm also became insolvent and was suspended by the Exchanges at Chicago and New York.

In April, Insull was called to a final conference with his creditors in New York, among whom were Owen D. Young of General Electric and several representatives of the Chase and Morgan banks. Young, a corporation lawyer of long experience, later testified that he found the Insull holding-company structure an affair so labyrinthine that it completely baffled his understanding. Further financing was refused point-blank for the man who had controlled the largest public utility group in America; he was also forced to resign from the high-salaried offices in his operating companies, such as Commonwealth Edison and People's Gas. Insull was a man overborne late in life by the passion of greed. In his desperate hours, driven by fear of losing his empire, he had committed what were alleged to have been irregularities in the use of funds of one of his operating utility companies; suits were levied against him by the Illinois State's Attorney on charges of alleged embezzlement and by the Federal authorities on charges of fraud; Insull was indicted. Aged and sick, he took flight to Europe rather than face trial before an outraged public opinion. There State Department agents pursued him in plodding fashion, seeking to have him extradited from one country after another. All through 1933 the newspapers followed his vanishing-and-reappearing act with excitement. He was arrested finally in Istanbul and brought back to face trial in Cook County, Illinois.

In effect, finance capitalists and bankers especially were put on trial for years *because they had lost so much money* for the public, though, in all but a few cases, they had done nothing unlawful according to the statutes at the time. The collapse of the Van Sweringens' holding company, Alleghany Corporation, was almost as costly to the public as the failure of Kreuger. One of their bond issues was in default; their $100 par preferred stock suspended paying dividends; the common stock, which Morgan had distributed to its "preferred list" of friends and which had sold at over $56, was down to thirty-seven and a half cents a share. It was generally known that the Van Sweringens' enormous railroad organization was actually under control of the bankers. When the Government's giant credit bank, the Reconstruction Finance Corporation, first opened for business in January, 1932, Oris P. Van Sweringen was "on their doorstep," as he phrased it, with applications for loans to three of the railroads he controlled, and they were among the first corporations to get help —$75 million—so that they were able to cover part of their most pressing debts. (The Missouri-Pacific Railroad, though helped by the Government in 1933, went into receivership.) However, the "rescue loan" of $39.5 million made to the Van Sweringens personally by the banking group remained unpaid.

The hearings on the operations of investment banks and securities exchanges were resumed in the summer of 1932 with Ferdinand Pecora, of New York, acting as examining counsel. The Senators representing Western farmer constituents—chairman Peter Norbeck of South Dakota, Smith Brookhart of Iowa, and Hiram Johnson of California—bore hard on the bankers who came before them as witnesses.

One subject of inquiry was the story of the great mass of bonds issued by foreign governments, cities, provinces, and corporations, amounting to more than eight billion dollars, which a select group of investment firms including Morgan's; National City Company; Kidder, Peabody; Dillon, Read; J. & W. Seligman; and Kuhn, Loeb, had placed in the hands of the American public between 1920 and 1930. On their books all of three billion were now in default. What was most shocking, as revealed by evidence before the committee, was that the leading underwriters of foreign loans, such as National City and J. & W. Seligman, had been warned both by officers of the State Department and by their own investigators in the field that the governments of nations like Peru and Bolivia were poor risks for large loans. Yet Seligman had not only persisted in issuing a $50 million loan at 7 percent to Peru, but had also paid a "fee" of $500,000 to the dictator Lleguia's son for acting as go-between. These bond issues were distributed to American investors after a very high "spread" of some 5 or more points was taken by the underwriter. The profits to the American banks were very high on such issues, which sometimes amounted to as much as $90 million. The bonds had been sold, moreover, by high pressure methods, by sub-brokers having little choice but to accept and distribute their quota and by the banks' securities affiliates, such as National City Company, Chase Securities, or Guaranty Company, as well as by the established underwriting firms, such as Kuhn, Loeb; Dillon, Read; and Seligman. By 1929 the National City Company, for example, had sixty-nine district offices in the principal cities of America and hundreds of bond salesmen ringing doorbells, offering not only foreign bonds but also National City Bank stock, then selling at between $600 and $700 per share. Under Charles E. Mitchell, the City Bank's affiliate had flooded the country with some $3 billion in new securities, a large part of them the bonds of dubious foreign regimes. So profitable had this business become that in 1929 Mitchell had been paid by bonus arrangement the sum of $4 million in addition to his salary.

Senator Brookhart, in the chair, called Mitchell to the stand and told him that as he had entered the Hearing Room he had been surrounded by distressed customers of the investment bankers, some of whose bonds were down to thirteen cents on the dollar! They had besought the Senator to "do something for them." What did Mr. Mitchell think about this? Mitchell answered in the sententious style of bankers of that day, "Mistakes . . . are among the penalties that have to be paid for freedom."

Russell C. Leffingwell, lawyer and Morgan partner, also former Assistant Secretary of the Treasury under President Wilson, submitted a written statement to the committee, in which he tried to extenuate the excesses of America's bankers in their foreign lending, holding that these had been in response to the urgent need to go forward with world trade and help rebuild the economy after so much of war's devastation.

At another hearing, before the younger Senator Robert La Follette's subcommittee on Education and Labor, there was discussion of the possibilities of economic planning for the reemployment of fifteen million jobless citizens. A number of university economists and union leaders proposed reducing hours of work and expanding public works. Among the leading financiers called to testify was Wiggin of the Chase Bank, who had been garnering rich profits for himself by secret bear operations in the time of catastrophe. Wiggin declared that economic planning was an "impossibility," that human nature would always remain the same, and that "once in so many years," periodic disasters were bound to overtake us and nothing could be done to stop them. "You think the capacity for human suffering is unlimited?" asked Senator La Follette. "I think so," replied Wiggin coolly.

The Senate subcommittee on Banking and Currency applied sterner methods of examination after May, 1933, when Pecora himself went to 23 Wall Street, armed with a subpoena, and took possession of pertinent documents from Morgan and Company's files. Lamont was outraged at this seizure, and he evidently appealed to Harrison of the Federal Reserve Bank of New York to prevent the correspondence of Morgan's with that institution being turned over to the Senate. But this Harrison could not promise to do.

The extensive hearings of the Morgan partners, including Morgan himself, Lamont, and George Whitney, were conducted with courtesy and in the presence of Morgan's distinguished counsel, John W. Davis. The exposure of the Morgan "preferred list" for the sale of what were temporarily valuable options on Alleghany stock created a considerable shock to the public when reported in the press, with its picture of a privileged financial oligarchy. It was considered significant that important political and military personages were included among the privileged, such as Secretary of the Treasury Mellon, Senator W. C. McAdoo, Secretary of the Navy Charles Francis Adams, General John J. Pershing, and John J. Raskob, then National Chairman of the Democratic Party. Further shock was registered when the untutored public learned that the extremely wealthy Morgan partners paid no income taxes in years such as 1929 and afterward, when they could apply paper losses in depreciated securities against salaries and capital gains by exchanges or "dummy" sales to their wives or to private corporations. These were common practices among the very rich even when income taxes were moderate, but indignation grew when the disgraced bankers Mitchell and Wiggin were shown to have employed similar means of tax "avoidance."

By 1932 even President Hoover had become convinced that a law regulating the securities exchanges and requiring truth in all statements of the character of newly issued securities must be enacted. The great lesson the legislators derived from the 1200 pages of testimony delivered before the Senate subcommittee was that investment banking and commercial banking must at last be separated. Such a provision, along with a truth-in-securities measure, was adopted as part of the Democratic Party platform in 1932, and in fact was approved by both political parties.

The aftermath of the Pecora Committee investigations— one of the most notable of Congressional inquiries—was the great fall in public prestige of bankers and of the professional financial class. Men had been wont to look up to them and to consult them as trusted and wise counsellors; but they had been shown to have exercised poor leadership in the crisis days, and at the end of Hoover's term were seen to have fallen to quarreling with their own political friends in the Republican Party.

A. P. Giannini was not called to testify in public about his huge banking group and holding company; and yet the danger of having a bank associated with a securities-selling affiliate is nowhere better illustrated than in his case. At the end of 1931 the satellite corporation called Transamerica owed its parent, now called The Bank of America, N.A. (of California), about $51 million, largely money lost in trying to "peg" the market in its own and affiliated corporation securities, and in bad loans or investments. Moreover the Western bank chain itself had been losing deposits heavily, more heavily than the big banks of New York. The Federal Reserve authorities now pressed The Bank of America to force its affiliate to liquidate or repay part of its big debt to the mother bank. The bank itself was also loaded with "slow paper," mainly acquired with the too costly purchase of the Merchant's Bank of Los Angeles. One of the most important holdings in the Transamerica portfolio was the parcel of 500,000 shares of the Bank of America of New York, the $400 million institution that gave Giannini his long-desired foothold in New York and promised realization of his dream of a nationwide banking system.

In February, 1930, A. P. announced his retirement—or at least he pretended to retire—and Transamerica came under the management of his new lieutenant, Elisha Walker, who became chairman, while Mario Giannini was named president. To Giannini's great dismay, Walker undertook to sell the controlling shares of Bank of America (New York) to the National City Bank, which promptly merged its branches into its own city-wide chain. In exchange, Transamerica received a minority block of City Bank shares, then selling at very low prices. It seemed a very poor bargain indeed. A bitter conflict now arose between Giannini senior and Walker, the Wall Street financier he himself had brought into his organization. By September, 1931, the elder Giannini had resigned his directorships in both Transamerica and Bank of America, while his son Mario hung on in both corporations but felt himself stripped of all authority.

Walker seemed to be pursuing a coldly rational program, trimming sail and lightening cargo in order to ride out the storm. The dividend paid by Transamerica and the great bank too was reduced and the stock of Transamerica fell below $10. The Gianninis protested at these measures, but a number of their principal associates, such as Mount, Bacigalupi, and Hale, supported Walker.

GIANNINIS LOSE RULE OF HUGE BANK CHAIN—ran the headline of a news story from San Francisco in *The New York Times,* September 22, 1931, as Walker announced the change of control. A. P. retreated to Europe for rest and repairs.

A. P. Giannini was by temperament one of the most overweeningly monopolistic of all Americans. He bought shaky banks at low prices and rich ones at high prices, and incessantly pressed on with his branch system toward the goal of achieving not merely a nationwide but a worldwide banking organization. In his regulated industry supervised by many state and Federal bureaucrats, he needed good political "contacts" to make sure that his mergers and corporate changeovers would be sanctioned; and so he made liberal pay-offs for those contacts in one way or another, not in the form of bribes of money, but with high-salaried jobs available to considerate office-holders who supervised his banks.

In truth he never exhibited the greed for money and securities that brought Insull and others low; he never held much of Transamerica or Bank of America stock in his own name. As Elisha Walker said on taking charge of affairs:

> The Giannini institutions . . . are operated for the benefit of stockholders and depositors. Mr. Giannini never thought of holding a large amount of stock himself.[1]

When the Van Sweringen and Insull holding companies crashed, their controlling owners were bankrupt; but when

Transamerica stock fell to 13 in 1930 and later even to 2 per share, Giannini was unaffected. He had scattered those shares in so many hands (nearly 200,000 stockholders), that he controlled his organization virtually by his "political" appeal, his *charisma* for the mass of small investors. Through the machinery of the strategic Proxy Committee of Transamerica, he had their names and addresses. Wherever they were (many centered in the Italian quarter of San Francisco), he could communicate with them and always rally a majority of proxies. In short, his power derived purely from "other people's money." He himself traveled light, living on his retirement fund of about $500,000, but sometimes drawing a bonus payment or retainer fee which was also moderate. Indeed during the struggle for control that developed in 1931, Walker was able to say correctly that he himself had become the largest individual stockholder in Transamerica. Walker's next move was therefore almost the *coup de grace* for the House of Giannini; he had the new board of directors relieve both father and son of their duties on Transamerica's Proxy Committee.

A. P. had some claim to a part of the management bonus payment of 1928–1929—aside from what he had given to charity—amounting to $791,000. The Walker-Monnet regime rejected this claim; then to add insult to injury they announced a drastic write-down of nearly a billion dollars in Transamerica's stated assets.

At sixty-one, living "in exile" at Bad Gastein, Austria, seriously ill and frequently in pain, A. P. looked very much like a worn-out tycoon, ruined by the defeats suffered between 1929 and 1931. His empire, formerly boasting over $2 billion in assets, sprawling across the United States, had suddenly slipped from his hands, the power won by a lifetime of labor seemingly lost forever. And thanks to the principles he had professed—by which he refused to line his own pocket as did some other bankers, at the cost of his own bank—he had left himself without sufficient means to give battle to his adversaries who, to his ever-suspicious mind, had carried out a long-premeditated conspiracy to grab Transamerica and plunder its assets through the process of reorganization. The Walker slate of directors, representing both Blair and Company and Lee, Higginson and Company, were not only strong through their ties with the higher circles of Wall Street, but, what was most galling, were in a position to use the resources of his own companies against him.

A. P. thirsted for vengeance. He was sick, relatively poor, and alone "against all the power of Wall Street," whose wrath he had provoked by his transcontinental schemes. To fight such a combination seemed a fatal choice; but anger always gave A. P. renewed strength.

In the late summer, shortly before the rupture with Walker had become known to the public, A. P. cabled his son: "I am waiting only to recover health and strength to give the dirty gang a real stiff battle when the right moment to strike arrives."

In September he was well enough to start on his long voyage home as secretly as Napoleon had returned from Elba. Taking a roundabout route, he traversed all of Canada unrecognized, restless at the length of the journey and seething with anger at the base ingratitude of former business friends and protégés, men he had made, who now had turned against him. He kept his movements secret to avoid premature publicity about the impending stockholders' contest. Stopping at Vancouver, he met privately with his son Mario, who had come north to greet him and bring the latest news from headquarters. Still incognito, he rode on to Lake Tahoe at the Nevada line, putting up at an inn where the Giannini grapevine, consisting of loyal followers who were employed inside the bank and the holding company, could more easily maintain contact with him.

How things had changed in two years since 1929. A. P. had spent most of that time in Europe taking the cure. Yesterday crowds had trampled each other to greet the mighty *condottiere* who was Giannini. Today he skulked about alone at the resort in the high Sierras, wondering if the people of his hometown, San Francisco, would receive him with stones instead of flowers. Yesterday thousands had acclaimed the financial wizard who had enriched them by persuading them to buy his stock. Today they had lost faith in his wizardry. At many a branch of the Bank of America, the stockholder-depositors would appear and ask mournfully, "Well, when is Transamerica going up?" (The stock had sunk as low as 2⅛.) And as mournfully, the bank officer would shake his head and silently exhibit a bundle of the shares in his own possession as if to say, "Me, too!"

One day as A. P. sat gloomily ruminating in the barber-shop of his hotel at Tahoe, a man came in who recognized him with surprise. It was Herbert Fleishacker, head of the Anglo-Californian Bank of San Francisco, whom Giannini regarded as an old adversary and the last man he would have liked to see. Within the hour, news of Giannini's "return from Elba" was flying all about, causing seismic shocks in Wall Street as well as Montgomery Street. At this, A. P. decided to come out in the open. He returned to his home in San Mateo and began the battle.

In a statement to the press he explained his resignation as a director of Transamerica and its constituent banks, declared that he disapproved of the Walker management, and charged that the Walker faction was "selling out" Transamerica's richest assets without the approval of the stockholders. The Gianninis called together old supporters and stockholders and quickly organized them into an opposition group that they proposed to lead in a proxy contest for control of the Transamerica board at the next election of directors early in 1932. Money to carry on the fight was raised in small sums by loyal stockholders in various towns throughout the Golden State.

What followed was a sort of revolution within the far-spreading Bank of America chain and among the investors in its holding company. By 1932 the "pied pipers" of the nineteen twenties were nearly all ruined or disgraced, and certain ones among them were headed for jail. Of the group of financial tycoons of his era, including Insull, Mitchell, and the Van Sweringens, A. P. Giannini alone fought on—and survived—using methods different from those of the other money men, the methods of the politician, or if you will, the demogogue.

As described earlier, Walker had installed principally Eastern financial men as directors of Transamerica and was engaged in liquidating its shrunken assets as well as he could, firing dispensable help and eliminating dividends, a deflationary action that was unpleasant medicine for stockholders and employees. Now some 75 percent of Transamerica's stockholders were Californians, and more than half of these of Italian descent. Upwards of one million shares of stock in Transamerica were held by the Bank of America's 6000 employees, many of whom owed their jobs to Giannini and looked up to him as a father.

The ownership of the holding company was widely scattered among nearly 200,000 stockholders, each having a small amount of shares, while the members of the managing group, including Giannini, owned but a small fraction of the outstanding shares. It was a perfect case, as described in Berle and Means, of everybody and nobody "owning" the business, while the managers controlled it with little money of their own, as "absentee owners," financially speaking. Walker might well claim that he was the largest individual holder—Transamerica stock was very cheap now. Giannini's response was to "go to the people," in newspaper advertisements and circulars warning that "Control of your corporation, which has been in the hands of Californians, *has now passed to Wall Street interests.*" Furthermore, A. P. did what probably no other banker ever did; he went barnstorming all over the state, holding stockholders' meetings in high school auditoriums and movie theaters, as if for a political campaign. At San Francisco's Dreamland Auditorium he drew 12,000 persons. His son Mario and other aides made torrential speeches damning the Wall Street bankers, while A. P., imposing in old age but shy on the platform, would utter one sentence of greeting, calling to people by their first names, then retire amid tremendous ovations.

In many of the 300 branches of the Bank of America, employees held secret meetings in the banks' lavatories; the loyal Italian-Americans among them would say: "We don't know Walker—look what A. P. Giannini did for our people! Before he came we were *dagos*; now we are *Americans*!" A. P. appealed to the pride of the large ethnic minority in the California cities. Like a consummate politico, he contrived to focus the discontent of his public away from himself upon the alien management from the East. The local newspapers described Giannini now as a latter-day "Populist" leading a crusade against the "plutocrats." As one of them described the affair:

> Back to the people of the West—back to the farms and wharves and associates of old—went A. P. Giannini, rallying his loyal stockholders. Farmer stockholders of the great valleys thronged to these gatherings.

On several occasions Walker struck back, charging that it was Giannini, the heedless optimist and boomer who had brought losses to the bank and holding company by his imprudent investments, while receiving $5,200,000 in bonuses during the three years from 1927 to 1930. Walker had taken charge during the worst of the depression; he was wielding a scalpel, even cutting away men's hope, and few liked what he was doing. Many stockholders said, "Under Giannini we would have a chance to come back." Meanwhile A. P.'s thunderous campaign against the "Wall Street racketeers" drowned out criticism of his own egregious blunders; the burning issue became "stockholders' democracy" against "absentee ownership," or "California against Wall Street." Also the cry was on for dividends against no dividends. (A. P. on occasion was sometimes charged by Federal Reserve officials with declaring dividends that had not been fully earned!) The outcome in February, 1932, was a thumping majority of more than 15 million proxies carrying A. P. back to his imperial throne. Walker wired his congratulations, and departed.

Giannini brought theater into everything he did; to signal the change of regimes, he had the main banking floor at the Montgomery Street headquarters, where Walker had partitioned the open floor into separate private offices, restored to its old plan, "Tear down those spite fences," he cried. "We are now going to do our banking in the open!" It is not surprising that Senators in Washington engaged in war with Wall Street avoided calling in the "Populist" among bankers for investigation and confined themselves to the "big money-center" of New York.

A. P. was a good hater, too; heads began to roll, including those of James Bacigalupi, A. J. Mount, and other executives who had joined forces with Walker. When A. J. Mount, a formed president of Bank of America, moved over to neighboring Oakland to run a bank there, A. P. after a while reached across the bay, bought that bank, and put Mr. Mount out of business again. (However, they became reconciled later.)

Giannini was firmly mounted in the saddle again, but his steed looked as famished as Don Quixote's Rozinante. The grim year was the year of "silent" bank runs—check withdrawals alternating with wide-open panics. The closing of the Bank of United States in New York, a branch system, hurt the Gianninis' Bank of America in New York as well as their system in California. Although all banks were losing deposits, the Transamerica group was losing them to other banks. A. P. faced the 1932 bank runs with typical bravura. He flew in small planes with bags of currency to branches in various towns and made personal appearances at points of trouble bearing silver and gold, shouting for all to hear: "Money talks!" In the time of danger he was happy again; his health improved, and he set a hard pace for the younger men on his staff.

In February, 1932, the RFC had begun business with Eugene Meyer as chairman and Charles G. Dawes as president. The Bank of America was among the first to ask for a loan, borrowing $61 million on collateral; even the holding company, Transamerica, managed to borrow $30 million from the RFC against mortgage paper after Jesse Jones, the Texas Democrat, succeeded Eugene Meyer as chairman. (Dawes himself was obliged to resign from the RFC, then he applied for and received a loan of $90 million to tide over his own bank, the Central Republic of Chicago.) In the year that followed, the Bank of America lost about one-third of its $1.1 billion in deposits and was under greater pressure than other big banks because it held proportionately larger investments in slow real estate mortgage notes.

During recent political campaigns Giannini had pretended to be neutral, for there had been some scandal over his "buying" a Governor of California in 1926. But he was angry at President Hoover, and ignored a personal appeal the President made by letter for Giannini's support in the Golden State. Hoover had ignored Giannini but had used as his personal adviser, Henry Robinson, one of A. P.'s strongest rivals in Los Angeles. On the other hand, Joe Kennedy, the Wall Street operator who had gone all out for Governor Roosevelt, offered a good contact with the man who seemed destined to become the new President. During the several years Kennedy had spent in Hollywood as a financier of motion picture companies, he had done some very profitable business with the help of the Bank of America. Through Kennedy, Giannini arranged to meet with the Democratic candidate when he came to speak in San Francisco and gave $10,000 to the campaign chest Kennedy was raising among his business friends. During the campaign Giannini also telegraphed accurate reports of the voting sentiment in California; after the election he was received by Roosevelt at Hyde Park. The two men discussed the banking crisis, which had become a raging panic sweeping the whole nation. After their talk Giannini said he felt hope that the new man in the White House would be a "people's president" and help "open things up."

In the spring of 1932 the big New York bankers had been at loggerheads with President Hoover over the investigation of the securities exchanges. In the winter of 1933, during the awkward change-over period between the retiring and the new president, they pressed Hoover to have the Federal Government take extraordinary measures against the bank runs spreading from one state to another. In Michigan, the Guardian Trust of Detroit, one of the two largest banks in the state, was on the verge of closing its doors. It had used up all acceptable paper in loans from the Federal Reserve Bank and the RFC, and could raise no cash to face the daily lines of depositors, because one single customer, the Ford Motor Company, refused to subordinate its claims for $7,500,000 on deposit. But for that, the RFC under existing rules could have been authorized to advance $50 million, enough cash to meet all conceivable demands.

President Hoover sent two emissaries, Secretary of the Interior Roy Chapin and Under Secretary of the Treasury Arthur Ballantine, to plead with the obdurate Henry Ford to give way. Though General Motors and Chrysler had already agreed to subordinate their own similar claims, Ford still would not budge. The Governor of Michigan had no other recourse than to declare a temporary bank holiday for the whole state. The runs spread to all the neighboring Midwestern states, Illinois, Indiana, Ohio, and there was the devil to pay.

In behalf of the Federal Reserve System, George Harrison now appealed to Hoover to declare a national bank moratorium as of February 17, 1933. This was a fortnight before Roosevelt was to take over; but Hoover could not obtain the President-elect's agreement to share responsibility for an action taken by his predecessor. Hoover refused to do anything, even on the Friday, March 2, when Harrison hurried to Washington to beg that he do something to stop the draining of the Federal Reserve's gold. He told Harrison that he "did not want his own last official act in office to be the closing of all the banks."

In nearly all the forty-eight states, and finally at the weekend in New York, bank doors were closed as the new President began his Inaugural address. The blunders and delays that preceded this event gave the dénouement of the bank crisis all the greater dramatic force when it came. Roosevelt not only inveighed against the "money-changers," but immediately after his address by emergency decrees ordered the closing of all banks, embargoed shipments of gold, and called for an immediate special session of Congress to enact emergency laws. Thus the Emergency Banking Act of March 9, 1933, was passed virtually without debate. Among other provisions the new law authorized the Federal Reserve Banks to give credit to member banks *at their discretion against all assets,* whereas hitherto such credit had been allowed only against government bonds and prime commercial loans. As George Harrison wrote in his diary, printed money was to be issued against "all kinds of junk, even the brass spittoons in old-fashioned country banks." The central bank authorities themselves were shocked at what they were led to do. Harrison's memorandum of the bank holiday went on:

> The first thing we realized was that we were actually out of money. Money in circulation, that is, hoarded money mostly (in the hands of the public), had jumped to the record figure of six billion by March, 1933. We had closed in the midst of a great bank run, and as far as we knew would reopen under the same condition. Should the panic continue for some time . . . there would not be enough Federal Reserve notes, secured by 40 percent gold under existing law, to meet all demands. This time it was decided that we not use Clearing-House scrip, as in previous crises, but real currency.

The Federal Reserve examiners were to estimate the "good assets" in a bank, issue sufficient credits, and certify such banks as they approved for prompt reopening—or if not approved, for closing in the hands of court receivers. Having actually run out of paper currency, Treasury officials located in some storehouse a pile of unused national bank notes in five and ten dollar denominations dating from the nineteenth century; these they decided to put to use quickly by simply overprinting on them "Federal Reserve Bank Notes." Nothing was said about their being payable in gold or silver. (Later, when calm was restored to the public, they were gradually withdrawn from circulation.)

Raymond Moley, who was then working closely with Secretary of the Treasury William Woodin as well as with Roosevelt, wrote afterward in his memoirs: "The most dramatic decision we made involved Giannini's Bank of America." This one bank still accounted for about half the savings and a third of the checking accounts of all California, a total of about a million depositors, mostly small, and its closure would paralyze business on the West Coast. It was now up to the veteran Governor John Calkins of the San Francisco Reserve

Bank, who had sometimes censured the business methods of the huge banking chain, to determine which member banks in his district were in condition "to withstand all withdrawals that could possibly be made." He could then allot credits and certify them for reopening, according to the terms of the Emergency Banking Act. President Roosevelt had promised that only "sound banks" would reopen; about 5000, in fact, were closed. The Bank of America, however, held some $200 million in real estate mortgages, which were not now very liquid; moreover there were heavy debts of Transamerica in the bank's portfolio, which Federal Reserve examiners had repeatedly objected to. Calkins evidently preferred that the hairline decision should be made in Washington, and sent his adverse report to Secretary of the Treasury Woodin. This report, it was said afterward, did not give recognition to some recent improvement in the bank's condition.

During the week of the Bank Holiday, Giannini had not been idle. Ever more conscious of the importance of political pressure, he had been setting out lines leading to the new President. He had also asked the two California Senators, Johnson and McAdoo, to keep a sort of deathwatch for the "people's bank" at the Treasury Department. Meanwhile the lawyer for William Randolph Hearst (who with McAdoo had ensured Roosevelt's nomination at Chicago) was actually encamped in the White House offices urging the bank's cause with Roosevelt's personal aides. Preliminary reports indicated that Secretary Woodin favored reopening; but on the last Sunday, before large city banks were to be certified, Giannini learned by telephone that Woodin, having received a belated memorandum from Calkins in San Francisco which judged the bank as "hopelessly insolvent," had reconsidered the affair and reversed himself. It was 6:30 P.M. California time when A. P. heard this black news, and he immediately called Secretary Woodin to expostulate with him. The Secretary finally promised he would take the matter up with "the man in the

White House," who had already gone to bed. Hearst's lawyer also sent urgent messages to Roosevelt in Giannini's behalf from the press lord of San Simeon.

Giannini's dream of a nationwide bank chain had been dissolved; he had fought his way back to control of the huge California institution he had been building up these thirty years; now he waited through the night to learn if it would all be finally destroyed.

After an all-night session at the White House during which other urgent affairs were ironed out at the last moment, the President spared the Bank of America. Shortly after dawn on Monday—at 8:00 A.M. in Washington—it was learned that the Secretary of the Treasury had had his mind changed for him again! That morning the 410 branches of the Bank of America opened for business as usual in the first echelon of large Reserve member banks. Roosevelt's Sunday night "fireside talk" over the radio succeeded in calming the public, whose money came flowing back from chimneys, cellars, and mattresses to the reopened banks. Once again the banks were to flourish, and none more than Giannini's. As Governor of New York, Roosevelt had recently witnessed the disastrous effects of the receivership of the Bank of United States, one of the larger branch banks with many small depositors, which many believed should have been kept open. In the case of Giannini's institution, the decision was affected by concern for all of one million depositors. But after Monday, March 13, 1933, Roosevelt's aides did not fail to remind A. P. that the New Deal had "saved his hide." Giannini, almost alone among big bankers, was an ardent champion of F.D.R. and a generous donor to Democratic Party campaign funds.

As earlier, he continued to be California's perennial boomer. His bank's frozen assets began to thaw out, and soon it began to expand again, buying more banks and pushing out new branches. Transamerica, loaded with foreclosed real estate and vast tracts of farmlands, became the world's largest farm owner. What did it matter? To the "big bull of the West," as some now called Giannini, the future value of California land was immeasurable. For sixty years he had seen the population grow more rapidly than in any other region; his faith in the Golden State was never diminished. It was indeed impervious to periodic reversals of fortune, and who can now say that he was wrong?

THE FALL OF THE ALMIGHTY
DOLLAR

The new President cut a dashing figure during the dark days of the economic crisis. His cheery radio chat had brought most of the nation's frightened depositors back to the re-opened banks to deposit the currency they had been hoarding. In the first hundred days Congress enacted the emergency and reformatory legislation, characteristic of the early New Deal, controlling banks, and farming and railroad reciverships; it also authorized public works spending, appropriations for the relief of the unemployed, and national planning for indus-trial recovery (the NIRA). The reopening of the banks and the stock market—which began to rise in spectacular fashion —was made even more festive when Congress restored to the people their long-desired beer.

The Senate's "Pecora Committee," as it came to be called, meanwhile, continued its investigation of the securities and investment field with even more scathing exposures of financial malfeasance. It mattered little at the time however; there was, at the beginning of his term, even a sort of love fest between Roosevelt and the House of Morgan. Indeed all groups seemed to recover spirits that had been numbed by terror; the rich and the middle classes had their banks and brokers going again, the poor had the dole, and there was also beer and circuses.

By the summer of 1932 manufacturing activity had fallen so low that there were shortages of articles of everyday utility. The declining movement had slowed; even the stock market, which was closed during the national "bank holiday," had begun to creep back from the lowest levels seen since 1893. (General Electric had fallen to $10 a share, General Motors to $5, and Standard Oil of New Jersey to about $20.) Our weak national banking system undoubtedly delayed a partial recovery that had already manifested itself in Europe a year earlier. At the time of the winter's bank runs in 1933 the stock market here stood at a measurably better level than in the preceding summer and no longer gave ground. On March 16, 1933, a day after the big (Reserve) city banks opened, the New York Stock Exchange and other exchanges opened for business.

On that day I went down to the Street and found the financial district so quiet it seemed like a ghost town. Many brokerage firms had closed down; the rest functioned with skeleton staffs. Just before the opening bell at 10:00 a.m. I entered the board room of one of the leading firms founded by members of one of America's "Sixty Families." A younger scion of that family, whom I had known for some years, was now managing partner of the firm. He greeted me good-humoredly as an "early bird." In a spacious room that could have held a hundred or more persons, I saw only two or three gloomy customers, who watched the opening in silence. I had brought with me some government bonds, the fragments of my small estate, which had been well liquidated in 1931, and asked the broker to sell them and invest the proceeds in ten different "blue chip" industrials. We bought some shares of General Electric, Union Carbide, and J. C. Penney Stores, ranging from $10½ to $20 per share, with a conservative margin of 50 percent. The broker looked at me as if I were quite a brave fellow. I counted strongly on the combined effects of currency inflation and Government deficit spending, which I believed would lift prices generally.

That day marked the beginning of a new bull market, the averages rising about 15 percent in a single session. The movement continued straight upward until July, when the market indices were approximately 100 percent higher than those of March 16; then stocks leveled off, or declined moderately. I was able, at any rate, to recoup a part of the losses I had sustained in the Crash.

In his assumption of wartime powers by the proclamations issued on March 6 and shortly afterward, Roosevelt had not only taken control of all the banks in the United States but also of the gold held in the Federal Reserve System; at the same time he placed an embargo on the export of gold. For the first time since the Civil War, the dollar had been cut adrift from the gold standard. Later an Emergency Farm Relief bill, calculated to raise crop prices, permitted the issuance of three billion dollars of greenbacks. The road to currency inflation was now wide open.

In the panic periods of past times, the nation's banks had somehow fended for themselves, sometimes killing each other off, sometimes organizing their own rescue parties under an improvised leadership of the strongest in the pack. But lately the banks had experienced phenomenal failures and reform was long overdue; the Federal Reserve System had proved unequal under existing law to cope with the crisis. Thus President Roosevelt became in effect the "dictator" of the banking field, control of which the big "money changers" had relinquished. What this amounted to was the beginning of the active phase of state capitalism under the New Deal.*

Roosevelt, heading the "crisis state" at the time of the bank holiday, might have been able to nationalize the banks, as two or three of the Brain Trusters urged. One of them, Professor Rexford Tugwell, recommended this course, proposing that the U.S. Post Offices, which received deposits then, be used as branches of a state-owned bank system. But while Roosevelt enjoyed innovation, he never entertained the thought of pursuing a consistent socialist program. His contention that he worked always to save the capitalist system was to be fully borne out.

The bankers were aware that they had put their heads into the lion's jaws and at first tried to be friendly. Russell C. Leffingwell, who was later to replace Lamont as head man at Morgan's, wrote the President in most complimentary terms that he had "saved" the nation by going off the gold standard. George Harrison, the top bureaucrat of the New York Reserve Bank, acted as the go-between for the Wall Street complex and the man in the White House. Harrison believed fervently in the "separation of the central bank and the state," by which he meant that the Federal Reserve must be autonomous. But Roosevelt's crisis government was now making deep incursions into its provinces under pressure from the angry farm bloc, together with silver and copper producers, who cried for currency inflation. The Treasury's increasing deficit also aroused Harrison's fears that the printing press

---

* It may be argued that the conservative President Hoover introduced the principles of state capitalism with the government's credit bank, the RFC, replenishing vital capital lost by private banks and railroads; but he performed his role with reluctance, and the RFC's "relief" loans to business organizations were more severely limited than under Roosevelt, who never shrank from exerting his full powers. State capitalism is defined as the system under which the government supports and controls and also owns, in part, capitalist enterprises.

would be used to cover the endless debt of the national government.

One of Harrison's first private visits to Roosevelt, in May, 1933, was for the purpose of beseeching him to postpone the greenback issue. This the President refused. Actually so much hoarded money was being redeposited in banks that only a small amount of the new greenbacks was circulated, and this was later withdrawn. The supply of hoarded gold was also being restored to the central bank by presidential dictate. Meanwhile the Reserve System again undertook "open market" operations in buying bonds, increasing bank reserves, and making money easier. That, coupled with the prospect of currency inflation, contributed not only to the recovery in the stock market, but also to a sharp advance in wheat and cotton prices—which made a happy springtime for the New Deal.

At the start the dollar had fallen moderately, to a discount of about 14 percent from its former parity with other currencies; but thereafter it tended to rise in the international money market, against the depreciated pound sterling which was held at about $3.50 after 1931. The next logical move was to open discussions with the British, seeking to stabilize the two currencies and to avoid a competitive race in devaluation. At the same time Secretary of State Cordell Hull was about to open a historic international conference, to be held in London in June, looking toward reciprocal trade agreements. Hence Roosevelt in May authorized Harrison to sail for London and negotiate quietly a preliminary understanding with the Bank of England people on the currency exchange rates, on which future trade would be based.

The prosperous nineteen twenties had been the heyday of the central or government bankers, who met together periodically in secret conclave (sometimes at romantic and secluded castles) to regulate the world's gold and monetary exchanges and even rates of bank interest. This breed of central bankers considered themselves experts in all matters of money or gold. They had their central banking "mystique"— indeed the Bank of England's Sir Montagu Norman hoped equilibrium and prosperity could be ordained by world monetary control. Since the movements of international funds necessitated by the huge German reparation payments tended to disrupt exchanges, Norman used to meet with Benjamin Strong of the Reserve Bank of New York and with the heads of the Banque de France and the Reichsbank to negotiate monetary agreements that had virtually the force of international treaties. After the adoption of the Young Plan of 1929, which reduced German reparations, the Bank for International Settlements, also called the "World Bank," was established at Basel, Switzerland, to clear payments between the government banks by simply crediting them on its books. Stock control of the relatively small World Bank was shared by the several European central banks and a number of large American banks engaged in international trade and finance. A retiring executive of the Chase Bank of New York became titular chairman, while an American lawyer, Leon Fraser, who specialized in international law and had been adviser to Owen D. Young during the Young Plan conferences, was appointed deputy chairman and its real manager. (In 1930 Fraser was named chairman.) The World Bank, under its American management, symbolized the United States' role as chief creditor.

I had known Leon Fraser in 1917 when he was a young instructor in political science at Columbia College and before he entered the Army to serve on the Judge Advocate's staff in France. When the war ended he had become a member of an international law firm in Paris serving American corporations and banks. After he returned to the United States in 1936 to fill a high post in Wall Street, I went to see him, and learned a good deal about how the international bankers had managed their affairs during the crisis years. Their well-intentioned plans to stabilize European and American exchanges had all been swept aside by the cataclysm of 1929. Even the reduced scale of German reparations continued to divert large sums to the United States, the main creditor of the Allies; but the American bankers lent the money back to the Germans by selling German bonds to our investing public. The British also made a good business of lending to the Germans at high interest rates, while borrowing the money in London at low rates.

The depression created greater unemployment in Germany than in any other European country. Bruening's government, Fraser said, found itself in straits and tried to effect an *Anschluss* with Austria in order to strengthen itself politically against right wing opposition parties in Germany, while at the same time it made arrangements to obtain a large loan through a long-term (foreign) bond issue. "However, the French suspicion of the Germans," Fraser went on, "and at the same time the discord that had arisen between the French and the British in 1931, caused abandonment of the plan for an international loan that might have saved the Bruening regime." The French drew money out of Austrian banks, forcing the suspension of the Kreditanstalt, Vienna's largest bank; this in turn tied up the German Reichsbank funds, which were owed to the British; and in a chain reaction the British were driven to suspend gold payments and devalue their currency. Then the economic situation of Germany became worse than ever; the masses of unemployed on doles and the renewed threat of money devaluation to the middle class were factors leading to the accession of Hitler to power, which, Fraser believed, might have been avoided if not for the undercover hostilities of the British and French financiers.

During five years in Basel, Fraser was in a strategic position to watch the unfolding of the European tragedy and to discover for himself, as he said afterward, that "the whole rotten structure of Victorian finance, which had grown up crazily in Europe, was doomed." Together with the central bank's money managers, he would run from one danger point to another. "We would set up a dam, and if it didn't hold, we would go and set up another somewhere else, though knowing it would also fail." The central bankers were the insiders who "knew in advance that their . . . accounts were going down, down, down." Fraser, by disposition a cool diplomat, was chiefly occupied in protecting the interests of American banks involved in Germany's "frozen assets."

To return to Harrison, he met with what was sometimes called the "World's Most Exclusive Club" in late May, 1934, when its members got together in a private room of the British Treasury Building in London. Professor O. W. Sprague of Harvard, the Reserve Bank's economic adviser, and James Warburg, an aide to Roosevelt, accompanied him. Sir Montagu Norman sat at the head of the table. At these palavers of the government bankers, Sir Montagu was rated as a "wizard." He also liked to assume the figure of a Mystery Man who traveled to secret meetings in disguise, even wearing false whiskers. But neither Sir Montagu's wizardy nor his whiskers, on this occasion, could save Europe's finances. The central bankers proceeded to work out the exchange rates of the dollar, pound, and French franc, within the proximate limits that President Roosevelt had told Harrison would be acceptable. At about the same time Secretary Cordell Hull's international conference had begun its meetings in London to try to stimulate trade through reciprocal tariff concessions. One of its American delegates happened to learn of the results of the "secret" central bankers' negotiations on currency and leaked this news to the press. At once the world market prices of wheat, cotton, and other farm commodities crashed, to the consternation of the Roosevelt Administration which had been struggling to raise them.

To the President back in Washington it seemed that the British were asking too high a price for agreement: they wanted the trade advantage of a depreciated pound at about $3.75 to $4.00 "more or less." He, however, was determined to keep his hand free to try more inflation, if it should be needed, and wanted the pound at nearer $5.00. Thereupon he reversed himself and in a brusque cable rejected the gentlemen's agreement worked out by Harrison. To the dismay of Secretary Hull he sent further orders via Raymond Moley that made it impossible even to frame some patched up agreements for the larger reciprocal trade conference. The White House also took the position that it "had not been informed about Mr. Harrison's visit to London." Harrison said in private that he felt as if he had been kicked in the face by a mule. He, Warburg, and Sprague all testified that the President had made a verbal agreement with them to accept a rate of $4.00 to $4.25 for the pound sterling.

After mid-July the 1933 boom in the stock market came to a sudden end; now there came reports of business activity slowing down again. The war of the dollar against the pound and other leading currencies was resumed. On August 29, 1933, the President, under his emergency powers, raised the Treasury's buying price for gold mined in the United States from $20.67 an ounce to all of $29.62, but the dollar still refused to go down proportionately in terms of foreign exchange markets as he had hoped.

According to the New Deal theorists, the value of leading commodities such as wheat and cotton ought to have been controlled automatically by the rise or fall of gold prices. Nothing of the kind happened; and so in October, 1933, Harrison was once more summoned to the White House.

In the Oval Room, as he related, he found the President surrounded by a large group of Treasury and RFC officials, among them Jesse Jones of the RFC, Henry Morgenthau, Jr., Farm Credit Administrator (but soon to succeed Secretary of the Treasury Woodin), and Professor George Warren of Cornell, represented to Harrison as an economic expert. Harrison, however, thought they were all economic chuckleheads. Professor Warren stood before a blackboard and gave a discourse which the President followed eagerly. Harrison had learned that Warren was a biologist who had once invented some feeding formula that induced chickens to lay more eggs; and he greatly feared the man would lead the country to financial anarchy. The Reserve Bank Governor argued that the professor's ideas and methods were wrong. The price of gold could not be raised unless concerted buying operations by the U.S. Government were carried out on an international scale.

The President responded: "My object is to raise the price of wheat and cotton. Otherwise we are going to have an agrarian revolution in this country." He was trying to do it quickly by bidding up gold; and it seemed to him the methods that the Federal Reserve proposed might take "maybe two years," and he did not have enough time. But since Harrison urged that the dollar's exchange value could not be effectively forced down in foreign money centers without gaining control of the international gold market—by working with Europe's central banks—Roosevelt finally came around, saying, "Very well, let George do it, since he knows more about it." The RFC would put up the money, and the Reserve Bank of New York would buy gold abroad in the markets it knew well.

By conviction Harrison was a hard-money man; now he found himself elected to drive the dollar off the gold standard! The year before he had been fighting the "battle for the dollar" under Hoover; now he would be working under Roosevelt to debase the United States currency and speed inflation. It was like asking a sworn teetotaler to swallow a bottle of gin. Yet the world was in crisis; it was better for the "Fed" to carry on such monetary manipulations than to leave them to some expert on chicken feed. Like all bureaucratic institutions, such as the military or the police, the "Fed" had its technical secrets; it "knew where the bodies were hidden," and where gold could be had for rupees or dollars. Harrison took a deep breath and said, "I am willing," but stipulated certain conditions that must be agreed to before he could undertake this job. First, he demanded a free hand to buy or sell gold without waiting for orders from Washington; second, "I would want to keep Governor Norman of the Bank of England and M. Moret of the Banque de France informed about what we are doing. That is the way we have always worked together in the past."

There were angry murmurs from the group of New Deal advisers. Harrison was under suspicion here; and even more suspect were those secretive foreign money managers. But Roosevelt spoke sweetly: Harrison had been picked to do the job, and "he ought to have the conditions he feels he needs."

Harrison moved up to the President's chair and whispered that he appreciated the trust the President had shown in him, then added: "It is my sincere belief that the plan may not work out as you hope, but I promise you I will do my very best."

What Harrison feared was that other nations would be competing to lower their currencies, or would raise tariffs, nullifying the inflationary effect of the gold buying. Day by day he bought gold that came in through all the highways and byways of the world. He was more close-mouthed than ever. Much of the business of a great central bank is hush-hush, and a leak of information about the gold business would have meant millions in profits for speculators. Now the dollar really began to sink. Secretary of the Treasury Morgenthau, whom Harrison considered an adversary, said to me later, "Although Governor Harrison was opposed to our policies, when he gave his word, he carried it out faithfully."

The President and Morgenthau actually set the price bid for gold each day, sometimes in frivolous sport, pitching a coin to decide what it would be. Harrison's account corresponds closely with that given in Morgenthau's diaries. For weeks on end the money market was in chaos. Governor Norman of the Bank of England grew frantic over the transatlantic telephone, but when the President learned of this he reflected only mischievous pleasure. Harrison found that Roosevelt, ill-versed in economics, understood with much difficulty how one trades in gold and that the trader must sometimes *sell* as well as buy the stuff.

At the end of January, 1934, the price of gold was pegged at $35.20 an ounce, setting the dollar at about 59 cents in terms of its former gold value. Bullion poured into the United States thanks to the profits gained by such revaluation; the Treasury's store rose to above $8 billion. Yet the gold purchasing scheme did not result in proportionately higher prices for farm products in this country; these were achieved quite a while later, after the Agricultural Adjustment Association's farm allotment plan, drought, and increased Government spending combined to raise values. Other governments used other methods to increase the return to farmers for their crops. The entire gold buying program was probably a miscarriage. In the end it made very little difference, since the weight of the United States economy in world markets was so important that other nations gradually adjusted their exchanges, tariffs, and prices to conform with the new dollar.

The bankers who had been so delighted with the Roosevelt of the crisis days in March became completely disenchanted with their quondam hero once he began the experiment in monetary devaluation. They held that it could not fail to spread confusion and fear of loss in the world markets. Those who had spent their lives with sound money as their stock in trade felt confounded at this seemingly useless debasement, which left them with what the former Governor of New York, Al Smith, dubbed the "baloney dollar." The wise men of the Eastern money centers were embittered. To a Giannini of California, however, who ran a bank mostly for small depositors and who hoped land, building construction, and mining would recover, the departure from the gold standard made little difference. Among economic experts, John Maynard Keynes virtually alone applauded Roosevelt's inflationary measures and his deficit spending. The "sound money" group of presidential aides—Budget Director Lewis Douglas, Assistant Secretary of the Treasury Dean Acheson, and the young banker James Warburg—made public their opposition to the President's monetary schemes, and resigned. The chorus criticizing Roosevelt as a "demogogue" rising from the bankers and financiers grew ever stronger. It was moderated somewhat in January, 1934, when the President announced that the dollar was pegged at fifty-nine cents in terms of gold and that purchases of foreign gold were to be halted.

At all events the bankers, during the early days of the New Deal, had lost face before the great public; and as a group they were definitely in the doghouse as far as Washington was concerned. As a consequence of the exposure to which they had been subjected by the Senate's Pecora Committee, the rulers of our most venerable financial institutions were nowadays stigmatized as "banksters" in the parlance of the New Dealers. Roosevelt himself pointed with pride to the emergency banking legislation of 1933 and other reform measures introduced in the investment business, claiming they had brought about the *transfer of the financial capital of the United States from Wall Street to Washington.*

In 1934 the Roosevelt Administration began drafting revisions of the Federal Reserve Act to give the (politically appointed) Reserve Board at Washington stricter control over the regional Reserve Banks. In truth these new controls were aimed at the Reserve Bank of New York, which held the effective power to direct the "open market committee's" bond-buying moves, to carry on deals in currency and gold with foreign banks, and thus to manipulate the nation's total money supply. In drafting this bill the principal adviser of the Administration was a young Western banker, Marriner Eccles of Utah, who, like Giannini, opposed the hard money policies of the Eastern bankers and also sought to strip the Fed's giant New York branch of its decisive powers. The "Eccles Bill," as it was called, proposed to make the Reserve Board at Washington the real head of the System, instead of "just a debating society"; it also became known that Roosevelt intended to install the monetary heretic Eccles as Chairman of the Board of Governors (as it would be called).

A stiff fight over the proposed bill developed in the Senate, with much of the opposition being directed by George Harrison. He spoke softly when he came to the White House, but he worked behind the scenes with conservative Senators of both parties to block Roosevelt's banking measures.

Deficit spending required that many billions of dollars be raised by the sale of new government bonds. It was mainly the Reserve Bank of New York that distributed such bond issues in cooperation with investment firms of Wall Street and La Salle Street. It also "managed" the market for these bonds by expert buying and selling tactics. Harrison, as impartial public servant, called on the new Secretary of the Treasury Henry Morgenthau, Jr., to offer his services in this field by furnishing advance estimates of bond market conditions and interest rates. But Morgenthau rebuffed him, dealing with him at arm's length, for he was suspicious of a man he considered the agent of the Morgan-Baker banks. Thereafter the Secretary handled the flotation of bond issues through the facilities of the Treasury Department. In explaining his policy he said privately. "If the big banks could have stopped the Roosevelt Administration from borrowing, we would have been licked right then and there." Although Morgenthau was a millionaire by inheritance, his own business experience had been limited to running a large apple farm neighboring Roosevelt's estate at Hyde Park. Harrison, for his part, thought this fanatical partisan of the President an ignoramus, and said that Morgenthau's suspicions that big bankers might not support the U.S. Treasury were ridiculous. At a time when business was slack, the banks were lending little and had no other alternative but to put their increasing surplus funds into U.S. bonds, even at the low interest rates prevailing.

During the Congressional election campaign of 1934, the controversy between the friends of business and banking and the new political powers grew fierce. Harrison felt much concern at the effect of all this public squabbling; and when the chance presented itself to bring about a truce, he leaped at it.

Early in October, 1934, he was at the White House discussing the new banking act, then being debated in Congress, when Roosevelt amiably invited him for a weekend cruise on the S.S. *Sequoia*. The mere rumor that George Harrison was to be Roosevelt's guest on a cruise caused tremors in the markets. As a matter of fact, Henry Morgenthau was also present.

The first day out Roosevelt began by saying to Harrison, "Now I want to talk to you about something—" and went on to complain of the hostile attitude shown by the banking community. "They oppose everything I do," he said, "even though it is with the intention of helping them." He had saved them, and now they were carping.

Harrison replied that not all the bankers spoke unjustly of the President, and cited Jackson Reynolds of the First National Bank of New York. Reynolds was known to have avoided many of the practices that had brought other bankers into disrepute; he had even voiced approval of some of Roosevelt's reform measures.

The President cried, "Then why in Heaven's name

doesn't Reynolds speak up?" Harrison explained that the veteran banker followed a rule of never issuing public statements. At dinner Roosevelt kept reverting to the subject of Reynolds, who he remembered had been his law professor at Columbia University twenty-five years before. Suddenly Roosevelt had an idea. There was to be a convention of the American Bankers' Association at Washington on October 24, and he himself had agreed to appear as its principal speaker. "Why not get Reynolds to come down and say some of those things at that convention?" Then Roosevelt might respond in kind and much of the ill-will between him and the banking fraternity might be dissolved.

Harrison was willing. Perhaps he could negotiate a historic concordat between the New Deal politicos and the embattled bankers. Reynolds was one of the truly Big Fish of finance. But time was short; surely the speakers' program had already been fixed. The President said that all could be arranged with the help of his own staff.

As soon as he touched shore, Harrison rushed to New York to lay the President's proposal before Reynolds. As an honest broker between the financial community and the all-powerful state, Harrison urged a "truce" that might bring business recovery. Reynolds was not sanguine. "I really don't like to do it," he said, "but it seems to me the most important speech I've been asked to make in all my life."

On the day before the A.B.A. convention, Harrison arrived in Washington with Reynolds in tow and steered him into the White House. There the speech that would introduce the President was submitted for Roosevelt's inspection. Jackson Reynolds, by repute an independent-minded old-school banker, was also a man of considerable learning and humor. His speech was a forceful appeal for cooperation between government and private finance, save for two passages in which he plainly had his tongue in his cheek. In one, he kidded the now mighty Roosevelt by recalling that while bankers had sometimes erred, Reynolds' former pupil had also shown some failings in his law studies. In another, a parable from classical history, he likened the warfare between the bankers and the Roosevelt administration to that of Hannibal's Carthaginians against the Romans of Scipio Africanus. After parleys for truce had failed, the two armies had virtually exterminated each other; Hannibal died in the field, while the Roman victor, Scipio, never got back from Spain.

The President, after a quick reading, appeared not to mind and gave the draft of the speech his blessing. That day a flock of bankers paid courtesy calls at the White House; and news dispatches carried rumors of the coming truce. In the evening the aged Reynolds retired early, while Harrison slipped away to some hidden retreat in Washington, where he could enjoy a game of poker with old friends. But within an hour the phone rang insistently, the Treasury's "bloodhounds" had tracked him down. Harrison was asked to fetch Mr. Reynolds and bring him to Morgenthau's office at once. Grumbling, he heeded the call.

Morgenthau and a group of Treasury aids, including Herman Oliphant and T. Jefferson Coolidge, were waiting for them like inquisitors. The Secretary, beside himself with rage, berated Reynolds, shouting that he had "belittled" and even ridiculed the President of the United States. The reference to Roosevelt's poor law-school record, he insisted, must come out; likewise the comparison between Roosevelt and Scipio. How could Reynolds dare to represent the bankers' association as a sovereign power dealing on terms of equality with the head of the National Government! An incredible scene followed, as Harrison recalls, in which Harrison and Reynolds, the dean of New York bankers—in this time of national crisis—disputed with Roosevelt's lieutenants over points of ancient history and over who won the Carthaginian wars. Harrison maintained that Morgenthau proved weak in Roman history, believing Hannibal had won that battle.

"Even a schoolboy should have known that Scipio, to whom Roosevelt was likened, had come out ahead of Hannibal."

Reynolds kept his temper, saying he had only come on the President's invitation, and offered to abandon the speech and go home at once. The affair was settled at length by Reynolds's agreeing to delete the offending paragraphs.

The A.B.A. convention at the Mayflower Hotel on October 24, 1934, had been held purposely at the Capitol city to signal a rapprochement, in fact a love feast, between the banking fraternity and the New Dealers. But it was noticed that when Roosevelt reached the platform he snubbed Reynolds. Reynolds had been expected to offer some defense of the bankers' side of the case; the esteemed bank he headed had not been accused of malpractice. But though Reynolds began by saying, "I do not mean to suggest any surrender," he was extremely conciliatory and at times humble; he admitted the bankers had been at fault in the nineteen twenties, declared they were now in a "chastened" mood, and ended by thanking Roosevelt for all he had done to "rescue and rehabilitate our shattered banking structure." It simply did not sound like the staunchly conservative and crusty old Reynolds. He even ventured that it was too early to have the Federal budget balanced when so many were impoverished and jobless.

Roosevelt's talk was mild and light in tone, though he did not neglect to remind the A.B.A. how its members had failed the country. He stressed, however, the program of "partnership" between banking and government which he felt he was carrying out. On the surface everything went off smoothly, and a truce seemed to have been effected. But some of the bankers were resentful of what seemed to have been a too-ready yielding to the President by Reynolds and the managers of the convention. Before they left Washington there was some grumbling among the delegates particularly when it leaked out that Roosevelt men had insisted on censoring Reynolds' speech, and that Reynolds and Harrison had humiliated themselves for fear that the President might refuse at the last moment to appear before the convention. When this became known, and was commented upon the newspaper columnists, the bitterness of the bankers waxed again. The American Liberty League had already been launched earlier in 1934 by conservative Democratic Party leaders to make propaganda in opposition to Roosevelt's reelection, and some of the big bankers joined its ranks. The warfare over the long-pending Banking Act (passed in 1935), which would reduce the power of the New York Reserve Bank, flared up again in Congress. Two years earlier, emergency banking legislation had given approval to statewide branch banking for national banks, to Giannini's great satisfaction. (He was able to put seventy-five more branches into the Bank of America.) Now he stood forth as the only one of the banking giants who supported the "Eccles Bill" in testimony before Congress. The big issue was the transfer of direction of the Reserve's open market committee from the New York unit to the Reserve Board at Washington. Giannini supported this measure in a blunt public statement:

> The group that has exerted the dominant influence has been the New York bankers. . . . Personally I would rather that this power be exercised by a public body in the public interest than by the New York banking fraternity.[1]

When this came to the President's attention, he wrote Giannini a letter expressing his grateful recognition of his help. There was much talk of Giannini's growing influence, which his Eastern rivals resented. At times Giannini found it expedient to treat with the President through third parties, such as Postmaster General Farley.

Giannini was again buying up banks in Nevada, Washington, and Oregon through his holding company Transamerica. He had hoped that an article of the new banking act would approve of interstate or regional branch banking within the Federal Reserve Districts, which often crossed over state lines. But this idea was finally dropped at the last moment at the insistence of Secretary Morgenthau and of Eastern banking authorities, who favored keeping branch systems within state limits. Giannini nevertheless persisted in lobbying for new bills that would favor his drive toward a nationwide chain. In the meantime he gave open support to Roosevelt's campaign for reelection in 1936, visiting him several times that year and on one occasion dining with the President at the White House. At the time it was believed that the Transamerica chain system could exert a decisive influence in an election year in California. In the late summer Giannini reported to Farley that he had made a tour of several hundred of his bank's branches, and he confidently predicted that Roosevelt would carry California "by at least 500,000 votes." The margin of victory proved to be almost twice as high.

In the old days bankers wasted little time on politics. But in the new environment of the nineteen thirties those who believed that they must manage to live in "partnership" with the government gave a great deal of time and thought to political action.

BROKERS IN UNIFORM

After the passage of the National Industrial Recovery Act in June, 1933, the managers of leading industrial corporations trooped to Washington to sign agreements, under the NRA "codes," shortening hours of labor and, in some cases, limiting production and fixing prices. The representatives of labor also came as prospective partners to these "industrial planning" codes to benefit by improvement in hours and re-employment and by added opportunity for union organizing. The farmers and the industrialists of food and tobacco were also regimented for agricultural planning under the Agricultural Adjustment Act. Then it was the turn of Wall Street and the securities exchanges to undergo reform and regulation.

One of the first of the New Deal emergency measures, the Banking Act of 1933, had ordered commercial banks to divest themselves of their affiliated securities corporations. Morgan and Company chose to remain a bank, separating itself from its underwriting department, and establishing a separate concern, Morgan, Stanley and Company, to manage its investment business under executives formerly attached to the bank. National City, Chase, and other banks acted in similar fashion. It was very much like the break-up before the war of the old Standard Oil Trust into thirty-three different corporations, whereby a monopoly was changed into an oligopoly. Some of the old investment banks, like Kuhn, Loeb, on the other hand, chose to give up banking and confine themselves to underwriting securities. But more drastic changes followed.

For many months a team of Roosevelt's White House aides were engaged, in consultation with members of Congress, in drafting an elaborate bill to regulate the securities exchanges, their general plan being to adapt in this country the provisions of the old British Companies Act. The principal authors of the draft were three young lawyers—James L. Landis, Thomas G. Corcoran, and Benjamin V. Cohen—who were advised by Felix Frankfurter of the Harvard Law School, Roosevelt's unofficial legal expert. In February, 1934, the draft of the Securities Exchange Act, known as the Fletcher-Rayburn Bill, was ready and sent to Congress by Roosevelt for passage. The measure proposed to ban all forms of stock-market manipulation and rigging; it would control the flow of credit for margin trading, and would set up a government agency to maintain surveillance over the markets and punish violators under the law.

When Wall Street learned what was in store, a great cry of protest arose from the men of stocks and bonds. The New York Stock Exchange's President Whitney issued press statements promising the undying opposition of the financial community. As hearings on the bill were opened under Congressman Sam Rayburn of Texas, Whitney arrived by special train, bringing with him a crowd of petitioners, who camped in Washington hotels for weeks on end. House and Senate members were deluged with letters and telegrams from the nation's banks and insurance companies. The brain trusters Corcoran and Cohen, who testified on the bill at the hearings, later described the concerted movement of opposition directed by Whitney as "the most powerful lobby ever seen in Washington," and declared that the bill's chief sponsor in the House, Rayburn, came under "extraordinary pressure." Rayburn, then the Democratic floor leader and soon afterward elected Speaker, was a man of moderate views, disposed to compromise, but Whitney's scare tactics put his back up. For weeks the Congressman knew no peace; and the opposition became so shrill that President Roosevelt had occasion to issue a public rebuke to the Stock Exchange contingent. Whitney in reply ranted before the Congressional committee that the New Deal was attempting to seize control of the financial district's machinery; he warned that it would bring disaster for industry and labor, possibly a "strike of capital." Earlier, Whitney had prevented member brokers from answering one of the questionnaires of the Pecora Committee; now he refused to allow representatives of Congress to examine the operations of specialist brokers on the Exchange who recorded and matched orders for buying and selling of securities. His own Board of Governors, however, had overruled him in the matter late in March, 1934, and permitted such an inquiry. The moderate element in Wall Street, in fact, had begun to bypass Whitney and work sub rosa with the Administration.

A succession of high-powered corporation lawyers and financial experts testified day after day against the bill. Corcoran, the vivacious young presidential assistant, distinguished himself in this debate by the thoroughness with which he had mastered all details and met every argument. He explained afterward that his colleague Benjamin Cohen, who was strong on research, foresaw all contingencies and briefed him before he took the stand, enabling him to make a brilliant exposition of the bill's complex provisions. He said later, "Rayburn and I stood alone against all the batteries of lawyers sent by Morgan's and the Stock Exchange—and we won out!" Judging from the publicity released by the Stock Exchange, one would have thought Corcoran and Cohen were political firebrands. Actually Corcoran was a cherubic young Irishman who had graduated from Harvard Law School and had begun practice with the old Wall Street firm of Cotton and Franklin. In 1932 he had been appointed to the legal staff of the RFC under President Hoover. Cohen was also a man of unimpeachably bourgeois background; a native of Indiana, now nearing forty, he had also studied at Harvard Law School and had practiced public law for the power commissions of Illinois and Wisconsin. He was moreover a man of independent means and knew enough about the securities markets to have liquidated his investments prior to the 1929 Crash. He had no leanings toward socialism, but he was a devoted disciple of Supreme Court Justice Louis D. Brandeis, an arch individualist who believed that the state should intervene in the world of private business only to right the balance between the needs of public welfare and the drives of "irresponsible power."

The moderate element in Wall Street, led by E. A. Pierce (one of the brokers with numerous branch offices), while agreeing to accept reform and control, elicited from the Government a series of compromises on technical grounds, which presumably would allow the law to work better. In its final form, the bill provided for a new Federal agency, the Securities and Exchange Commission; it was to be composed of five members appointed by the President who would administer and police the markets.

At the time of the great hullabaloo over its passage, I asked Ben Smith for his view of the measure, off the record.

He exploded: "That law was long overdue—people could get away with murder in the market." He was for it, and he thought the Old Guard in the Exchange, headed by Whitney, had made things worse by opposing it so stubbornly. On the other hand he guessed that it would effect little change. Men would go on speculating, winning and losing. Those seasoned operators, Ben Smith and Joe Kennedy—both of whom had made large donations to the Democratic Party in 1932—had known in advance what was coming in the way of reform, and professed to welcome it. But they could not forbear having one more caper in the old market before the Government police moved in.

After Roosevelt took office, when the tide began to rise again in the Street, Ben Smith turned to the bullish side. Kennedy, who actually believed he had made Roosevelt President, had received no Cabinet appointment, but he had an inside line to what was going on in Washington. In the early spring of 1933 it was known that the end of prohibition was drawing near; bottles would be needed, at first for beer, later for whisky and gin. Kennedy therefore became a participant in an important pool that would operate in the stock of Libbey-Owens-Ford Glass Company. Smith on the other hand devoted his arts to the stock of American Commercial Alcohol. The directors wanted the price of their stock raised to the level of 40; they offered Thomas Bragg an option on 20,000 shares at 20, near its current level, and Bragg brought in Smith as the pool's manager. He bought and sold and "churned" the market with wash sales, so that its activity aroused interest, and he was able gradually to raise the price to 40, while stealthily reducing his original holdings. Excitement gathered about this stock; it traveled up through the 60s, the 70s and made a final desperate leap to 89, when Ben unloaded his last shares. This was in July, when the "Roosevelt Bull market" suddenly broke down. American Commercial Alcohol experienced a collapse and wound up below

30. These wild gyrations attracted the attention of the Pecora Committee in the late summer of 1933. Although everything done or undone was still lawful then, the Senate Committee invited "Sell-Em Ben" back to the witness stand. He, however, was on a journey to Indonesia, from which he did not return until it was too late for him to testify.

The operations of Joe Kennedy in the pool for Libbey-Owens-Ford also caught the attention of the Senate Committee, and its record, like that of Smith's pool, was spread out in detail in the Congressional Record as one more horrid example of skullduggery and market-rigging.

In this case the cream of the jest was that Libbey-Owens-Ford manufactured chiefly plate glass, not bottles. But the gullible part of the speculative public, dreaming of "repeal" stocks, confused its business purpose with that of the Owens Illinois Glass Company (which did make bottles). Elisha Walker, the man whom A. P. Giannini had recently driven out of the Transamerica Corporation, noticed that Libbey-Owens-Ford was depressed in price, and on learning that the company needed cash, he arranged for the pool to take an option on 125,000 shares of its stock at a price well below the current market. Joe Kennedy's share was about one-fifth of that block. Amid tremendous trading generated by market riggers the stock of Libbey-Owens-Ford rose nearly 50 percent within a few weeks, and the pool made a substantial profit.

Joe Kennedy's reputation in Wall Street was that of a "loner"; he would take part in a pool of Smith and Bragg, but he also operated secretly on his own. In R. J. Whelan's informed biography of the elder Kennedy, it is demonstrated that he was one of the toughest operatives in the Street and regarded as a bit too ruthless even by his hard-boiled associates, Smith, Bragg, et al.[1] (He was at the same time, in private life, an affectionate father who knew how to interest and stimulate his talented sons.) In his pool operations—though not in the Libbey-Owens-Ford business—he generally concealed himself by means of an agent or a dummy corporation, for he counted on receiving some high political appointment. In business, as in politics, Kennedy deployed all the arts of the born manipulator, and thus he was able to become the founder of a dynasty of money and political power. He used his Boston family's important political connections and his own money to raise himself to the highest circles of the Democratic Party; then he used his political contacts to make more money. Roosevelt's speech writer, Rexford Tugwell, recalled clearly how his drafts for public addresses by the presidential candidate in 1932 were often shown in advance to Kennedy (as well as to Baruch) at Roosevelt's request. Later, Kennedy also became very intimate with the President's eldest son James; while traveling with James Roosevelt to London in September, 1933, he was able to win a very profitable franchise for Scotch liquor, in the face of stiff competition, by displaying his close connections with the Roosevelt family. Liquor would provide a great leap forward for the Kennedy fortune at the time when he was out of the stock market and (temporarily) in government service.

Roosevelt's liberal followers were astonished when, in June, 1934, only a few months after the little scandal of the Libbey-Owens-Ford pool, it was announced by the White House that Kennedy was to be appointed chairman of the newly established Securities and Exchange Commission! Most people had expected that Landis or Pecora would have that office; but it was known that Wall Street hated Pecora, and Baruch, on being consulted, gave his approval to the choice of Kennedy, who was keen to have the job. One wag among the New Dealers remarked that "naming Joe Kennedy as chairman of the SEC was like setting a wolf to guard a flock of sheep."

To his intimates Roosevelt explained that the eminent plunger had made his pile and had promised to stay out of the market. He "knows all the tricks of the trade," Roosevelt added. There was also the political debt owing Kennedy for his donations to the Democratic Party chest, an important consideration. The Wall Street community was amused at finding Joe Kennedy in the role of reformer and cop, but made no objections. He was Irish, one of the Street's *nouveaux riches;* when he had once tried to do business with the younger Morgan, he had been snubbed; and it was known that he bore no love for the hierarchs of the financial community.

Up to the last moment Whitney had fought for the autonomy of the Exchange and repeatedly declared that the SEC law would destroy the free market. But once the law came into force he reversed himself completely and announced that the New York Stock Exchange would cooperate "one hundred percent" with the Commission. (Some thought Whitney's abrupt reversal comic.)

The SEC marked a decisive change in the relationship of the Government to the economy. Some held that the provisions of the law were innocuous or depended on their application by the Commissioners and their being tested in the Courts. The law indeed moved into untrodden ground, legally speaking; its main purpose was to require "truth in securities," that is, in dealings in securities. Registration of all corporate securities listed on Exchanges—and later the unlisted as well—was requisite, and with it explicit information about the corporation, far more than ever published hitherto. Options to syndicates, or pools, on blocks of stock at prices more advantageous than the current market were prohibited; and insiders or directors were forbidden to use their knowledge of their company's affairs for short-term profits in trading. Pool operations and rigging were barred, and short selling was limited to sales of one-eighth of a point above the last sale. There were even clauses in the law that forbade a man's "claiming ignorance of what his wife was doing in the market," or, in other words, evading responsibility by transfer of shares to a wife or child. Finally, violators of the law were made subject to fines of up to $10,000 and/or terms of imprisonment. Thus it was expected that the free market would no longer go unbridled as before.

Would the securities market be rendered more "artificial," as some claimed? Would the window and orphan be safer than before in making investments? Nothing in the law prevented a person from losing money. But the fact that there was "the cop at the corner"—that is, the SEC's detectives and experts watching the ticker tape for signs of unusual action or manipulation—would be a deterrent to crime. For the rest all would depend on how the government men implemented their broad authority.

Joe Kennedy had sworn before Roosevelt that he would serve as chairman of the Commission with entire devotion to the public interest. Moreover he was flanked by Pecora and Landis, New Dealers, and two other good men who were Republicans, former judge Robert E. Healey and George C. Mathews. No one doubted that Kennedy had a quick brain and ability as an administrator. At once he went to great pains to assure the financial fraternity that the SEC had come to improve Wall Street and not to bury it. He himself was not the sort to frighten the old bulls and bears. In mid-August, as he began his work, he said: "In a large measure, we would have the Exchanges do their own policing. They are in much better shape to do this than have the government send in a staff."

Stockbrokers, however, were not only frightened, they were heartbroken. The affairs of the Street had shrunk sadly in 1934. After the new law was passed, the market, which had lately become so dull that traders and clerks had to devise games to while the time away, staged a short declining movement. In truth the issuance of new capital securities was at one of its lowest levels in modern times, which was bad for business and employment; so great was the lack of confidence. Turnover was less than half the volume of 1933. It is plain that the old investment banks, such as Morgan and Kuhn, Loeb, were bitter at the Roosevelt Administration, no less than the great commercial banks. Some ardent New Dealers charged that a form of "sabotage," a "strike of capital," as Whitney had threatened, was being carried on by the financiers. Kennedy, aware of this tension, proceeded at the start to allay mistrust and bring about reconciliation.

After the new regime began, arrangements were sought for the five Commissioners, whose headquarters were in Washington, to pay a visit to the floor of the New York Stock Exchange and observe its operations with their own eyes. Permission was granted after some delay, and the great day of the visitation was set for September 18, 1934.

They arrived at Broad and Wall on the appointed morning, accompanied by members of their staff, and gathered in the office of Richard Whitney, who with studied politeness offered to serve as their guide. Some advance preparations had been made for the government men's tour of the trading floor. Members had been warned that they were to desist from the schoolboy larks they usually indulged in during a dull market session. Brokers had been known to slip a live mouse into a specialist's coat pocket, or place a fake gold brick atop a trading post; some floor brokers would throw paper pellets at colleagues, but now all that was out. It was intended that no overt incident mar the occasion, for there was a die-hard faction among the floor members who, if not disposed to do bodily harm to the Washington authorities, were certainly equal to thumbing their noses, or whistling or shouting at them to vent their displeasure.

The opening gong at ten saluted the entrance of the "Federal cops" (as the Street thought of them) under the protective wing of Mr. Whitney. For those dog days the floor was crowded, one hundred and fifty more brokers than usual were on hand, all of them staring at the Commissioners, while the Commissioners stared back, or shifted their feet. The tall

Mr. Kennedy, well known in these parts, appeared bland and disarming; Mr. Pecora, the sharp-witted inquisitor, was debonair; while the long-jawed James Landis, suspected of being a New Deal "extremist," wore his characteristic frown, and was described by one financial reporter as looking sourly at the people in the "enemy camp." The Commissioners moved about inspecting the various specialists' trading posts, marked "Steel," or "Telephone," or "American Can," and also the high-speed telegraphic mechanisms for receiving and sending orders and for recording prices and quantity of sales. After a while the brokers went on about their business as usual; the market was uncommonly dull. No one joked with the Commissioners, who left saying that they were impressed with the Exchange's spirit of cooperation.

Once returned to Washington, where they used temporary quarters in the old ICC Building, the SEC equipped a room with New York Stock tickers and a Curb Exchange ticker, as well as a Dow-Jones financial news ticker. The tapes were arranged so that they passed across a table under the eyes of Federal agents, while each minute a clock device stamped the time upon them. This was to enable the Sherlock Holmeses of the SEC to watch for signs of suspicious activity—abrupt rises or declines, or large quantity trades. The experts, it was said, "could detect pool operations in fifteen minutes."

The new regulatory law applied to numerous lesser Exchanges all over the country; hence the SEC soon established regional branches in San Francisco, Chicago, and four other key cities, with the most important of these branches in downtown New York. Beginning with a staff of a hundred auditors, lawyers, economists, and secretaries, the SEC soon had over four hundred persons checking quotations, studying the registration papers of some five thousand listed corporations, and also conducting investigations in the field more or less discreetly.

Under Kennedy the Commission, whose powers were

both very broad and vaguely defined, proceeded with much prudence; for it was feared that a rude show of power might upset important applecarts. At a time when the financiers were still bitter at Roosevelt and his "rubber dollar," the underwriting of new capital issues needed for plant and construction was undoubtedly blocked. Each new bond or stock issue now required that investment firms register it with an accompanying statement of the character and history of the corporation, the risks involved, and the terms of its sale; and their registration form was to be approved by the SEC. The underwriters, therefore, wanted reassurance that after they had "registered" their issue they would not be taken to jail for some violation. Like Jesse Jones at the RFC, Kennedy urged the brokers to "be smart" and take the Government in as "partner." Meanwhile he instituted very few prosecutions, and these affected only some bucket shops and petty thieves selling "blue sky" stock in the unlisted market. In the first year, action by the Justice Department was called for only in thirty-six cases; while four times as many prosecutions were recommended in the second year, after Kennedy resigned.

The investment bankers did not even know what would happen to the dollar, or the claims of gold-bond holders, until the Supreme Court ruled in favor of the Government's revaluation. Then at last one of the "independent" investment banks, Salomon Brothers, floated an issue of $43 million of Swift and Company bonds, which was big money for those lean times; charging a low fee, they also undertook to sell the bonds directly to the public and to out-of-town banks, instead of through a syndicate of sub-brokers. The issue was successfully distributed; and 1935 showed a large advance in new underwritings to a total of over $2 billion worth, as against less than $500 million the year before. Soon the investment business and the stock market were rolling again toward another bull market, even under the increased policing of the SEC.

Kennedy tried to prod the New York Stock Exchange to

impose (through its own Governors Board) a more rigorous auditing of brokers' procedures; but here he was frustrated by Whitney's delaying tactics. However, a dissident group of brokers, those with numerous branch offices catering to small accounts, worked covertly wth the SEC to frame rules of supervision by outside accountants, rules which were imposed two years later when Whitney went out of office.

Kennedy, the rising millionaire and self-proclaimed "President-maker," enjoyed his place and the publicity it brought him, but felt he could only afford to serve for a year. His divided soul pined for action in the marketplace and its quick money, and at the same time he longed also for high public office, the higher the better. Though he practiced extreme restraint, he had made a good start with the new system. It was important also that he encouraged Landis, the former Harvard Law School professor who was to succeed him as Chairman, to explore the legal and administrative grounds for the SEC's regulative action. After 1937, legislation by Congress, such as the law pronouncing a "death sentence" for public utility holding companies, defined more clearly and strengthened the corrective power of the SEC.

When I visited the New York financial district in the autumn of 1934 everything seemed outwardly unchanged among the cliffs and canyons south of Fulton Street. The Trinity Church graveyard was tranquil; the "pillbox" of J. P. Morgan still squatted across the street from the ornate Stock Exchange Building; and the ticker tape flowed steadily like Old Man River.

At the beginning of the new regime some old-timers sulked and growled. One man vented his bitterness at a law which would compel insiders of a corporation to turn over their market profits to their corporation treasuries, while they must bear any losses they sustained themselves. "That, I say," he exclaimed, "is downright confiscation, or our constitution is nothing but a scrap of paper!"

Some of the veteran brokers complained that the securities markets were put in a strait jacket as they struggled for long months to fill the registration forms of listed stocks. One Street denizen remarked that the "brokers were now in uniform," an allusion to a famous film of the period about young girls being tortured in a German boarding school by a sadistic headmistress.

Others, however, who operated many-branched houses for small investors, said that the SEC law would be recognized in time as "the greatest thing that has ever happened to Wall Street."

Ben Smith ruminated sadly at the changed order of things:

> I saw the handwriting on the wall. I had made money. I got out. The Exchange was 'way behind the times. It was supposed to regulate itself—it did, but never enough. A man could make millions literally, you know as well as I, without putting up a dollar of his own. It was too good to last. The market will never be the same again.
>
> If I can't go in and create a little action in a stock or sell it short for a turn—[here his hand gestured, like a musician at the piano trying a chord of music]—then what's the use? Take Telephone: suppose I want to sell it a little. I must now go short only on the rise, at a price an eighth above the last, instead of being able to pound the thing with selling orders on the way down, and then cover. But there's always a "daddy" for every important stock on the list; and if I go short, the "daddy" can put it up without limit and squeeze me, cut me to pieces. And there are the detectives in Washington who watch the ticker.

Smith had turned to working over special situations for the long term, selecting a stock for accumulation, operating as a director, or as an insider, but unable to trade more often than once in six months. The thrill of the old game was gone for him.

There was also complaint by professional traders that

restrictions on trading made market movements less "natural" and elastic than before. After "strings" of large blocks of shares appeared on the tape, there would be no followup. For example, they reported that upon news that American Telephone was to be investigated as a monopoly (which everyone knew it was), this very widely held stock broke badly, falling more than ten points in two days, as the public stampeded to sell. But no short sellers appeared to buy back stock at a profit they had sold during this declining movement, which would now provide a cushioning effect. Yet others believed that the bred-in-the-bone operators, blessed with patience and indomitable cunning, would find ways to evade the new rules and the new policemen. (Indeed the frightened market of 1934 was succeeded late in 1935 by one permeated with the old bull-market fever, so that it ran ahead full speed—to be halted only by the big crash of 1937.)

Smith said he found surveillance by the SEC mild enough. In one instance the Commission's "bloodhounds" pounced upon an obscure gold-mining corporation listed on one of the lesser Exchanges to inquire about the suspicious rise of its stock during five weeks from 25 cents to $3.75—a gain of 1300 percent! And who was at the bottom of this affair? None other than Kennedy's old friends Sell-Em Ben Smith and Tom Bragg. Smith told about the investigation with great good humor.

The New York agents of the SEC came in to make their inquisition. "We had gone into the mine in 1933, a year before the new securities law was passed," Smith related. "Though its provisions were not retroactive, we volunteered to show the SEC's agents our books and records. They were young lads, very polite, and were under orders from Joe Kennedy not to 'get gay.' " Some accountants came in to help them; but they all seemed rather awkward. The promoters, it turned out, had put up only their own money to bring gold-bearing ore out of their mines, and news of this, becoming known in the Toronto and New York mining-share markets, had caused the stock to rise. No rigging was charged in this case; the SEC agents apologized, saying "we just wanted this record for our files," and gave Mr. Smith and company a clean bill of health. He grinned broadly over the affair; but still there was the suggestion that the encounter had shaken him up a little.

In other cases, where the SEC sleuths did catch some blue-sky operators manipulating a worthless stock, the mere threat of a court suit put a stop to the operation; such persons generally preferred to have their stocks delisted and removed from public trading, if the suit were dropped. Public exposure itself acted to ruin the chances of such schemers.

Brokers were "in uniform"; Big Government was intervening everywhere and threatening to raise taxes higher and higher for the rich. I asked Sell-Em Ben if he were unhappy about the New Deal reforms and taxes, and he replied with a grin that he had his investments placed at points all around the world, and his bank accounts too were scattered between New York, the Bahamas, Indonesia, Australia, and Switzerland. As for taxes, he said with feeling. "Anything the Government can get out of me in the way of taxes they are entitled to!"

8

THE RAILROAD KING FROM
TEXAS

The unending dramas of wealth begetting and wealth losing
went on in the markets under a new political environment
much as before; the players used more ingenious means and
a different vocabulary, and paid more respect than hitherto to
the social police. It will be recalled that Giannini, who adjusted himself very well to the rules of the New Deal, continued to expand his great banking chain while attacking the
old "money trust" of the New York bankers. After the nineteen thirties old-time capitalists seriously questioned the
likelihood of men getting rich quick, or again founding dynasties like those raised in the late nineteenth century by the
Carnegies, Rockefellers, and Harrimans. Taxation alone made
such achievements "impossible," as one aged financier asserted in a tract for the times entitled: *It Can't Happen Here
Again*.[1] Yet seekers after wealth and power appeared one after

another and made their bids for great stakes. An instance more remarkable perhaps than any other is the case of Robert R. Young, sometimes called "the daring young man from Texas," who managed in 1937 to seize control of the huge Van Sweringen railroad empire with 23,000 miles of track and three billion dollars of assets, all bought for what is proverbially known as a "song."

The Great Depression of the nineteen thirties for the owners of paper wealth was a time for taking losses. But it was also an open season for hard-eyed bargain hunters who knew how to turn other people's catastrophes into coin. In those lean times private yachts, cast-off sunbursts, dried up swimming-pools, landed properties, or mountains of surplus razor blades could be purchased for prices that seemed absurd. One collector of seemingly worthless securities, Floyd B. Odlum, was able to gather together in the financial junkyards the materials for an imposing investment trust. Robert R. Young's tastes ran to broken-down railroads. "From . . . 1937 until the day he died in 1958, he kept Wall Street in a state of turmoil. . . . He waged unrelenting war on the major investment banks, insurance companies and law firms," a biographer of Young has written.[2] Allying himself with the New Deal, he made himself known as a "populist" in the financial world, with the mission to "save capitalism from the capitalists," according to his own declaration. Too small a group of men had assumed control of the great corporations, he said, and he must find some way to "diffuse" the power of the Morgans and their associates. These high resolves and principles were announced to the world, however, after Young found himself in the midst of battle, heavily engaged by his adversaries. In the beginning his ideas were more modest and conventional, those common to the acquisitive class.

It was known that he had worked for the Du Pont chemical company during World War I and later had been employed at the General Motors headquarters in New York;

but he had left General Motors to set up his own investment firm, which boasted several of the millionaire executives as its clients. He had weathered the Crash of 1929 in very good form by selling short. Thereafter he made it his business during the years of depression to pick up some good things among the ruins; here the shares of a broken-down motion picture concern, or there the very low priced shares of some railroad that might have a potential value. In 1932 he was able to buy a seat on the New York Stock Exchange for a record low price of $30,000. At that time his attention was chiefly attracted to the securities of the Van Sweringens' Alleghany Corporation; it was insolvent, and its common stock going for less than a dollar; its $100 par value preferred was selling at less than $10 per share and paying no dividends. Young and his brokerage partner, Frank Kolbe (a former financial analyst for General Motors), estimated that there was a large leverage potential in those shares and especially in the more limited issue of preferred stock. This he bought in some quantity for himself and for his General Motors clients, President Alfred P. Sloan and Vice Presidents Donaldson Brown and John Thomas Smith, winding up with a block of 20,000 shares under his control. The shares had almost no value then; but Young calculated that if recovery set in and the collateral stock pledged behind the Alleghany bonds should rise, value would rapidly "telescope" the price of the preferred shares. Moreover voting power adhered to the cumulative preferred stock until dividends, suspended for several years, were paid up. (Within the Alleghany portfolio there was still a controlling block of 800,000 shares of Chesapeake and Ohio, a rich coal-carrier, paying dividends even in depression days.)

In 1933 Young went to see Oris P. Van Sweringen and asked that his group of investors in Alleghany preferred stock be given representation on the company's board of directors. Actual control, however, lay in the hands of the company's bankers, Morgan and Guaranty Trust, who brusquely turned down Young's request for a directorship. Young never forgot that rebuff, to him an act of injustice, since his group owned one of the largest stockholdings in Alleghany. Having become a professional of the market, Young desired the position of an insider in control of a "special situation" instead of remaining a passive speculator. As he continued to accumulate the cheap Alleghany preferred stock for himself and his clients, his judgment was borne out when the stock began to rise gradually and in 1936 sold as high as 60. His own calculations allowed for a potential value of more than 100; and he kept a close watch on developments in the Alleghany affair.

The Morgan banking syndicate had been carrying the Van Sweringens for five years with their "rescue" loan of $39.5 million and accumulated (unpaid) interest charges of over eight million more. In the meantime, the Missouri-Pacific, one of the largest of Alleghany's subsidiaries, had gone into receivership, along with seven other smaller roads within the system. The RFC had helped several of these railways with loans. But Congress was preparing new railway legislation and was about to conduct an investigation during which there were likely to be embarrassing questions about the nation's leading banker controlling one of the largest railway systems indefinitely. Since the prospects for recouping the money sunk in the Van Sweringen loans seemed poor, the bankers found it obligatory to foreclose. An announcement that the collateral underlying this loan would be disposed of at auction was inserted as a small newspaper advertisement by Morgan in the late summer of 1935. It looked like the end of the road for the once celebrated Van Sweringens. Robert R. Young sent Kolbe to attend the auction, while he waited at the end of a telephone line to hear the results.

The historic sale was held on a Monday, September 30, 1935, in the dingy auction rooms of Adrian H. Muller & Sons on Vesey Street facing St. Paul's churchyard. Muller's place was known in Wall Street as the "graveyard of securities"; it was a locale full of old furniture, cheap pictures, and bric-a-brac, illuminated by a dirty skylight and some glaring arc lamps. The audience of about four hundred persons, however, looked like a selection from America's social register of finance, mixed with some journalists, messenger boys, and street loafers who happened in. There was the handsome, bored-looking George Whitney representing Morgan's; their lawyers from White and Case and Davis, Polk, Wardwell were also on hand; and a Midwestern group including pudgy, round-faced Oris Van Sweringen, one of his aides, Colonel L. P. Ayres, and George A. Ball, a glass-jar manufacturer from Muncie, Indiana, evidently a new ally of the Van Sweringens. The plan now put into operation was apparently to sell out the Van Sweringens' Alleghany shares carrying control of the railroad combine to a non-banking group, which accounted for the presence of Mr. Ball.

A whole empire was going on the bargain counter under the auctioneer's gavel, amid heaps of battered picture frames, broken desks, secondhand chairs, and books, in an old auction parlor. The Alleghany holding company embraced a railway system that sprawled across the heart of industrial America; in the same basket also were railway terminals and freightyards, office buildings, real-estate developments, ships, trucking companies, armored cars, coal mines, hotels, a department store, and finally "Daisy Hill," a big dairy farm with a peach orchard, the home of the Van Sweringen brothers outside Cleveland. Most of these various properties were insolvent at the time.

At the given hour, 3:30 p.m., the auctioneer began to drone his announcements of packages being offered for sale. The key parcel, called Group 1, contained 34,000 shares of Alleghany cumulative preferred stock and a bundle of 2,-064,000 shares of Alleghany common quoted in the market at $1.37 per share. At each offering one of the Morgan's lawyers would make a bid in a perfunctory way, and Colonel Ayres, acting for Van Sweringen and Ball, would bid a trifle more. "Two million eight hundred and three thousand," said Colonel Ayres. No one opposed him and the parcel carrying control went to the Midamerica Corporation, newly formed by Ball to buy in the bankrupt corporation. Van Sweringen, who had looked tense until the sale was made, relaxed and smiled when no opposing bids came from other quarters. With some other parcels of securities, the total sum realized by the bankers came to about $3.1 million which revealed to the public the full loss of the Morgan syndicate.

As the auction ended people came forward to congratulate Van Sweringen. Somehow, without money of his own, he had managed to snatch back his "empire." It was one of the Van Sweringens' most brilliant maneuvers: they had sought out Ball, well known to them, and persuaded him to put up the cash necessary to buy control of Alleghany for a new holding company, which the Van Sweringens would manage for him. Having been shown a view from the mountain tops of millions of dollars in future profits, the old canning-jar manufacturer had agreed to give the Van Sweringen brothers sole and exclusive control of Alleghany's railway holdings, by granting them an option running ten years to buy it all back at what it had cost plus 5 percent interest. To be sure, there was the added provision that the Van Sweringens in the years to come were to pay off the huge creditors' claims against them, now totaling some $70 million most of it owed to New York and Cleveland banks. At any rate, Alleghany and the Van Sweringens had a chance to come back in a big way, as Young had calculated.

During the industrial recovery of 1935 and 1936, dividends from the holding company's railroads increased to such an extent that by December, 1936, Alleghany was able to resume interest payments on its bonds, and these were taken out of the friendly receivership imposed by the trustee,

Guaranty Trust Company. The value of the Alleghany preferred stock holdings of Young and his clients at that period had risen by about 500 percent.

For the money lords of banking and railroads, however, the whole political and social environment had changed greatly since 1933, and in a sense was unfavorable to them. In their time of crisis the finance capitalists particularly had turned to the RFC for help; now their prime creditors, the Congress and the Administration, held them, as it were, under durance. They were no longer free to manipulate or pile up paper profits in any old way, as in the nineteen twenties, and recoup their losses. In earlier times the "robber barons" ignored the protests of the public and settled things among themselves; but under the Roosevelt Administration, Morgan and Company felt it necessary to give up control of the Alleghany system, pocket their huge losses, and expose them to the public. By 1935 the prestige and influence of Morgan's had fallen greatly, and soon was to fall even lower. Under the New Deal the plutocrats felt themselves at bay. Not only were the banks more severely regulated than others by the Federal Government, but the public utility interests were then desperately fighting against the proposed "death sentence" for utility holding companies, which was finally enacted late in 1935.

In the Senate a subcommittee of the Interstate Commerce Committee, under Senator Burton K. Wheeler of Montana, had begun a searching probe of the railroads and prepared bills covering reorganizations and receiverships, in which bankers like Morgan and Kuhn, Loeb had formerly acted with a free hand. The Wheeler Committee—whose chairman was the formidable prosecutor of the public figures involved in the Teapot Dome oil reserve frauds—harried the Van Sweringens by calling them repeatedly to the witness stand in Washington to reveal all the details of their various corporate schemes. Even the small investors nowadays were up in arms against the great underwriting banks and the railroad barons, as illustrated from my own experience at that time.

A few days after the auction sale of the Van Sweringen securities, I happened to visit my friend and neighbor, Charles A. Beard, the historian at New Milford, Connecticut. There I met another friend named Max Lowenthal, who had a summer home near the Beards. He was then in his middle forties; a native of Minneapolis, he had graduated from Harvard Law School with distinction and had been a corporation lawyer in New York as well as counsel to important labor unions. Over the years he had also held posts as an investigative lawyer for various Federal government commissions under Presidents Wilson and Hoover; more recently he had aided the Pecora Committee. When we met at the Beards, he was serving as legal counsel to Senator Wheeler's subcommittee on railroads. As both Beard and I had some souvenirs of the Van Sweringen wreckage in the form of defaulted Alleghany bonds, we asked Mr. Lowenthal what that forced sale really meant. He had had much experience of such matters, and two years earlier had published an informative book on railroad receiverships managed by Kuhn, Loeb and Company entitled *The Investor Pays*.[3]

"The same banking crowd that financed and advised the Alleghany combination, until it reached its present condition, will stay in control," he explained, "as trustees and preferred bankers." The new owner was only a "dummy." The financing of these moribund railroads, he went on, offered nowadays the most important source of "gravy" for the bankers; and the same bankers who had helped mismanage the roads so that they were overburdened with debt would continue to manage those same roads through receivership and reorganization. They would reduce the bonded debt in some degree and give the bondholders equity shares paying no dividends, at least for a long time ahead; and for these services they would again exact large fees.

It turned out that Beard had five bonds of the Missouri-

Pacific Railroad (part of the Alleghany chain), while I had one; they were now worth about fifteen cents on the dollar. Their bankers were already forming plans for reorganization; they had begun to circularize the bondholders and would soon have most of them lined up to approve of the proposed receivership plan. And later on there would no doubt be a receivership again and more millions in fees to the bankers.

Beard and I looked at each other sheepishly and laughed. "Why we chuckle-headed investors are being fleeced again," Beard exclaimed.

Lowenthal, a man given to bland humor, went on: "Think of it, the Morgan partners and their associated banks believed that the more money the Van Sweringens lost for them the more they were obliged to lend them. And when it got so they owed more than they could ever repay, fifty million dollars, then the Morgans decided to take good care of the poor Van Sweringens: they provided the insolvent brothers with a salary of $100,000 a year—for the bankers were so *kind*, so sorry for them that in this case they resolved to throw good money after bad!" Lowenthal had us shaking with laughter, although the fun was partly at our expense.

Beard then proposed that we lodge some protest before Congress. This led to the impromptu formation of our Missouri-Pacific Railroad Independent Bondholders' Committee. I agreed to be a member and nominated Beard as chairman. We found the president of a small bank with a few Missouri-Pacific bonds in its safe, and he willingly joined our committee. With the help of a volunteer lawyer, we prepared a petition to the Senate Subcommittee on Railroads setting forth the wrongdoings of the Van Sweringens; and as a consequence Senator Wheeler invited Beard to testify before his committee.

Beard, a man of distinction, and a great platform speaker to boot, made an impressive witness at the Senate hearings. Citing chapter and verse, he testified that the Van Sweringens had milked the Missouri-Pacific's treasury and then falsified its records; in their blundering efforts to support their Alleghany stock during the Crash, they had unloaded weak properties on "our" railway, resulting in further loss. Now the same wrongdoers and their "preferred" bankers were trying to put over their own reorganization plan. In the name of our independent committee Beard petitioned the Senate to investigate the fraudulent transactions of the railway's officers, which were carried out at the order of the Van Sweringens.

Our little committee's testimony had an effect out of all proportion to our importance and received wide coverage in the press. We were a David assaulting the financial Goliath. The Wheeler Committee now had grounds to begin a searching inquiry into the Van Sweringens' and other railroads. The masters of railroads were plainly made uneasy by these exposures, and the Morgan group was also embarrassed; they had the reputation for hitting very hard in such contests, but now there seemed little fight in them. Meanwhile lawyers for our committee and for other investors in the Missouri-Pacific filed injunction suits against the proposed "Morgan plan."

Senator Wheeler, still wearing his guise of a Western Populist, thundered at the disgraced railroad financiers, while the subcommittee's investigations extended themselves year after year, throughout the thirties. But at an early stage of these affairs, in December, 1935, Mantis Van Sweringen, the younger of the brothers, died of a sudden illness. The elder Van Sweringen brother struggled alone to hold together the loosening chains of his empire during the year that followed, and frequently rode back and forth in his private train between Cleveland, New York, and Washington, where he was often called to hearings. About a year later he too died, at the age of fifty-seven. He had been on his way from Cleveland to New York by overnight train, for he was planning to call at Morgan's in the morning. But on arrival at the yards of the Lackawanna in Hoboken, he had felt ill and retired to rest a while in his sleeping car. When attendants returned, he was dead of a coronary thrombosis.

Upon the death of the last of the Van Sweringen brothers, the complex option agreements they had drawn up with Ball for taking back ownership of the Alleghany Corporation were now void. Possibly Oris Van Sweringen had labored under increased excitement at the time because, while he was being harassed in Washington, the stock market was rising strongly again. Ball was in his late sixties; he knew nothing about managing railroads and now said he was minded to sell his bargain-counter securities at a good profit. At this point, in January, 1937, a few weeks after Oris Van Sweringen's death, Robert R. Young, who had been watching from the wings, came forward with an offer to buy the whole package of Ball's holdings for $7.5 million. Behind the daring young broker were his wealthy clients, the inner-circle executives of Du Pont and General Motors: Alfred P. Sloan, Pierre S. Du Pont, Donaldson Brown, and John Thomas Smith. The Young syndicate also included himself, his partner Frank Kolbe, and another client, Allen F. Kirby, heir to a large fortune derived from the Woolworth chain. Young's own firm was to take a one-sixth share of the syndicate's package.

Old Mr. Ball was agreeable to the sale; but before it could be settled there was a little contretemps. The GM executives, particularly Donaldson Brown, decided at the last hour to "dump" Young; they considered him "brilliant but unpredictable," and found him obstinate in dealings with them. On the other hand, the GM people were notorious for forcing hard bargains on those who had the privilege of doing business with them, such as parts suppliers or car dealers. Young, who was nothing if not aggressive, had once threatened to go to court against the Du Ponts rather than have his fair share of a bargain scanted. The Alleghany business was all his idea, and yet they proposed to dismiss him with only a broker's fee.

Before taking this action, Brown and Smith had the forethought to ride down to Washington and consult Senator Wheeler about their buying the former Van Sweringen holdings. Wheeler, at first, seemed not unfavorable, but the Committee's lawyer, Lowenthal, said "Haven't you boys a big enough company to play with in General Motors?" There was the hint of an antitrust suit if the GM group bought control of one of the largest railroad systems; Smith, GM's corporation counsel, concluded at the time that "they could not stand the gaff of an investigation," and so they withdrew as prospective partners in the enterprise.

On first hearing that the GM group had planned to cut him out, Young, who was vacationing at Palm Beach, Florida, hurried back to New York to start litigation. But soon he was assured that he could take over the whole deal for himself, if he could manage it. This would need seven times as much money as Young had. Where in the world would he find it?

He undertook new negotiations with George Ball on behalf of his brokerage firm and the man who was now his principal client, Allen P. Kirby. Ball agreed to take 4 million in cash and a collateral note for $2,375,000, payable in two years and secured by a pledge of a large part of the same Alleghany common stock they were buying. The multimillionaire Kirby readily agreed to pay three-fourths of the cash needed and signed a note for the rest with Young, in whom he had the most implicit faith. Kirby had inherited a large estate, which he found had been poorly managed by great trust companies of New York, and had turned to Young as his financial counselor. He had had very little actual business experience; as for Young, he knew nothing about operating railroads but was willing to learn, and he had supreme confidence in himself.

The little Texan was one of the most overweeningly ambitious of the new breed in Wall Street. Like Joe Kennedy and Ben Smith, he had no great fear of the regulatory action of the government and intended to live with it; like them too he had no respect for the House of Morgan, whose tremendous bungling in the financing of the Van Sweringen railroad ventures was now public knowledge.

On May 5, 1937, the nation's newspapers announced that the unknown Robert R. Young had bought control of the ramshackle Van Sweringen empire and was to become chairman of the Alleghany Corporation. The next day Young, never a shrinking violet, called a press conference at his small Park Avenue apartment in New York, gaily dispensed cocktails to reporters and photographers, and told all the world what he would do to rehabilitate the decrepit railways and win back dividends for all the "Aunt Janes" among the investment public. At forty, Young was small, slight of figure, with a round, bumpy head, pale blue eyes, and hair prematurely gray, and was described as resembling "an underpaid college instructor." His voice, however, was strong and confident; he was quick-thinking, well-informed, and well-spoken, the reporters found.

In Wall Street, one of the Morgan executives was reported to have said "Anyone who buys into Alleghany ought to have his head examined." A day later Young and his associate Kirby were having their heads examined at hearings in Washington before the Senate Subcommittee on Railroads. Other times, other ways: to be a railroad baron one needed no longer the approval of the two or three great investment bankers, but that of the U.S. Senate.

Towering over Young, Senator Wheeler dealt with him just as if he were another one of those finance capitalists, those absentee owners who juggled the nation's railways with a view to shaking down profits. On the witness stand Young admitted to knowing nothing about the industry, and he acknowledged that, thanks to the attenuated holding-company device, he had been able to buy control of huge assets for a relatively trifling sum.

Was he not just another "shoestring speculator"? the Senator demanded. Was it not true that he had used only $254,000 of his own money to gain control of the Alleghany system, following the buy-now-pay-later plan?

SENATOR WHEELER: *There is the possibility, with the control of three billion dollars worth of roads . . . as you well know, to make money in a hundred different ways. For one man to have power of life and death over such a combination, and subject to so much temptation, is surely a bad thing?*
YOUNG: *Yes, it is a bad thing.*

In response to questions as to his object, the Wall Street operator avowed, strangely enough, that he thought such holding-company "monstrosities" as Alleghany should be closely regulated, or eventually done away with. He declared that he had seen the errors of the Old Guard in the financial world and was resolved to avoid them. "We are obligated to no one—we are absolutely independent," he said, " . . . I have nothing to conceal." He promised he would clean house, simplify the Alleghany corporate structure, reduce its debt, and thus do a thorough job of reformation. In fact he would do that better than the Government could do it. "We are going to beat you to it!" he exclaimed.

Senator Wheeler then reminded the witness of the controls exercised by favored investment bankers over the railroads and of their practice of financing the roads through private negotiations instead of open competition. Wheeler observed that many evils flowed from the situation of the bankers being both confidential advisers and wholesalers of the road's securities. What, he asked, did Young propose to do about that?

Young replied boldly: "It is certainly our intention to

open things to competitive bidding. We expect to shop around and sell our bonds in the best possible market, and if they have to be opened up to competitive sale, we will do so."

This declaration of fiscal independence was widely reported in the press and sent a seismic shock throughout America's financial community. It meant that Young was ready to "snap the old Van Sweringen chain," as he said, break up long-standing banker relationships, and open the underwriting of railroad securities to independents in finance, instead of handling such business on a preferential basis. And that was the business that gave most of the railroad gravy to firms like Morgan, Kuhn, Loeb, and the big trust companies.

Upon returning to New York, Young received word almost immediately that Thomas W. Lamont of J. P. Morgan and Company would like to see him for lunch. Young then did something unheard of: he declined Mr. Lamont's invitation on the ground that such a meeting would be "politically embarrassing" at a time when he was being "hounded" through a Senate investigation.

An invitation to lunch with the chairman of Morgan and Company still had something of the nature of a command. At seventy, Lamont was one of the elder statesmen of Wall Street, the friend of Presidents, prime ministers, and literary celebrities; his manner was usually urbane. But on this occasion, when the interloper Young came to the Corner, Mr. Lamont laid him on the carpet and thoroughly "spanked" him, as Young remembered it afterward. What he had said before the Senate committee in Washington had been carefully noted, and it was not liked. Young was reminded that Morgan had not only been financing but also advising America's railways for seventy years, especially the Alleghany group, and Lamont insisted on their being informed about his plans for improving things. In Washington, Young had had the happy notion of representing himself as a financial "reformer"; but he had not committed himself definitely to anything. Now, at 23 Wall Street, he "made himself humble for the good of the cause," he said later, granting that Morgan's and Guaranty Trust were "Rome" and that "all roads led there," including railroads. He contended that he had to change the old ways of running things in these times, but he would keep the railroads' regular bankers informed of developments. Lamont, however, had not been satisfied with that; he said "We not only want to keep informed, we want to guide you."

In other nations rail transport systems had been built up at about the same period as those in the United States under the ownership and control of emperors, Mikados, or republics, and they ran well enough. In the United States railways privately owned, but loosely regulated by government, became the sport of finance capitalists and investment bankers. Promoters like the Van Sweringens, using other people's money, had built out of them a fantastic pyramidal structure of holding companies, largely for the purpose of doing something that could not be legally done by railroads without those corporate disguises. And so R. R. Young, the "sharpshooter," had been able to seize control of the same transport system by paying only a pittance for the holding company at the top of the pyramid. At the hearings in Washington he had spoken as one exalted by the crusade he had enlisted in: to cleanse the financial stables, to help restore the faith of the poor investors. While Young was testifying before the Wheeler Committee, Lowenthal was heard to remark, "This man Young seems just like an evangelist—perhaps a self-deceived evangelist!" Then he added, "But it's the evangelists who are making all the money nowadays!"

I asked Lowenthal why anyone in his right mind should fight for control of a debt-ridden, almost bankrupt holding company, several of whose subsidiaries were in receivership. He replied. "Think of all the *perquisites!* Those roads must run thousands of cars every day, and spend millions on coal, engines, wooden ties, and even paint. Even the insolvent 'Miserable-Pacific' keeps large deposits in banks and wields business and political influence in a dozen states."

The ploy for financial evangelism looked as if it would pay off pretty well for the "crusader." Young was not just a dreamer; he had the training of an accountant at GM and had taught himself a great deal about corporation law. In May, 1937, Young and Kirby were elected directors of the Alleghany Corporation, Young becoming chairman. He was in full charge by agreement with his partner Kirby—who would have the ownership of the bulk of the two million Alleghany common, owing to his larger cash investment.

The Alleghany empire, however, was a veritable corporate jungle with its interlocking holding companies (one lying upon the other) and its seven railways, not to speak of two hundred affiliates in coal mining, real estate, trucking, shipping, and railway terminals. More than one who sought the gold in this vast corporate wilderness were destined to come, like the Van Sweringens, to a premature end. The holding company's controlled assets were all too heavily mortgaged, while its own equity was also hypothecated. Alleghany itself had a debt of $80 million in a series of bond issues that would begin to fall due in 1944; interest on those bonds exhausted all dividend income; and $20 million in arrears of interest and dividends were owing on its debentures and preferred stock. Until these obligations were covered, there would be nothing for the common stock, of which the Young syndicate had bought nearly two million shares for cash and notes.

The Alleghany might be dead broke, but it still held working control of one of America's richest railways, embodied in 800,000 shares of Chesapeake and Ohio that were pledged against Alleghany's bond issues. There was also the Nickel Plate that rambled through the Middle West (paralleling the New York Central and the Pennsylvania) and together with the Chesapeake and Ohio made up a large Eastern trunkline. The C&O in turn controlled the smaller Pere Marquette, which looked to profit from the reviving automobile industry in Michigan. These three roads were connected with the Erie to the East and with the long Missouri-Pacific to the West.

Young had gotten control of this $3 billion transport net with its 40,000 workers, its land, its terminals, and its affiliates, through the cheap shares of the Alleghany, by using only $254,000 actual cash of his own and borrowing the remainder to make up his own million-dollar down payment. He proposed to merge certain of the rail properties, liquidate some of the real-estate holdings, and reduce debt in the more favorable climate of the 1937 bull market. He knew that because of the leverage factor a moderate recovery in the affairs of the underlying railway companies would make for bigger gains for the holding company. Thus Young might become a "king" of railroads like Harriman, who also had started as a Wall Street sharpshooter.

He now dissolved his brokerage firm, opened a small office for the Alleghany Corporation in the Chrysler Tower in New York, and then had himself and Kirby elected as directors of the Chesapeake and Ohio. Attending his first board meeting of the C&O at Cleveland, he mounted to the thirty-sixth floor of the Union Terminal tower and seated himself in Oris Van Sweringen's sumptuous office. Here were the headquarters of the several roads of the Alleghany system, whose officers and directors used to meet together on the same day. On days when mists flooded in from Lake Erie the place seemed full of the brothers' ghostly presence.

Although Young labored under great nervous tension, he had a strongly logical spirit and was clever at figures. He would take up a pad of yellow foolscap, and reducing masses of financial detail to a simplified pattern, set forth his calculations and extrapolations in neat figures. But the trouble was that the Van Sweringens had made of the Alleghany a corporate fantasia that refused to perform reasonably. From the beginning of the adventure Young was faced with trouble and danger, and a succession of lawsuits derived from the Van Sweringen regime.

I felt the keenest curiosity about Young as a self-avowed reformer in railroad finance. The Missouri-Pacific Independent Bondholders' Committee, of which I was a member, had helped create a favorable political environment for his plans. For several years I followed his battle for financial survival in the newspapers with the purpose of some day writing about him. When I got in touch with him about my intentions, he responded cordially, granted me extended interviews, and opened to me all the documents bearing on his contests with the railroad bankers. I acquired a more intimate knowledge of him than of any other among the new breed of capitalists, and it afforded much light on how they operated in the era of the New Deal. Some things Young revealed to me I might never have learned from any printed texts on the workings of our economic order.

Robert Ralph Young was born on February 14, 1897, in Canadian, a village in the Texas Panhandle with a population of some 1500. On his father's side his forebears were English who had arrived in America in the eighteenth century. Young has been called the descendant of Texas cowpunchers, but his father and his maternal grandfather quit cattle raising at an early period to go into business together as small-town bankers, operating the First National Bank of Canadian. In his boyhood Robert Ralph, the youngest of three sons, was accustomed to outdoor life and became adept with rifle and revolver.

He was mettlesome and mischievous as a boy, and though an excellent student at his grammar school, he got on badly with his father, who had old-fashioned notions of discipline and played the stern parent. His mother, however, was loving and imaginative; the child of Texas pioneers, she would enchant him with tales of Indians and Mexican raiders. Sitting by the fire in the evening she often read to the boy and cultivated in him the love of good literature, especially poetry.

There was a lively gang of kids in the village of whom the small, skinny Robert soon became the leading spirit. Because he was physically inferior to the others and had a disproportionately large head surmounted by a mop of yellow hair, giving him a rather odd appearance, he tried to dominate his fellows by proposing the boldest and wickedest pranks and by using his ready speech as well. While she lived, his mother kept his mischief within bounds. Her early death, when he was but eleven, was for him an immitigable disaster.

After his mother was gone, his father, unable or too impatient to control the boy, decided to place him in an orphanage in Denver. Robert did not stay there very long; he made his way back, but for him it was a traumatic experience, judging from what he said to friends later on. For a while he lived under the heavy-handed regimen of his father, who used to hold "trial" over him, and fine him by cutting his allowance whenever he was detected in some boyish wrongdoing. At length his father, who had remarried, packed him off to a military academy in the East, where he would be subjected to strict discipline. It did not seem to make him more tractable, though he showed the potential of a good student and wound up at the head of his class. Entering the University of Virginia at seventeen, he felt the attraction of literature, but gave most of his time, as he related afterward, to "such extracurricular activities as poker, crapshooting, billiards, and bull sessions." In his second year he "cracked up," as he remembered it, missed his mid-year examinations, and became a dropout. Worse still—when he was scarcely nineteen, and without waiting for paternal permission—he married. His bride was a Miss Anita O'Keeffe, whose mother then ran a boardinghouse at Williamsburg. She was a great beauty, like her talented elder sister Georgia, who was destined to become one of the most famous American artists of her time. But the young husband was penniless; after a few weeks he rode home to Texas to face his father, who did not feel kindly toward him but at least offered him a job in the family's bank. This the youth refused with much spirit, declaring he would never work under his father, and returned to his bride in Virginia.

While a student at the University of Virginia, he had seen an announcement of summer jobs open to college students at the Du Pont powderworks. The war in Europe was going on in 1916, when Young applied and was given work "cutting" rifle powder at one of the Du Pont mills in New Jersey, earning wages of 28½ cents an hour. After about six months of this, when his employers found he could read and write, he was promoted to a supervisory job with the status of a junior engineer. In some notes he wrote for an autobiography, Young related with evident satisfaction that when the United States entered the war, he was exempt from the draft as a skilled munitions worker. (It seems that his military academy had fixed in him a lingering hatred of army life, which grew later into opposition to war itself. But with a moral inconsistency always marked in his personality, he saw no wrong in making ammunition.)

Marriage and regular work cured Young's restlessness— his own term. The attachment between him and his wife, who was a little older than he, helped; and when in 1918 their first and only child, a daughter, was born, he became deeply attached to her as well. After the war he was transferred to the Du Pont's main office in Wilmington, where he worked as an auditor under Treasurer Donaldson Brown.

With a small inheritance of $5000 that came to him at the death of his grandfather, he took off from the firm of Du

Pont in 1920 and engaged in an independent business venture based on a food processing scheme, of which he was manager. It collapsed within six months, and Young was so flat that after a while his wife had to mend his only presentable suit of clothes so that he could go on looking for work. Another inheritance of some two or three thousand dollars emboldened him to take some fliers in the stock market; he quickly lost all that sum as well.

During his evenings he had been devoting himself seriously to a correspondence course in business management, and by displaying his added theoretical knowledge, he finally obtained an administrative post at the Allied Chemical and Dye Corporation in New York. Not long afterward the Du Ponts, who had taken control of General Motors from W. C. Durant, called Young back, at a higher salary, to serve as assistant treasurer in the New York headquarters of GM. There Young stayed for the next seven years, eventually earning as much as $35,000 a year, including bonuses, while "receiving a training in corporate finance and accounting that could have equalled in almost no other job in the world."

At GM the independent-minded Young, who impressed his associates as "brilliant," if temperamentally difficult, won the notice of John J. Raskob, reputedly the financial brain of the Du Pont organization. It was Raskob who was said to have urged them to invest in General Motors and also to have initiated GM's installment plan. When he undertook to direct the presidential campaign of Governor Al Smith against Hoover, Raskob was obliged to retire as GM's vice chairman. In 1929 Raskob, now deep in the stock market, formed his own investment trust, Equishares, and invited Young to join his staff.

After his first misfortune in the stock market, Young, who had studious habits, determined to learn all he could about the game. To this end he had memorized the contents of Poor's lengthy *Manual of Corporations* so that he had the

rating and business record of a thousand or more corporations in his head. In time he became a sharpshooter, speculating in the market with unvarying success and accumulating
some capital of his own. By 1929 he was able to invest $100,-
000 in Raskob's trust.

He left GM to join Raskob because he felt that to climb
further in the giant corporation and become "a thirty-seventh
vice president" he would always have to exhibit "a lack of
independence." Moreover he was tired of all the bother of
"committees" in a bureaucratic organization. Meanwhile his
abilities as an analyst won for the young man the respect of
his elders, such as Pierre S. Du Pont, who, on his advice,
shifted $15 million from stocks into high grade bonds in
1929. In the October crash Young turned bearish, sold
selected stocks short and made his first big killing. "The first
million," he said.

After October, 1929, "my views became respected as a
financial forecaster," he wrote later. Young calculated that the
depression would be long with us but that Raskob, an inveterate optimist, would not listen to his bearish views.
Raskob, he thought, nowadays seemed to keep company with
the gambling element in Wall Street, such as Mike Meehan,
the broker, and Joshua Cosden, the oil man, and lost nearly
all of his personal fortune in the crash. After a year or so,
Young parted company with Raskob and formed his own
brokerage firm in partnership with Frank Kolbe, a fellow
worker at GM. They used research methods to counsel their
rich clients, among whom were Donaldson Brown and Allan
Kirby, and improved their fortunes during the years that
followed, until Young felt strong enough, early in 1937, to
make a giant leap forward and strike for control of Alleghany.

From the very beginning of the adventure, there were
only headaches: the Alleghany Corporation faced insolvency
unless interest could be met on its debenture bond issue, the

$25 million 6s of 1950. Two of the holding company's biggest railways, the Erie and the Missouri-Pacific, were in receivership; the Nickel Plate, though in fair shape, had a large bond issue coming due that had to be paid off or refunded to avoid receivership. Alleghany still had title to a big block of shares of Chesapeake and Ohio, which earned and paid a $3 dividend, and this road's treasury held the shares of the other affiliated roads. But while the Alleghany "owned" them, it did not fully possess anything, for the valuable C&O shares were pledged as collateral against Alleghany's $80 million of senior bonds. Now those bonds had written in their indenture a rigid clause requiring that the value of the collateral pledged for them should be 150 percent of the face value of the bond issues; but if the collateral, mostly C&O common stock, fell to 140 or 120 percent, then the trustee, the Guaranty Trust Company, had the authority to take voting rights over the collateral, thus controlling both the Alleghany Corporation and the Chesapeake and Ohio Railroad. When the market was strong and C&O sold at $60 or over, everything was lovely; but when it slipped below 50, the Guaranty Trust could impound all dividends, and Young and Kirby could just go and whistle.

There was nothing the Van Sweringens had done in the way of corporate construction that was not devious. Alleghany did not own the Chesapeake and Ohio shares directly, but instead owned a dummy, the Chesapeake Corporation, which held those shares; and again Midamerica, another dummy, as topmost corporation, owned the Alleghany shares. Young therefore devised a consolidation plan that would dissolve the several go-between corporations into one, Alleghany, which would simplify the structure and also serve as a means of improving market and collateral value. He then undertook a soliciting campaign among the bondholders to have the restrictive clauses changed, so that the owners of Alleghany's common stock would have a freer hand to deal with the corporation's fiscal problems. He also proposed to merge several of the affiliated roads into the stronger C&O. But at his first move to dissolve the useless Chesapeake Corporation, strong opposition arose, his old group of GM clients (Donaldson Brown among them) held a large block of Alleghany preferred stock and obtained a court injunction restraining him.

In August and September, 1937, the stock market underwent a tremendous fall, as steep as in 1929, and C&O stock fell to 38, which was considerably less than the coverage required for the senior bonds. Young learned that the Guaranty Trust intended to impound all cash from railway dividends, and even cut off Alleghany's small office expenses and salaries, in order to protect the interests of the company's bondholders.

The market crash of 1937 caused enormous paper losses for Young and Kirby only a few months after they had begun their big venture, and Young was heavily in debt. W. C. Potter, chairman of the Guaranty Trust, now made it known that he intended to dislodge the man whom he qualified as a mere "shoestring speculator" from command of Alleghany and from his directorship in the C&O. Within the Alleghany's board, the titular president, Charles L. Bradley, a holdover from the Van Sweringen's regime, started the attack on Young. Young displayed his fierce temper during on uproarious meeting and had Bradley fired. (Not long afterward Bradley died of a heart attack.) The fall of the market, however, forced Young to postpone his consolidation plan indefinitely.

Now it was Senator Wheeler's turn: he haled Young down to Washington and berated him for making plans that would discriminate against his preferred stockholders. But the Senator's real purpose—now as an opponent and would-be rival of Roosevelt—was to scold Young for giving large sums of money to the Democratic Party's fund raising campaign.

Sheepishly Young admitted having forked over $15,000 for James Farley's souvenir campaign books.

"You're a bigger sucker than I thought you were!" roared Wheeler. Young had only acted in conformity with the rules of the new breed of finance capitalists who flourished under the New Deal—Giannini, Joe Kennedy, and Ben Smith—to make liberal donations to the party of Roosevelt so long as it was politic to do so.

Young and Kirby had bought their railroad empire to "enjoy and possess" it; at times it seemed real enough to them; at others it became weirdly unreal, and seemed to vanish into a Looking Glass world. Young's course moved from swift triumphs to sudden disasters, and his moods from hope and joy to black despair. The "damn bankers," as he called his opponents at Guaranty Trust and Morgan's, were now preparing to drive him from the Chesapeake and Ohio board of directors. The lust of battle was always strong in Robert Young, but like other tragic heroes he had his weak spots: he faced the world with a hard cold mask, but suffered sorely under tension. With all the storms swirling around him in the autumn of 1937, he suddenly underwent a complete nervous breakdown and lapsed into a state of melancholia.

Since the middle nineteen twenties, when he was at GM, he had arranged to spend part of each summer and weekends at Newport, Rhode Island. By 1937 he had rented a large house on Bellevue Avenue, one befitting a railroad magnate, that overlooked the sea. Edward Stettinius, son of a Morgan partner, who had been Young's classmate at the University of Virginia, lived nearby. One Sunday morning while walking along the cliff path that fronted the big houses on Bellevue Avenue, he stopped in at Young's, entering by the garden. Through a window he saw Young sitting in his library, staring before him as if sightless, with a large revolver on top of the desk by his hand. Stettinius made his way in, took the revolver away from Young, and had him put to bed. For three months Young remained secluded, part of the time in a rest home under the care of a psychiatrist, with no one but his wife and nurse permitted to see him.

He had been addicted to writing poetry in his youth; now in his paranoid state he wrote in a cadenced free verse a poem that while not distinguished for originality of expression depicted well his desperation:

> *Sad are my thoughts, for I am forty,*
> *Sad as the drifting leaves this autumn day . . .*
> *Until today it seemed my path led upward,*
> *But now I find myself upon a constant downward slope*
> *Which gains in pitch, until I see*
> *Dim, distantly a void*
> *From which departed friends have turned tired faces,*
> *And love has lost its zest,*
> *The quest for fortune ended,*
> *While none but liars house the halls of state.*

His loyal friend, Allan Kirby, had not deserted him. Though urged by Young's opponents to cease being the angel of the tempestuous Texan, he had answered that he would "play along with Young." He came to Newport, and being unable to see his friend, left him a message of good will. On learning of this the sick man was greatly cheered. At the end of December, with health restored, he came out of seclusion and went forth to give battle to his adversaries.

In later years Young often remarked that his principal troubles in 1937 and 1938 flowed from his first statement at the Senate Committee hearings of a resolve to establish the rule of competitive bidding by underwriting bankers for his railroads' bonds. Thenceforth, he maintained, the great bankers of New York's money center, who had long operated as a "monopolistic financial clique, had turned against him.[4]

He may not have been wholly committed to financial reform; but now, faced with the implacable enmity of the bankers, he was driven to espouse competitive bidding with his whole heart—though, when practiced, it had a fairly revolutionary effect on the business of underwriting corporate securities. He began to believe fervently that he and Kirby were no mere money-grubbers but had made their venture, as he declared at the time, "with the purpose of getting much, if not most, of our return in the satisfaction of doing a big job. How could our dream of consolidation and constructive public service materialize without an effective voice in C&O? We would be truly left holding an empty bag."

At heart Young was no reformer. Nevertheless he determined to use methods and avow principles that made him appear for a number of years as a "Texas Populist" in Wall Street, a New Deal crusader who had risen against the "money-changers." He convinced Kirby that they must wage a sort of holy war, must appeal to public opinion and political authority against their powerful opponents, who were "plotting" to impose their "absentee ownership" over the group of railroads that rightfully belonged to Young and Kirby and the army of small stockholders they were going to lead. Only by public exposure, only by the pitiless use of publicity as their one great weapon—which would injure the banking interests more than anything else—could they hope to win their fight for control. Kirby vowed he would back Young to the limit.

Oddly enough Young never stopped to think that he and Kirby also were absentee owners, who by means of the Van Sweringens' tricky corporate devices were able to bid for control of a huge railroad system. Young talked as if he meant to do away with the Alleghany Corporation, which would have been logical; but after a while one heard nothing more about that. Indeed he conserved the holding company (a great device for using other people's money), and found it very useful years later in a fight for control of a still larger rail system, the New York Central. At any rate, Young always hereafter identified the cause of the "Aunt Janes" with his own "mission," and could never see it any other way. He was a Saint George fighting the dragons of Wall Street.

On a Monday in April, 1938, the Chesapeake and Ohio was to hold its annual stockholders' meeting and reelect directors. Young asked the Guaranty Trust for authority to vote Alleghany's C&O shares, which they had already impounded, and he was refused. He then filed suit in Federal Court at New York for an injunction restraining the bank from voting Alleghany's shares of C&O. His affidavit charged the giant trust company with "violation of its trust duties" and with serving a monopolistic combination of banks headed by Morgan and Company. The Guaranty's chairman replied to Young with the aplomb of one commanding a three billion dollar fortress, calling him a purveyor of falsehoods. The temporary injunction Young had won was quickly voided, but his lawyer immediately went on to the U.S. Court of Appeals to have it extended. Young was nothing if not litigious. Lawsuits darted from his brain like lightning from the brow of Jupiter. He would brush aside the doubts of lawyers and order them to open fire.

The power of Morgan's was still considered immense, and their people were formidable in a fight. Many thought the young broker was mad to contend with such foes. But their prestige was now really fading. Young related afterward that one day in March 1938 when he was still hesitating over undertaking a civil suit against Guaranty Trust, he read in his afternoon newspaper the story of the arrest of Richard Whitney on a charge of embezzlement and grand larceny! Whitney, the floor broker of Morgan, "hero" of 1929, and leader of the Old Guard in the Stock Exchange, was done for. This reflected badly on Morgan and Company, whose executives must have known for some time the secret of Whitney's troubles, coming as it did not long after the exposure of their tremendous losses on the Van Sweringen loans. Young calculated that they would never be as strong again as they used to be, and he determined to go ahead with his fight for control of Alleghany.

Several weeks before the stockholders' election and the scheduled board of directors meeting was to be held in Richmond, he had launched a strong campaign to solicit the proxies of the Chesapeake and Ohio Railroad's 60,000 stockholders in his favor. Teams of professional solicitors from their "boiler rooms" telephoned lists of people day and night; they also mailed out proxy forms, circulars, and copies of those public letters which Robert R. Young dashed off in his own hard-hitting style. The railroad's operatives and executives continued to run the trains as before, in routine fashion, conducting themselves as neutrals during this noisy contest. Young however made it appear in his literature that his committee represented the present "management side" while the Guaranty-Morgan people sought to put over new and untried personnel. When by April 18, 1938, the proxies were counted, Young's committee had won more than 41 percent of them, a surprising display of power, while the Guaranty Trust had only 30 percent. Since neither side had a quorum (proxies for half the shares), as the bylaws required, the stockholders' meeting was postponed. To gain time was just what Young was hoping for.

Jubilant, he turned up at the big rambling Jefferson Hotel in Richmond like a conquering hero to be honored at a banquet given by C&O railroad officials and other local notables as the man who had "saved" the C&O. The speech he gave was spirited. "We have just begun to fight," he cried. Everybody gave the Rebel yell, and Young remembered the occasion as "the greatest day Richmond had known since Fort Sumter was fired upon."

The adversary, given to preserving a dignified silence in public, now departed from tradition to make angry rebuttals to Young's statements in paid newspaper advertisements, and began to wage the war of the proxies with all its power. Earle Baillie, head of Seligman and Company's investment trust, which owned a block of C&O shares, turned up as a candidate for Young's directorship. Baillie was a genial Wall Street veteran and something of a board room orator; he brought impressive financial strength with him in the next round of the proxy contest. Young saw that the engagement would be long and hard. After an exchange of broadsides, Young's lead in the race began to melt away "like a cake of ice in the Texas sun," he observed grimly. Driven to seek compromise, he felt himself lucky to hold his seat on the board of directors, to which Baillie, the ally of the Guaranty Trust, and two of his associates were added. Thereafter Young constituted what Baillie called "only a one-man minority" within the C&O directorate. Still he had made a strong showing against America's most powerful financiers; his fight for the C&O had rocked Wall Street and made him a popular figure in the newspapers.

The joy of battle was always strong in him; he was never happier than when he found himself bombarding the adversary's corporation lawyers with his own battery of lawyers. Indeed he spent millions "having the law" on his opponents, employing men of the first rank, but also contributing much through his own resourcefulness in legal affairs. Besides invoking the power of the law, his other weapon was publicity; he brought the pressure of public opinion to bear upon his adversaries in press releases and frequent paid advertisements. And inasmuch as he intended to keep telling the world that he was fighting the monopolists of railway finance, he tended to associate himself with the Roosevelt Administration, with the SEC, the Anti-Trust Division, and also with the Wheeler Committee in the Senate. These, along with the small investors and the liberal public that was critical of the old order, he saw as his natural allies.

He was never a radical zealot, however. To associate him

with the Populism of Bryan and La Follette, as does his biographer Joseph Borkin, is to misconstrue Young's really
schizoid personality. An empiricist, he had in fact no consistent political or economic faith. In a statement before the
ICC, he said that a study of the New Deal's reform laws and
the Justice Department's growing antitrust docket had
brought him to the belief that "the ability to adjust oneself
to public opinion as expressed in government will continue to
be a virtue in private management." He believed in the
freedom of the small financier to seize control of a large corporation if he could do so; and he contended that the establishment of the railroad-bankers stifled free enterprise and gave
fuel to radical agitators on the left. In his boyhood Young
had been a rebel "against the father"; in middle age he re-
belled against the "fathers" of Wall Street, in the interests of
himself and his own group of finance capitalists.

His most brilliant invention was the stratagem of combining the "missionary" spirit with profitable long-pull market investments. Yet he was no ordinary market operator, for
even the caustic Senator Wheeler ended by praising Young's
"honest, constructive work" in rehabilitating the Alleghany's
combination of roads.

For five years a bitter struggle raged within the Alleg-
hany-Chesapeake organization between Young's faction and
that of the "damnbankers." On the board of the Chesapeake
and Ohio the opposition had the majority, together with the
holdover personnel from the Van Sweringen regime, and
Young seemed the weaker party; but from his position in the
key finance committee of the road, he continued to deal hard
blows to the establishment financiers.

A $30 million bond issue of the C&O came due for re-
funding in the autumn of 1938. As the next quarterly meeting
of the directors was to be held in November, its preferred
bankers—Morgan, Stanley and Kuhn, Loeb—prepared in a

perfunctory manner to underwrite the refunding issue—a prime mortgage bond—at the same terms as they had given formerly, a 3½ percent bond at 95½ percent of par. In other words the investment bankers' fee was, as before, at about a 4½ percent discount to themselves.

Harold Stanley appeared for the Morgan's investment firm before the C&O directors at Cleveland, and with him came Elisha Walker, in behalf of Kuhn, Loeb, of which he had lately become an active partner. Then the two gentlemen left the room while the board discussed their proposal.

Young meanwhile had struck up a friendship with Cyrus Eaton, the veteran Cleveland financier, still heading Otis and Company. Eaton had come down in the world since 1929; his large investment trust had collapsed, but he himself had not been personally liable, and he was making a comeback without any help from the New York money-center banks, whom he regarded as his enemies. Eaton too now favored reform and competitive bidding. He had brought in the independent Chicago investment firm of Halsey, Stuart, and joined with them in making a low bid for the C&O bond issue. This bid Young now suddenly drew from his pocket at the directors' meeting, saying that Cyrus Eaton and Harry Stuart would underwrite the $30 million 3.5 percent bond at 100 even, which meant that the railroad would receive $1,350,000 more than they would through the Morgan-Kuhn, Loeb syndicate. Nevertheless the majority of the C&O directors indicated that they proposed to stay with the regular old bankers and refuse the better offer. Earl Baillie argued that Mr. Eaton was a man "in poor repute." Young replied that Eaton's reputation was just as good as Morgan's. Then he took up the cudgels for the principle of competitive bidding, declaring that a considerable sum of cash would be lost to the railway if it were not adhered to, and that he as a stockholder, and the Alleghany Corporation as the largest C&O stockholder, would sue the directors individually if they voted to reject the low bid and take the higher one. As he finished his tirade he sprang from his chair and pranced about the room chanting, "Morgan will not get this business, Morgan will not get this business!" The opposing directors asked for time out to consult their lawyers by telephone about the legal actions he threatened. Young promised to throw the book at them, along with the Justice Department, and the Senate's Committee on Railroads. The directors soon came back to the table and capitulated.

This was the start of *competitive bidding* in railroad finance, to which Young had resorted as a move in his war against the old banking establishment. In the course of the next year two high grade bond issues for affiliated railway terminal properties were also lost, as a result of Young's intervention, by Morgan's and Kuhn, Loeb and again distributed successfully by Eaton and Stuart. The old railroad bankers were losing a lot of "gravy" and it hurt. Young's fight to introduce fair bidding won him new laurels and caused the Federal Government to move in 1939 through its Power Commission and through the SEC to introduce competitive bidding for bond issues of electric utilities.

The bloodless struggle continued, like a chess game with life-sized figures, played for big money stakes and real financial power, while Young gained in confidence from each winning play. Baillie, however, gathered supporters in the Middle West, including John B. Hollister, the law partner of Senator Robert Taft of Ohio, and with a sudden thrust the Baillie group had Young dropped from the executive and financial committees of the C&O. Several months later, in January, 1940, Baillie launched a campaign to win a clear majority of the stockholders and throw Young out of the board at the next election.

The Texan countered by setting up a strong propaganda organization directed by young Randolph Phillips, a crusading newspaper reporter who had lately served as an investigator under Wheeler on the Senate's Railroad Committee. Thereafter Young and Phillips bombarded the stockholders with circulars denouncing the "Wall Street party," and they sent their proxy-soliciting crews after the full list of C&O's stockholders right up to the eve of the next Richmond meeting, when directors would be named. The two warring factions then moved into the Jefferson Hotel again, with Young and his party occupying one whole wing and Baillie and his associates stationed on an upper floor of the long building. All night long, emissaries of the two opposing generals trotted back and forth bearing demands and counter demands. Finally, at three o'clock in the morning, Young's lawyer, Carl Newton, presented an ultimatum to Baillie, demanding that his faction agree to the election of three new "independent" directors, or Young and Kirby would levy suits against the directors and the trustee and call for more government investigation. By some well-aimed legal attacks on the trustee bank's handling of the Alleghany portfolio, Young had recently weakened the position of the Guaranty Trust and made it disposed to withdraw from the struggle. Baillie was at last driven to assent to a compromise arrangement which was advantageous to the Alleghany party.

Several months later Earle Baillie suddenly died of a heart attack. The running corporate battle over the Alleghany empire left its trail of dead: the two Van Sweringens, their associate C. L. Bradley, and now Baillie. Nor would he be the last. At all events, Robert R. Young's fortunes rose again. By waging a new campaign to solicit bondholders' consents, he succeeded on August 30, 1941, in removing the restrictive clauses of Alleghany's bond indentures—those requiring 150 percent in collateral value—and thus finally freed the holding company from the interference of its trustee, Guaranty Trust. Thereafter three "independent" banks of New York—Manufacturers', Marine Midland, and Continental—became trustees for the bond issues, and their officers, who favored Young's cause, became directors of Alleghany and C&O. At last Young and Kirby were masters in their own house, able to vote the full block of C&O shares in their holding company's portfolio.

Newton, one of the corporation lawyers who served Young, styled him an "ideal client," a man who would willingly go as plaintiff into long, costly, and stubbornly defended court suits, and would have the nerve to fight them through to the bitter end. The legal history of Young at this period shows him as a man moving through a labyrinth from one hidden apartment to another until he emerges in the open air at last. Various suits were conducted simultaneously, although on different fronts of the "war." It will be recalled that Young and Kirby had a personal note for $2,375,000 payable to George Ball within two years of their agreement to buy the Van Sweringen securities; the due date was May 5, 1939. As collateral for the note they had pledged 1,200,000 shares of their Alleghany stock; this they would forfeit and with it all control of their holding company if they failed to pay their note.

In the autumn of 1938, with Alleghany common worth half of what they had agreed to pay, they had decided to renounce the collateral rather than throw good money after bad. But Young had conceived of another brilliant coup by which they might retrieve their position.

Ball's faction on the board of C&O had joined with Baillie in opposition to Young; Ball had also circulated rumors that he would soon be back in control of Alleghany. Young was a good hater, and he had learned to dislike the old glass-jar king. "By a lucky chance," he related afterward, "I had learned in May, 1938, that the SEC was quietly investigating numerous market transactions in the Alleghany preferred stock executed for Mr. Ball in 1936 just before he sold control. I then had our own investigators and lawyers look into these transactions to see if there had been any unlawful wash-sales or market-rigging operations."

On the strength of such information, Young and Kirby instituted an unprecedented suit in Federal Court in Indiana against the venerable manufacturer for the tremendous sum of $8 million, charging that Ball had violated the Securities Exchange Act of 1934 by fraudulently manipulating the market in Alleghany's securities at the time when he sold it to Young's syndicate. During the long court process that followed the 1.2 million shares of Alleghany stock pledged with Ball were placed in escrow by the court pending its decision in the long, drawn-out trial, and neither side could vote them. Young was therefore able to retain his several corporate offices. During the trial, evidence was presented of unlawful action by Ball to "rig" and inflate the value of securities being sold; though his lawyers dragged the case through the courts for three years, up to March, 1942, Ball was at last obliged to settle out of court by handing over to Young and Kirby $4 million in Alleghany securities. It was the largest suit levied under the SEC law; its adjudication put Young and Kirby back in possession of the "empire" at even lower cost than they had ever dreamed of—almost nothing!

YOUNG BACK IN POWER

ran the headlines in the newspaper financial columns. With infinite delight he now had his enemies removed from the Chesapeake and Ohio's board of directors, while his lawyer and friend, Carl Newton, was elected president. Then he himself at last assumed the seat of the chairman of the railroad at the head of the long table.

Young and his lawyer, neither of them railroad men, took over the management of the great coal-carrying C&O which also held control of the Pere Marquette, the Nickel Plate, and the Wheeling and Lake Erie, making it the third largest trunkline in the East. In truth the C&O, staffed with able technicians, seemed to manage itself in routine fashion, and prospered as war began in Europe and traffic swelled. With his tidy mind of an accountant, Young worked to reduce the roads' debt burden and eventually to consolidate them.

I once asked Young what he thought of James Burnham's theory of the "managerial revolution," which held that engineers and expert managers were the predestined class that would one day take command of our industrial and governmental system. Young intuitively liked the idea of a managerial elite, rather than a crowd of "socialistic" politicans and bureaucrats, in charge of affairs, but then he reared up and said he had no respect for engineers and technical men; most of them, especially in the railroad field, performed only routine tasks. "Go down and see our operating vice president, old Mr. Schmidt," he said, "and see what you can make of him." I found a big stout veteran who directed the transport of mountains of coal day by day, but knew almost nothing else, and seemed fairly frightened to death by little Robert R. Young.

Young was able to merge the Pere Marquette, important because of industrial Michigan, into the C&O; but the absorption of the Nickel Plate was blocked by the Interstate Commerce Commission. The Erie and Missouri-Pacific roads, whose nearly worthless stock Alleghany owned, remained in receivership; but the C&O trunkline and Nickel Plate flourished during the war, and their common stock rose substantially in value. Thus Alleghany Corporation, under Young's charge, was able to sell part of its railroad stock portfolio at favorable prices and retire about 80 percent of its bonded debt of $77 million. "Who would have believed that the Alleghany bondholders would be paid off at 102½ cents on the dollar?" Young said in 1944. The holding company was at last out of the woods.

What was phenomenal about Robert R. Young's career

was that he used the ideology of liberals and New Dealers as his weapon against the Old Guard, employing methods of mass propaganda, and newspaper and radio publicity to enlist the support of crowds of small investors and speculators. To his opponents at Morgan's and the old First National Bank, he was a reckless "demagogue" within the financial system, who in his contests with them, was ever ready to call the Roosevelt Administration, the SEC, and the Justice Department to his aid. However the Interstate Commerce Commission, established in 1887 to regulate the railroads, remained a stronghold of anti-Roosevelt appointees (except for its one liberal member, Joseph B. Eastman). Now the conservative ICC, under a new act of 1940 severely restricting railroad holding companies, began to move against the Alleghany, carrying on investigations and hearings to determine whether its control of the C&O, its most important possession, was unlawful. These proceedings, as usual with this bureaucratic Commission, dragged on for nearly five years, but Young, resourceful in legal battles, was well able to cope with them. They were to end in 1945 in a kind of compromise which changed things very little.

By then Young had become a millionaire eight or ten times over.

That Young was not consistently a reformer, nor democratic by disposition, is suggested by his conspicuously expensive style of private life and the locale he chose to live in —Newport, of all places. Decorous, quiet old Newport had been the haunt of the rich and the superrich since the late nineteenth century; the old-money people liked it because it was a community where you did not need to see poor or envious persons, except for the servile class. More recently it had come down in the world; its elaborate cliffside mansions had a look of decay, for they had been battered by hurricanes and left unrepaired. During the depression the livelier element of society had scattered to many different points on the socialite map, especially to Long Island. There were still, however, a few old Astors, Vanderbilts, and Drexels about, as well as a few aristocratic Bostonians.

Young said he liked Newport's quiet; it was out of the way, in fact so inconvenient to get to that people who wanted to "sell" things could not reach him easily. For years he spent three or four days each week in Newport. For a while he had rented cottages but by 1935 he felt he could afford to lease "Beechwood," the palatial estate of Vincent Astor, situated on the cliffs overlooking the sea. Young evidently fancied being neighbor to the descendants of the old money lords, railroad barons, and liver-pill kings of yesterday; and Mrs. Young was socially ambitious for her debutante daughter. The old families of Newport, however, tended to ignore these new rich who tried to crash the gates. Indeed the old families were turning seedy during the depression and the New Deal, and they were worried about servants and taxes. But all Newport sat up and took notice when the Youngs staged their coming-out party for Eleanor Jane Young in August, 1936. It drew about five hundred persons, many of whom used to be called the *real* right people.

The Victorian-style Astor residence was redecorated for this occasion by Mrs. Young, and a special supper room and lounge was constructed on the terrace for several hundred guests; there were rivers of champagne, colored balloons festooned the air, big floodlights lit up the lawns, rocks, and nearby ocean, and two orchestras continually played dance music. Newport was astonished at the extravagance of the affair—some estimated the Youngs spent $70,000 for that one party—and attributed it to Young's success as a "stock-gambler." All this conspicuous expenditure seemed odd behavior for a professed reformer. Young explained it away by saying he did it all for his wife and daughter, and "cared nothing about money." He was actually an abstemious person who drank and ate little in his later years because of his high blood pressure.

When troubles beset him in 1938, he had to cut down his scale of living for a while, but in 1942 he was up again and purchased the big estate of one of the Drexels, which had cost $200,000 to build in 1890, for only $38,000. It was one of the sensational bargains in resort mansions created by the misfortunes of the rich in wartime, when taxes were high and servants scarce. "Fairholme," as the estate was called, needed a large staff and $75,000 a year for maintenance.

In truth Young lived rather quietly amid all this splendor. For a time he had given up all social life after the tragic accident that befell his daughter. Described in the society columns as "one of the madcap members of café society" of that period, "Cookie," as she was called, was flying home in a private plane late one night in the autumn of 1941 when a sea fog came up, and the plane crashed in the water off Newport. She and her companion, an amateur pilot, were killed. Her father loved her perhaps more than anything in the world; after her death he told friends he "had nothing left to live for." For several months he remained in a state of depression. Long afterward one felt an undertone of melancholy in him, and he often appeared either grim-visaged or withdrawn.

In 1942, during a winter vacation in the Bahamas, Young and his wife met the Duke and Duchess of Windsor; the ducal couple liked the Youngs, and the following summer came to spend a week at "Fairholme." Their arrival set all Newport agog with excitement; the Youngs gave up their seclusion and held a round of luncheon, cocktail, and dinner parties such as the decayed resort had not seen in long years. The Windsors' visit made a high-water mark of social success that opened many doors previously closed to the Youngs.

His business associates shrugged their shoulders at his sumptuous way of life. Kirby, far more affluent, lived modestly in a New Jersey suburb. One of Young's eminent lawyers, after repeated visits to Newport, remembered the company in the Youngs' drawing room as stuffy, and the conversation as dull, though Young himself could be vivacious and sharp-witted. Meanwhile critics of Young pointed out that his sybaritic way of life did not sit well with his professed doctrines of business reform and his much publicized pity for the underdogs of the investment world. Although his railroad's main business was coal carrying, coal dust seldom got into the hair of the fastidious Young. He concerned himself with financial policy and political and public relations, to which he accorded the highest importance. His favorite office was the library of his house at Newport, its windows overlooking the bay, where he sat with the account books and reports of his railroads before him.

Once, at least, sometimes twice each day, Young would go out for a three-mile walk along the cliffs above the sea, carrying a pair of binoculars with which to stare out at seagulls and cormorants in the harbor. Commodore Vanderbilt used to keep the affairs of New York Central in a "cigar box." Young said, in the same spirit, that the business of the Alleghany holding company was very simple; he had it all in his head as he walked. Very often he walked alone, leaving a note of his itinerary so that he could be found quickly for an important message. His position during this period was an enviable one: he enjoyed the repute of one serving the public interest while steadily enriching himself. His imposing style of life was only another way by which the small man "crushed" other people.

In the autumn of 1944 Young invited me to attend a quarterly directors' meeting of the Chesapeake and Ohio Railroad. As it was almost unheard of then for any journalist to be admitted to a board meeting of one of our giant corporations, I was eager to go, and my notes of the time bring back glimpses of the man in action.

Regularly, in the third week of each month, the combined directors' meeting of Chesapeake and its three sister roads (though not yet legally amalgamated) would be held at the same time in the same room at the Cleveland headquarters. A day or two before the meeting Young would set off from Newport to meet several close associates at the Lackawanna terminal in Hoboken, where they would board the Chairman's private railway car. The group included his secretary Raymond Morfa, a former professional football player, who later became the president of a small Western railroad; also Carl E. Newton, the boyish-looking lawyer-president of C&O; and Joseph P. Routh, engineer and president of the Pittston Company, Alleghany's coal-mining subsidiary. At suburban Morristown, the train would halt and Allen Kirby, the wealthy silent partner of Young, would climb on board to complete the party. These men, all over six feet tall, seemed to tower over the little "emperor." However his brisk manner, sharp glance, and deliberate, incisive speech gave him a commanding presence in his circle.

The old-fashioned "palace car" was quite comfortable and had its special charm. It had a spacious dining lounge and full-sized bedrooms for each guest. But Young was apologetic, saying:: "Humph, the railroads have been asleep; we have the style of the gaslight age in our sleeping cars. We'll have to change all that when this war ends."

The talk of the group was that of familiars; it touched on modernizing rail passenger service, which many thought was already doomed by the competition of airlines. Young, however, had no use for airplanes. They also considered the program for the directors' meeting the next morning.

Joe Routh, the merry Irishman in the group, who had been raised on the lower East Side of Manhattan in Al Smith country, began in challenging style. "The trouble with you Bob," he said—and Young looked a bit annoyed—"the trouble with you, I say, is that you let your directors talk too much. I sit on my directors and don't give 'em a chance." Young gave a faint laugh.

I noticed that after some cocktails the burly Routh attacked his dinner like a wolf, and I remarked, "You must have a good conscience, Mr. Routh, you eat hearty."

He exclaimed with a laugh "Hell, I haven't got any conscience; you can't afford one of those things with these boys around here."

Young put in for my benefit, "Joe Routh always sounds off, you mustn't take him seriously."

Routh rejoined, "Yes I'm Irish, and impulsive, while Bob Young always thinks before he speaks." Routh was being rather sharp at his jesting; he was no fool. Did he imply that some of the atrocious insults Young had visited upon his opponents were uttered with calculation?

Young turned to Newton and took up the problems raised by certain antagonists, "What have they got against me?" he asked. And Newton replied frankly, "They say you are a willful guy—and by God they are right." Young scowled for a moment, then brightened up and said "I guess I am a willful guy."

Arriving at our destination in the morning, we stopped at the Hotel Clevelander, one of the group of high-rise buildings the Van Sweringens had put up in the nineteen twenties. The luxurious furnishings of the C&O's executive suite and conference rooms, high up in the tower, recalled the "Babylonian" style of 1929. There were present a crowd of railway executives and business agents among whom Young moved about, taking in their proposals quickly, answering them precisely, for his memory was very sharp. Veteran railroad executives in those days were generally a lot of old mahogany, but the new chief had been promoting younger men from the ranks.

One of the older faces, and one of the most unforgettable, in this crowd, was that of Cyrus Eaton; it was deeply lined and expressed much innate refinement; with his thin aquiline nose he recalled the physiognomies of wise old prelates in Italian Renaissance paintings. The Canadian-born financier was in fact Quaker bred. As a young man one of his first jobs had been that of private secretary to John D. Rockefeller, Senior, from whom he must have learned a few things. At any rate it was evident that Young deferred to his counsels.

The C&O board was wholly unlike what one would have expected to find in one of the "blue chip" corporations. Besides Young and his clan and the railway operating men, there was a group of Midwestern and Southern capitalists who were substantial stockholders. There was also present a contingent of three bankers from New York, only one of whom wore the Morgan collar—a young vice president of the Guaranty Trust. One of the "independent" bankers, head of the Marine Midland Trust, bore the famous political name of his grandfather, James G. Blaine, and he remarked that he was thoroughly accustomed to being abused here as a "damn banker." Still, no railroad moved very far without bankers. This board was composed somewhat in the manner of the Grand Council of the Venetian Republic, whose doges each represented different and even rival interests within the body politic. Eaton ranked here as an enemy of all that was Wall Street.

A horse of another color was a director named Lowell Erminger, a white-haired lawyer from Chicago who represented the McCormick-Deering family holdings in C&O. Chairman Young, in a flattering speech, introduced me to the forty persons representing the combined companies as a "distinguished guest" who planned to write the story of the Alleghany System for *The Saturday Evening Post;* he even mentioned my old book *The Robber Barons* in a favorable light.

At this Erminger jumped up and sputtered something about their need to "be careful" of what they said "with a writer present," and asked whether Young had arranged to approve whatever I would write in advance of publication. Young answered crisply that he understood I would write "independently, without interference from anyone," and he believed I would be accurate. Erminger subsided.

Following this there was a methodical discussion and voting on some technical and financial proposals bearing on new light-metal trains, advanced (gas-turbine) engines, and automatic switching controls for freight yards. Then President Newton reported on C&O's radio advertising budget for the popular program, "Town Hall of the Air," which would allow for free debate on vital public issues.

The suspicious Erminger again rose to warn the directors of the danger of "complete freedom" in such a public forum. "Will speakers be permitted to attack the railroads, or advocate the cause of the Soviets?" he asked. I found it hard to keep my face straight. Young and Newton both rebuked Erminger, and even called on me for my opinion of such a forum, if I cared to give it. I ventured that the "presentation of two sides of a question often tended to cancel out the arguments." An executive of the C&O then gave the directors his assurance that the "Town Hall of the Air" would not offer a platform for radical utterances. "We will know beforehand what is going to be said." After the meeting Young made some excuses for that "old-fashioned" director; but I laughed and said that at any rate he was candid. (I might have added that I had always suspected that extreme conservatives cared nothing for freedom of speech but had never before heard any of them say so.)

In Cleveland I used part of my time to drive to the city's outskirts and look over the immense properties once developed by the Van Sweringens and now being sold off against old bank debts. Alleghany Corporation had some claims on whatever was left—after the satisfaction of mortgages and notes—in the way of department stores, land, hotels, and terminals. Among the important parcels at Shaker Heights was the Van Sweringen estate, "Daisy Hill," a seven hundred-acre farm adjoining a bustling suburb, which nobody could now buy for development since it was wartime and residential construction was banned. The place and its buildings had therefore fallen into neglect. The brothers had built themselves a monstrous Swiss chalet out of an oversized dairy barn to which they attached other buildings as wings going out in all directions, so that the crazy structure had the area of a city block. On an upper floor were living quarters with the simple bedroom where the brothers used to sleep; they tended to seclude themselves both in the years when they were very rich and later, as if they were afraid of people. On the main floor there was a ballroom designed like the grand salon of a ship, but no one ever danced there because the ballroom was only finished after the Crash, and the brothers never had much social life anyway. Below the ballroom floor, in what had been the cellar of the barn, there was a gigantic swimming pool decorated in another and outlandish architectural style—a sort of 1929 Byzantine—with square, green-colored columns along the walls. By 1944 the water in the pool had turned to a stinking green slime.

Amid all this gimcrack luxury those poor brothers who had never learned or did not dare to have fun, lived mostly alone and played out their elaborate financial chess games. What a foul stench rose from the vast basement pool. Standing there one contemplated—like Gibbon in ancient Rome —the ruins of an empire in America. The Van Sweringens had walked as kings in our business society, but now their glory was gone; the flimsy monuments they had built were waiting for the wreckers' iron ball. How quickly oblivion had overtaken them. A doom also seemed to hang over the later "pursuers and possessors" who came after them and tried to snatch the gold out of their bedeviled empire. As I left that miasma-ridden "chalet" of the Van Sweringens, I wondered if Young would ever have much joy from the power he had assumed, and for how long. Even now he was hardly a man who exuded the joy of life.

I would not have wished to miss R. R. Young while he was around: his ascent to a commanding position in our industrial society was as spectacular as Harriman's in the eighteen nineties. At the Cleveland directors meeting I saw how quite a trail of wealthy speculators and investors had formed around Young and followed him in his ventures. One of them said: "Bob Young is a kind of genius. He has come up the hard way during the depression and the New Deal. The enemies he has made are the stuffed shirts." Another of his followers said that he "was one of the few men who bucked the System in Wall Street and survived!"

With his associates he was often "difficult" and contrasuggestive; in his opponents he sought to inspire fear. When in a heated discussion he would make a fierce mug, his light blue eyes blazing with anger. At times, one of his friends said, "he would freeze up until he looked like some maneating fish that would swallow his opponents at one gulp."

It is significant that in his living room at the Newport house he had hung up beside the fireplace a small but valuable oil portrait by the French eighteenth-century master, Jacques Louis David, representing Napoleon I as a young man. Like the diminutive subject of that canvas, Young too pined for still greater conquests. New ambitions possessed him. There were battles to be fought with more powerful antagonists than before; and once engaged in struggle his oft-depressed spirits revived strongly.

"Anyone who has an active mind must keep it engaged in important things instead of minor things," Young observed sententiously in the course of a press conference.[5] He continued to generate excitement and drama in the obsolescent railroad industry. After the war the nation's rail transport clearly entered into its decline. Not only passenger business but freight was being taken away by private automobiles, trucks, buses, and airplanes using roads and airports that were subsidized by the taxpayers. But Young, as one commentator wrote, "dreamed a great dream" of a modernized passenger service borne by locomotives and cars of light metal and advanced design. Once more he embarked on a "crusade," calling on the great public to help him rehabilitate the old irresponsible management of the "railroad bankers."

In 1946 the Pullman Company was being split up as a consequence of a government antitrust suit, and while its owners chose to retain their business of manufacturing sleeping cars and dining cars, they undertook to divest themselves of their servicing on the different railways, which they found unprofitable. Young now came before the ICC with a proposal that the Alleghany Corporation should buy in the Pullman service for 75 million dollars and reorganize it so that through trains would carry passengers from coast to coast without delay or change from one railroad system to another at the Chicago or St. Louis terminals, as was then the rule. To bring pressure upon the ICC Young tried to expedite things by having the C&O insert a half-page advertisement in the newspapers of fifty-five cities under the heading:

A HOG CAN CROSS THE COUNTRY WITHOUT
CHANGING TRAINS—BUT YOU CAN'T!

The advertisement, Young's own idea, was illustrated by a striking cartoon showing a smirking, self-satisfied porker looking rested and refreshed stepping down in California from the boxcar that had carried him directly from the East. In this advertisement it was also claimed that "The Chesapeake & Ohio and the Nickel Plate again Propose to Give Humans a Break."

The "Hog Ad" of March 4, 1946, was reprinted by virtually all the press and talked of all over the country, but it left the ICC unmoved. Young's proposal was rejected in favor of the Railroad Buying Group's plan to divide up the Pullman service among the major railroads.

In 1945 I had been told by Henry Sturgis, vice president of the First National Bank and its representative as director on several Eastern railroads, that Young was secretly buying the stock of the New York Central. "Young is bored with the C&O, which just carries coal, and is after something more glamorous." Young confirmed this, telling me that he was going to "cure" the Central, as he had "cured" Alleghany.

The Central was the country's second largest trunkline; it was the historic "Vanderbilt road" and boasted the crack "Twentieth Century Limited" on its Chicago line. In 1929 the stock had sold as high as $275, but later it had fallen to 13 or less. After enjoying a boom in World War II, it had wound up with its equipment run down, burdened by an enormous bonded debt, and a declining traffic. But where others saw only a receivership in the future, Young saw rich assets in the form of terminal real estate and "air rights," which gave scope to new skyscrapers. Early in 1947 it became generally known that Young had bought large amounts of stock of the Central for himself and Kirby and was buying still larger blocks for Alleghany and for the C&O Railroad. In a press interview Cyrus Eaton declared that the New York Central was now really a "Robert R. Young property." Young's next step was to apply directly to the veteran president of the Central, Gustav Metzman, for two seats on the road's board of directors, for himself and for Kirby.

The Vanderbilts and Morgans had been selling out their shares; Harold S. Vanderbilt had only 73,000 left, or about one percent of the outstanding stock, while Young's syndicate held more than a million shares. The blue ribbon group of Eastern financiers and industrialists, who composed the Central's board of directors, at first appeared to bow to Young and allowed his group two directorships—provided that the ICC approved of the arrangement. Young suspected that they were confident the ICC would block his election. He had attacked that agency before; and now, before they could move against him, he assailed them again in an address before five hundred newspaper correspondents at the National Press Club in Washington as "tools of Wall Street," who kept the railroads of America "enslaved." It was as if he sought to frighten the ICC and the Central's bankers into submission by giving them a foretaste of rhetorical bombardments to come. Indeed, his whole career was a story of fierce law suits and controversies that had left a trail of outraged opponents and broken business friendships.

A merger of two of the country's most important rail systems could not be effected without the ICC's approval as being in the public interest. Young had caused the Commissioners of the ICC to get their backs up; they had their toughest examining lawyers question him and his associates at great length as to how a consolidation of the C&O and the Central would help the Central, or relieve the roads of alleged banker control. "I think our mere presence there would relieve it," Young said without any pretense of modesty.

The roads he controlled, he argued, would contribute heavy coal tonnage to the Central and would strengthen its finances. But much evidence was introduced to show that the Central would lose as much from the diversion of traffic by other roads, and would gain nothing financially. The examiner in his summation of the hearings pointed out that the applicants would be violating the Clayton Anti-Trust Act, and moreover that they seemed willing to:

> take great risks (as trustees of the C&O stockholders) with the company's funds, speculating on their ability to get on the New York Central's board. . . . Little regard for the public interest . . . or the private interests of the stockholders of the Nickel Plate was displayed by . . . the applicants.

The ICC's lawyers argued that the C&O and the Alleghany had been led to expend large sums of cash out of their treasuries and also to dispose of valuable securities to buy Central's inferior shares in order "to indulge . . . Young's

personal ambition to . . . be in on the New York Central.[6]
The Commission voted down the whole plan; Young was
blocked for the time being.

The Korean War intervened, and heavy traffic rolling
across the country helped the weak railroads. Young never
ceased to plan a renewal of the contest for the Central. In the
meantime he was profitably occupied in other directions;
after a prolonged court suit of many years' duration over the
Alleghany's rights in the bankrupt Missouri-Pacific, that road
emerged from receivership, and Alleghany won back in new
stock a large part of the sum lost by the Van Sweringens. The
holding company also gained control of one of the largest
mutual funds, Investors Diversified Services, and saw the
value of its holdings in this company appreciate by some 800
percent! At the end of 1953 Young and Kirby each owned
100,000 shares of New York Central, while the C&O had
accumulated 800,000 shares at an average cost of about $20.
For propriety's sake this large block had been placed in
trust by the C&O with the supposedly neutral Chase National
Bank. From time to time Young circulated rumors in the
corridors of Wall Street that they would soon be moving in
on the New York Central. The directors of the Central, foreseeing another proxy war looming up, that year elected a new
and younger railroad expert, William White, to succeed Metz-
man as president, and White prepared for the fray.

In earlier times the wars of the railroad barons were
fought in the marketplace, and the ammunition they used to
corner a stock was money. Now the rules of the game were
somewhat changed. The six and a half million shares of Central were distributed "democratically" in small holdings
among 40,000 stockholders and numerous brokers who held
shares in their own names for numerous margin accounts.
Thus victory was to be gained not merely with dollars but
by waging a struggle before the court of public opinion, by
winning over "the hearts and minds" of the stockholders, and

by precipitating a mass movement among them in favor of one or the other contestants. This was a game at which the "financial demagogue"—as his opponents named him—greatly excelled. Young would use his vituperative rhetoric in advertisements in the newspapers, in press releases, or in brochures appealing for proxies; he would send out battalions of doorbell ringers supported by crowds of telephone solicitors; and finally he would dramatize the affair before an immense audience through the newly arrived medium of television.

Since he took over Alleghany, Young had shown an insatiable craving for publicity; while he used professional advertising and public relations men, he really acted as his own press agent, never asking his lawyers what he should say, talking to reporters with an air of frankness and candor while passing on to them sensational news about the alleged "crookedness" of his adversaries. My own series of articles on him happened to be the first attempt at an estimation of the man and his career.[7] Though my critical reflections on him did not spare his feelings, he wanted nothing better than to be introduced to six million readers. From that day he was a hero to the daily press, and the news weeklies (like *Time* in 1947) devoted to him leading articles and cover pictures. The railroad magnates and financiers who wore the Morgan collar tended to remain silent under public attack. An emissary of Morgan and Company, however, did approach Kirby on one occasion to urge that he and Young desist from their offensive statements in public, but Kirby replied, "Publicity is the only effective weapon we have, and we are going to use it."

In mid-January of 1954 Harold S. Vanderbilt telephoned from his Palm Beach home to President William White of the Central to report that Young had dropped in and informed him of his decision to dispose of his Chesapeake and Ohio stock and buy New York Central. "Young wants to be chairman and chief executive of the Central," Vanderbilt added. A few days later it was announced that all the Alleghany directors on the board of C&O, including Allen Kirby, had resigned, and that Cyrus Eaton had been elected chairman in Young's place. Alleghany was now free to acquire control of another carrier. Soon afterward Young rode up to New York and invited Mr. White to lunch with him. Declaring that he spoke in the name of the largest stockholder group in the Central, he offered to retain White as operating president after Young had secured the chairmanship. He also proposed to have the company's bylaws altered so that the chairman rather than the president would be the chief executive. Meanwhile he assured White that he would have ample opportunity to profit handsomely through stock options as the value of the railroad would undoubtedly rise after Young had taken over.

White delayed making any response to these proposals, saying that they must wait until the next board of directors meeting. Their meeting took place on February 10, and the directors announced that they had voted unanimously against electing Young and Kirby to the board; they also rejected Young's other proposals as being against the best interests of the New York Central.

Young now mobilized his battery of lawyers and his army of professional solicitors and began to canvass the Central stockholders for proxies supporting the election of his slate to the railroad's board. President White, who proved to be an intelligent and hard-hitting antagonist, also prepared in the same way for the general stockholder's meeting in Albany on May 26, 1954. The Central's management diverted its entire advertising budget of $1,250,000 for proxy soliciting, while Young spent about $1,500,000 of Alleghany's treasury for the same purpose.

Had they used the old-time methods of Morgan and Harriman in 1901 to "corner" the stock, they would have been subject to criminal prosecution by the SEC. Thus the battle for the proxies—in these days of the so-called "people's capitalism"—twined into a political election campaign, a sort of popularity contest. Young pitted himself not only against the Morgan-Vanderbilt interests but also against the Rockefeller-controlled Chase Bank, where the C&O's 800,000 shares of Central had been trusteed, by ruling of the ICC. Percy Ebbot, chairman of the Chase Bank, had been expected to play neutral. However he was also a member of the Central's board of directors, which had unanimously voted to exclude Young. Young now feared that Chase would use this big block of shares, acquired by Young with the C&O's money, against his party. Young's problem was to win back voting rights of those 800,000 escrowed shares, which would be decisive in the contest.

In his extremity Young contrived a brilliant stroke. He had recently engaged in some profitable business ventures together with those new money men from Texas, the oil millionaire Clint Murchison, and his associate Sid Richardson, whose combined wealth approximated half a billion dollars. Through a friendly broker he now proposed that the two men buy the 800,000 shares of Central from the Chesapeake and Ohio Railroad at $25 per share, and vote the shares for his slate of directors, in which they were to be included. Because of all the news about this "battle of giants," Wall Street had become wrought up and the depressed Central Stock had already begun to rise in the market from 20 to about 26. Young's offer to Murchison and Richardson was tempting: they were to put up virtually no money of their own; the Alleghany and Allen Kirby would lend them about two-thirds of the sum needed (20 million dollars) during a period of ninety days, and some banks would supply the rest. The buyers would also be given the option of turning back 600,-000 shares at what they had cost to Alleghany Corporation and to Kirby. It amounted to what is called in the Street a "put"; that is, the buyers would be insured against loss by being able to put back most of their stock at the contract price, while being given an opprtunity for a quick profit of some 10 million dollars, and all this on credit! The Texas oil drillers readily agreed, and the big block of 800,000 Central was removed from the hands of the Chase Bank.

When the Central's lawyers learned of this remarkable transaction, they tried to obtain court injunctions against Young and his friends, and had the affair investigated by the ICC. Senator Herbert Lehman at the ICC hearings in Washington argued that it would be improper for persons who had not put up a cent of their own to vote such a large block of railroad shares. Others denounced Young as a false friend of the small investors; like the bankers he denounced, Young had given away valuable options to men possessed of hundreds of millions. To this charge Young answered that what he had done was entirely lawful, and that his "big deal" had been to find two persons as buyers who were so rich that none could question the legitimacy of the transaction.

As the stock market boiled with excitement, New York Central rose as high as 43. The speculative fraternity of Wall Street were betting in favor of Young and the bull movement he had provoked. In voluminous advertisements Young aimed to arouse the greed of the public by reminding them that Central's stock in the nineteen twenties had sold at 275 per share and paid $8 in dividends, he suggested that it might even pay more once the "dead hand" of bankers and insurance companies was removed. President White replied for the management in advertisements heaping ridicule on Young's claims and warning the public that it was being misled. The SEC also intervened to stop publication of Young's more extravagant claims. But nothing could restrain what *Fortune* magazine in a May, 1954, article of exposure called the "Sound and Fury of Robert R. Young." As often before, he threatened everyone opposing him with court suits and publicly denounced what he called "The Little White Lies of Mr. White." He even made a television appearance on "Meet the Press" in the course of the campaign. Most important was the entrance, at a final stage of the battle, of an auxiliary force of three hundred vacuum-cleaner salesmen, employees of a company of Sid Richardson's, who rang the doorbells of thousands of proxy owners.

About half of the 6.5 million shares of the Central were then in brokers' offices, most of them held in margin accounts for speculators. This element had begun to play for the rise and cared little if the stock was rotten to the core so long as people wanted to buy more of it at advancing prices. There were also thousands of blue-collar workers employed by the Central who had small holdings of its stock; they voted strongly for continuing President White in office. The large branch houses on the Street, such as Merrill, Lynch and Bache, voted their anonymous margin accounts overwhelmingly for the Young party, as did the habitual market plungers. This vote, together with the Texas oil men's block of 800,000 shares, gave Young a wide margin of victory at the Albany meetings—as the speculative element had foreseen.

It was Young's greatest conquest, though scarcely a "Populist" triumph. He was now fifty-seven, at the very height of his public fame and financial power, but he was also enjoying all the hurrahs as he turned to the task of salvaging the New York Central. To help him he had taken the step of installing as the new operating president of the road, Alfred Perlman, the first Jew to occupy such an office. Perlman, a Massachusetts Institute of Technology engineer, had compiled during twenty years the most brilliant operating record of any American railroad executive and had risen to be head of the Denver and Rio Grande Railroad. (After careful study of the trunkline, Perlman persuaded Young to drop his favorite schemes for modernizing passenger service and concentrate all efforts on increasing freight business.)

Young's powerful adversaries in the recent contest had had full knowledge of the Central's precarious condition, which he could not have had. When he marched with his staff into Grand Central Terminal, the headquarters of the great road, with its 12,000 miles of track, 90,000 workers, and two billion dollars in assets, and seated himself in the armchair at the head of the table beneath the portrait of Commodore Cornelius Vanderbilt, he too had come to understand that the company was really insolvent.

During two years the road's income was sustained by nonrecurring Federal tax benefits. The stock rose again for a period, and Young, filled with hope, advised friends to buy more of it. But in 1957, a year of recession, traffic went down and Central faced heavy losses, its stock gradually declining to 13½. Young was then harassed by a whole series of law suits instituted by former associates with whom he had quarreled, derivative suits arising from disputes over the management of Alleghany's assets. One difficult legal contest directed against him by Randolph Phillips, formerly one of Young's intimate aides, tied up a large part of Young's fortune (a new issue of Alleghany's convertible preferred stock) during two years. The Alleghany Corporation and Kirby had been obliged to take back the 600,000 shares of Central stock at $25 from Murchison and Richardson, in accordance with their agreement of 1954, at a very heavy loss.

Young was said to have been greatly troubled by these setbacks and by rumors circulating in Wall Street that he was in straits. He was also greatly embarrassed at being unable to show himself in New York during this period for fear of being greeted with a subpoena to appear in court. In January, 1958, Central's earnings for the previous year showed a steep decline; the directors, meeting with Young at Palm Beach, voted to pass the dividend, and he, deeply humiliated, did not object. Like other men in the public eye he received many anonymous letters, some of them from the "Aunt Janes" who had lost money in Central. He still had a million or two in reserve funds, to be sure, some of it in his wife's name, and the suits which had tied up his largest stock holdings were expected to end in his favor, as they did, though too late.

He had seemed to his friends at Palm Beach not only depressed, but unusually quiet and withdrawn. On Saturday, January 25, 1958, he sat alone for a while in his library at the Palm Beach mansion, then went down to the billiard room in the basement, took up a shotgun, and ended his life.

The condition of the New York Central was terribly flawed; the best hope of Young and his helpmate Alfred Perlman was to consolidate the road with the mammoth Pennsylvania Railroad, Young and Perlman to withdraw thereafter. But the Pennsylvania's earnings were also declining steadily. Their plan was not to be carried out until 1968; and two years after that, the amalgamated Penn-Central wound up as the largest bankrupt in all history. It is certain that the Penn-Central affair was grossly mismanaged from beginning to end. However, the question has been raised whether the situation could have been saved even by the best of managers. The whole economic and political climate had changed for the old Eastern roads. Moreover the values and the very vocabulary of late capitalism have barred the way to constructive change in our great corporations of vital public necessity.

9

THE MONEY LORDS AND
THE NEW RULES

To revert to the earlier period under discussion, the nineteen thirties (when Young was just setting off on his imperial adventures), it should be noted that the Roosevelt Administration began with the express purpose of saving the private enterprise system. The salvaging of the banks had been accomplished by generous emissions of state credits via the RFC, as well as by severer regulation. The finance capitalists, especially their Wall Street fraternity, complained loudly of the Government's corrective measures; but they were the ones who had most neglected their fiduciary duties. Yet the prevailing attitude of the New Deal toward capital—a mixture of theoretical programs and improvisations—was truly benign, in fact that of a generous partner. This was particularly evident in the initial effort to stimulate recovery in the industrial sector.

247

The NRA introduced national planning under trade agreements called "codes," which were drafted by the different trade associations and administered mainly by representatives of business. The whole scheme for control of production, for stabilizing wages, and for eliminating "unfair" competition, while granting immunity from antitrust prosecution, was conceived originally by President Gerard Swope of the General Electric and by the U.S. Chamber of Commerce; it was modified somewhat by granting labor a vague "bill of rights," the NRA 7(a) clause providing for workers' representation by unions of their own choosing. (This privilege was effective only where labor was well-organized, and was nullified by employers of the mass production industries where independent unions were almost non-existent.) The whole plan was derived from the experience of the War Industries Board of 1917–1918; and Roosevelt chose as the NRA's administrator Bernard Baruch's business assistant, General Hugh S. Johnson, who had sat under him as the Army's representative on the War Industries Board. Johnson declared at the start, "This is not an experiment in dictatorship, it is an experiment in cooperation." Most leaders of big business, such as Gerard Swope of General Electric and William S. Knudsen of General Motors, gave voice to the high hopes they reposed in the NRA, which encouraged cartel organization in the various industries. The giant oil corporations likewise cooperated eagerly with a parallel program under Secretary of the Interior Ickes for curbing "hot oil" supply by excessive drilling; the food and tobacco industrialists similarly cooperated with the AAA to curtail crop acreage and raise prices. The Government expenditures of up to $5 billion a year for public works and relief were also useful in furthering recovery.

The operations of the NRA, however, proved unexpectedly complicated inasmuch as hundreds of different lines of trade were to be brought under the somewhat uneven controls of their industry codes. Several of the largest employers, such as Henry Ford, consulted their lawyers and flatly refused to comply with such programs; Sewell Avery, head of the great Montgomery Ward mail order concern, was another who resisted the NRA, though his concern benefited enormously from the Government's help to consumers.

In Washington there was a free-for-all as representatives of large and small businesses congregated in the capital to have their quotas of output, prices, and wages established to their liking. In Johnson's advisory committees one encountered regularly the heads of the giant corporations: Pierre S. Du Pont, Gerard Swope, W. C. Teagle (Standard Oil) and S. Clay Williams (Reynolds Tobacco). Indeed the agrarian Senators Borah and Nye were driven to make a series of set speeches denouncing the President and the NRA as the instruments of unlawful monopolies.

It was the rally of the labor movement, long dormant during the nineteen twenties, that most frightened the large employers. The unions were threatening to organize the assembly-line industries of motors and rubber, and also steel, where only management-controlled company unions were tolerated. Though the NRA won a partial success in having jobs shared, and "Iron Pants" Johnson hung up the Blue Eagle emblem at many points throughout the country, businessmen and the nation's newspapers reflected feelings of vexation or disappointment at the working of the government's program; important groups held it to be unconstitutional and awaited the lowering of the boom on the NRA by the Supreme Court, which took place early in 1935. Few regretted its passing; it had become notorious for its inept compliance machinery and suggested to many persons the procedures of corporate fascism.

Americans had no long tradition of obedience to a central government bureaucracy as did the Germans, who at that very time were carrying out a far more thorough reemployment program under Hitler and Finance Minister Schacht, which, to be sure, was based on arms production. At all events recovery in the United States lagged behind that of Europe in the nineteen thirties. It will be recalled that the heads of our big money-center banks had been thoroughly frightened by the Roosevelt experiment in devaluating the dollar in 1934; and that capital investment slowed down a great deal until the currency appeared to be stabilized. After that came the strong organizing drives of union labor in the mass-production industries under the CIO, accompanied by sitdown strikes in rubber and motor factories. Again the leaders of business showed anger and alarm as the Roosevelt Administration and Congress supported laws such as the Wagner Act, which sanctioned collective bargaining by unions of the workers' own choosing. By now the dominant business groups, fearful of the immensely expanded power of the Presidency, had assumed a complete adversary relationship toward the New Deal and particularly toward Roosevelt. The Liberty League, launched in 1934 by conservative Democrats and millionaire Republicans as a purportedly "educational movement," became a nationwide propaganda organization two years later, with the avowed purpose of splitting the majority party and preventing the reelection of Roosevelt. Funds were supplied liberally by John J. Raskob, former national chairman of the Democratic Party, the Du Ponts, the Rockefellers, and the Mellons. It held large public demonstrations at which business leaders tried to intervene actively in electoral politics. Often in the past, business leaders had appeared indifferent as to who might be elected President, confident that neither candidate could cause them grief, but now they pursued a form of class politics, with their spokesmen disseminating extreme statements about the "alien ideology" of the New Deal and its "sinister professors" who beguiled and misled an artless Franklin Roosevelt. These extravagant charges reflected well the nightmare fears that assailed men of capital in those days.

A thoroughgoing survey of the nation's economic status made several years later by the Temporary National Economic Committee showed, on the contrary, that as of 1939 very little had changed. Even in the financial field the bulk of new issues of securities from 1934 to 1937, in the amount of 10 billion dollars, were underwritten by the investment firms that had been segregated from Morgan's, the National City, and the Chase Banks, and in the field of high grade bonds 65 percent of all issues were underwritten by Morgan, Stanley, and the rest by firms like Kuhn, Loeb or Dillon, Read or First Boston (made up of former affiliates of Chase and First National of Boston). There was some change of outward form, but the faces were the same. In the typical mass production industries concentration had advanced strikingly in the nineteen thirties, as exemplified by the three major automobile companies which made 93.4 percent of all American automobiles in 1935.

The New Deal had introduced some modest changes in the social equilibrium by making the national government responsible for the welfare of the lower classes; by 1939 it had increased government expenditures by approximately 70 percent over those of 1929 and redistributed a part of the national income for the benefit of the unemployed. This deficit spending was never enough in the view of J. M. Keynes, who held that it should have been three times as large in order to attain full employment. Meanwhile the New Deal actually encouraged monopolistic industry; the same corporate lions, though somewhat chastened in spirit, still towered over the nation and clung to their lions' shares of the market.

The Austrian economist Joseph Schumpeter, who served at that period as a consultant to leading American corporations, observed that their directors appeared to him overly frightened and disheartened by the " revolutionary" New Deal policies. Though Schumpeter professed himself a cham-

pion of private capitalism—especially in its heroic age of
venture and innovation—he held that "the New Deal policies were . . . not incompatible with the effective working of
that system." In Europe he had seen so-called Socialist governments extract a great deal of what Marx defined as "surplus value" from capital and yet still leave room for private
profit. In his judgment, American business leaders found it
difficult to adjust themselves psychologically to the rapid
change of the government attitude toward them. The private
sovereignties of property and business had been too long
accustomed to an untrammeled freedom in America's "para-
dise of capitalism." When this freedom was abridged, business initiative became subdued and recovery remained sub-
normal. (A few years later, however, there arrived suddenly
the emergencies of wartime and its much heavier tax bur-
dens and controls, yet the men of business then performed
in excellent style.) [1]

In the relatively prosperous year 1937, unemployment
was much reduced; the President claimed credit for the New
Deal's "pump-priming" and promised to cut public spending
and balance the budget. There had been a surge of speculation for the rise in commodities as well as stocks, but Government economists gave warning of a new collapse and recession. The Federal Reserve tightened bank credit, and
prices began to fall swiftly, business activity slowed, and unemployment rose again to ten million.

In cutting spending for relief the President had yielded
to the appeals of his more conservative advisers, who desired
to strengthen the government's credit. Now he and his aides
were greatly displeased with the big industrialists who at the
first good opportunity had gone to excesses in accumulating
inventory and raising prices, which seemed to contribute to
the severity of the recession after the autumn of 1938.

At this period a new economic theory aroused the interest of the New Deal intellectuals, that of "monopolistic

competition" (or imperfect competition), which held that "administered" market prices in industries firmly controlled by cartels caused the malfunctioning of the free enterprise system, tending to create underconsumption and prolong the downward cycle. This seemed an apt description of the situation in a country, which as Schumpeter wrote, "had the best chance of recovering quickly," but failed to do so. The same men who had earlier conceived the NRA program now proposed to unloose a general attack upon the industrial trusts that had been favored before. The Roosevelt Administration also reversed itself by resuming deficit spending for relief and at the same time by beginning criminal prosecutions for conspiracy under the Sherman Antitrust Act of 1890. The object of this new crusade was to preserve and strengthen "the system of private enterprise for profit." It had an old-fashioned American Populist, rather than a collectivistic, spirit. Admirable politician that he was, Roosevelt held to no consistent credo; but he had a long lingering suspicion that big business was "on strike" and merited chastisement. As he stated in a commendatory note on the TNEC program, its thesis was that the free enterprise system "had not failed, but that it has not yet been tried."

A new favorite of the President had risen in the Justice Department: Professor Thurman Arnold of Yale Law School, a ruddy-complexioned, breezy Westerner from Wyoming, who had been educated at Princeton and Harvard, and who had served as an officer in the AEF in France. Appointed Assistant Attorney General in charge of the Antitrust Division, he hired a strong team of lawyers and in less than a year had begun the prosecution of more trusts than had been called to account in forty years, among them corporate monsters such as General Motors, General Electric, Alcoa, and Du Pont. Nor did Arnold spare certain labor unions in the building trades, which were indicted for conspiracy and featherbedding.

A man of wit, a forceful writer in the field of corporate

and public law, and author of a famous book, *The Folklore of Capitalism* (1936), Arnold represented the campaign against the monopolies to Roosevelt in a most attractive light. He looked beyond the mere prosecution of trusts, he claimed, to the end of liberating new competitive energies wherever dominant corporations retarded the progress of technology in order to protect their obsolete capital. The earlier awkward attempts of government at economic planning, he argued, "had created only confusion and bitterness and the constant backing and filling that went on in those years." The business groups had fought back in all the legislatures and courts and "the country was filled with the resentments aroused . . . by extreme theoretical positions in conflict." Antitrust enforcement would be far preferable politically to Government control of business and would revive competitive enterprise. Arnold's ideas won the ardent support of the President, and for two years he was the pride and joy of the second New Deal. Roosevelt relished the fierce assaults of the Justice Department on some of his big business adversaries. At the same period the TNEC, jointly appointed by the President and the Senate, under the direction of Leon Henderson and aided by Thurman Arnold, carried on a thoroughgoing inquiry into the various concentrations of economic power in industry and banking.

As he was engaged at the time in his struggle to keep control of Alleghany and Chesapeake and Ohio, Robert R. Young, together with his ally Cyrus Eaton, joined in the antimonopoly crusade. Both men gave impressive testimony before the TNEC touching the banking monopolists in the railroad field. Several years later Young again joined with the Department of Justice in an antitrust suit against the alleged cartel of two trade associations, the Western Association of Railway Executives and the American Association of Railways, which were charged with "collusive rate fixing, and agreements to limit service and suppress technological improvements." From the New Deal in its later antitrust phase, independents such as Young gained tremendous support.[2]

For A. P. Giannini the new antitrust crusade was no help—indeed it spelled sheer disaster. Up to then he seemed to have enjoyed the favor of the Administration; he had been able not only to expand his branch system in California, but had accumulated important banking properties in four neighboring states through Transamerica, his bank's holding company, which still survived in this Age of Reform. Meanwhile the Bank of America's deposits had risen to almost two billion dollars, making Giannini's banking combination, with its outstate banks, the largest in the country. But he had never abandoned his great dream of building an interstate chain within the West Coast Federal Reserve District, and eventually a nationwide concern. To this end he had lobbied persistently to have a clause sanctioning interstate branches incorporated in Eccles's Banking Act of 1935. Though he was disappointed when this was denied him, he nevertheless had stumped for Roosevelt's reelection in 1936.

It was inevitable that the Washington Administration and the Federal Reserve should regard his banking empire with apprehension. One of Roosevelt's advisers, Chairman Leo T. Crowley of the Federal Deposit Insurance Corporation, said, "If you let A. P. on the loose he'd have 1000 banks under his belt before you could say 'stop.'" The bank chain's reserves of cash did not seem to match its growing deposits. It was also loaded with great blocks of real estate still depressed in value and was known to have sustained losses of as much as $40 million in the bank's Los Angeles units (whose former directors had loaned themselves money and lost it). Although the Bank of America had been absorbing operating losses in 1933 and 1934, Giannini resumed paying annual dividends, declaring that it was one way to overcome fear. The Federal Reserve objected to the payment of those dividends which, in the estimation of their own examiners, were unearned. Moreover this one bank chain, as Crowley reported to Secretary of the Treasury Morgenthau, with its armies of small depositors in California, held half of the total deposits insured by the FDIC in its early years.

In 1936, as the stock market recovered, it was reported that the Gianninis had gone back into the business of selling securities with all their old vim. Once more a "boiler-room" type of agency sent salesmen hawking Transamerica stock all over the country, while a pool rigged its price in the market, so that the holding company's stock gradually rose to $18 a share from the low of $2 in 1933. The SEC sent a discreet warning to the stock-selling organization, a subsidiary of Transamerica, and the pool in the stock was quietly dissolved. The same rigging business was carried on thereafter by another agency that was not connected with Transamerica. "After having sold so much stock to the public, A. P. had a gnawing desire to see it all come back," one of his intimates said at the time.

As the recession of 1937 to 1938 made itself felt throughout the country, Treasury Secretary Morgenthau grew uneasy about the Giannini bank. The Treasury's Controller of the Currency, whose department examined and regulated national banks, therefore sent an order to the Bank of America demanding that it reduce its dividends so as to build up reserves. Giannini replied by telegram: "By God that dividend is right." It was not easy for Government functionaries to punish a bank with over a million depositors.

In an attempt to mollify the government examiners, the Bank of America (sometimes called "the world's largest farm owner") tried to lighten its burden of foreclosed real estate paper by "selling" sizable parcels of it to its corporate alter ego, Transamerica, and loaning Transamerica the money for this purpose. It was a way of doing what the law wanted it to stop doing. Clark Beise, the national examiner for the Controller of the Currency, judged these arrangements still unsafe, inasmuch as insufficient security was given in return for the loans; he therefore pressed the bank to raise more capital by selling $7.5 million of preferred stock to the RFC. The Gianninis however were unwilling to have it known that they were forced to borrow again from the Government and kept putting it off. Eventually they reached a compromise agreement with the Federal officials, by which five million dollars was transferred from surplus capital to reserves against losses on real estate collateral. Not long afterward Mr. Beise, the Federal official who had helped work out the compromise agreement, was invited into the bank as a high-salaried executive vice president; toward 1954 he became acting president of the Bank of America. In the days of intensive state regulation and assistance to big business, there was a good deal of shifting of manpower between the camps. It was decidedly more profitable for the underpaid regulatory personnel to change their roles and enter private business.

One of the most curious aspects of the operations of the growing welfare state under Roosevelt was its tendency to align a group of the intellectual elite vested with important bureaucratic powers against the formidable private business blocs they were authorized to regulate and sometimes even to police. Thus we have seen "Tommy" Corcoran fighting for the SEC law against all the powers of Wall Street. Later Corcoran, on leaving the Government service, became the highly paid lawyer for the kind of corporations he once helped to regulate, especially those having important business in Washington, such as the gas pipeline interests.

On another front the "death sentences" for utility holding companies was to cause the breakup of Morgan's Commonwealth and Southern Corporation, some of whose operating companies were to be absorbed by the Tennessee Valley Authority, headed by the young lawyer David E. Lilienthal. There was an element of the grotesque in the spectacle of the $10,000-a-year Lilienthal defending the TVA against the $200,000-a-year man Wendell Willkie, the Morgan's advocate, who had most of the press, a powerful lobby, and the conservative wing of Congress behind him. "Honest Harold" Ickes was constantly in fear that some of his staff would go whoring after the rich corporations, and with good reason, for here and there an underpaid official would resign and turn to counseling the same private interests he had been regulating.

Willkie himself remarked in an article published in *Fortune* in 1935 that the only reason why an able man worked at low pay for the government was "for the purpose of building himself up for a private job later on at a better salary." Therefore he suggested that a good way to influence such persons would be to let them understand that their resistance to compromise with private business views might impair their future chances for lucrative employment outside the Government. In his memoirs covering that period, Lilienthal recalled that Willkie, in dealing with him, performed in the style he described as now threatening him with everything in the book, now suggestively calling his attention to the plums of future business jobs. All this evidently had no effect whatsoever on Lilienthal's conduct while in office, but he himself admits that he felt strongly the lure of the cash and the fleshpots the men of the big banks and private utilities enjoyed. (After directing successively the Government's two multibillion dollar corporations, the TVA and the Atomic Energy Commission, Mr. Lilienthal did end up in the service of one of the biggest of the international investment banks.)[3]

At the SEC in 1938, William O. Douglas, the young law school professor who had recently succeeded Landis as chairman, pressed the New York Stock Exchange to draft a new constitution calling for sterner regulation of brokers by its own governing committee and for thoroughgoing inspection of their books. Douglas, who was a favorite of President

Roosevelt's, threatened to go to Congress for more drastic regulation of the securities exchanges. Although Whitney had been replaced as president of the Exchange, he retained a boss's control of its Board of Governors and during two more years had successfully opposed the examination of the members' books by outside auditors. But now the Exchange's authorities even had Whitney's books and records examined by outside accountants, because of his failure to deliver certain securities, and his insolvency, which he had long covered up, was revealed. The scandal of Whitney's trial and conviction for embezzlement of approximately three million dollars left in trust with him helped bring about a new regime in the New York Stock Exchange.*

Douglas also instituted the first criminal suit against an Exchange member under the SEC law. Next he turned and struck at Giannini's Transamerica Corporation by opening proceedings to delist its stock from leading markets, charging that it had been making false and misleading statements about its financial condition. The Government agency entered forty items of complaint against the holding company, the gist of it all being that it exaggerated its profits and minimized its losses; the SEC further charged that Transamerica concealed the names of various subsidiaries, through whom it carried on market rigging and manipulation of its own stock. The most damaging allegation concerning one of these subsidiaries, Pacific Coast Mortgage Company, controlled by A. P. and associates, was that in 1936 it had operated an insiders' pool which garnered profits of $1,620,941,

---

* By 1937 Whitney had been reduced to borrowing money on personal loans from members of the Exchange. Shortly before his arrest by District Attorney Thomas B. Dewey, the man with the facade of an old school financier approached Ben Smith for a loan. Smith testified: "Whitney came up to see me and told me . . . he would like to borrow $250,000 on his face. I remarked that he was putting a very high value on his face, so he said his back was to the wall . . . I said he had a lot of nerve to ask me for $250,000 when he didn't even bid me the time of day. I told him frankly I didn't like him—I wouldn't lend him a dime."

while unloading Transamerica stock on the public. It was the sort of thing A. P. had often accused other ornery bankers of doing! Californians laughed wryly when they read about it in their newspapers under headlines such as:

A. P. GIANNINI ACCUSED OF FRAUD

A. P.'s bellows of wrath, it was said, could be heard for several blocks up and down Montgomery Street in San Francisco. He was furious because he had not been informed in advance of the SEC's sudden thrust against him. (Often the SEC managed things quietly to avoid disrupting market values.) But he denied everything. Accompanied by a whole battery of lawyers, lobbyists, and publicity men, he marched on Washington in January, 1939, and prepared to give battle not only to the SEC, but also to Secretary Morgenthau, whom he suspected of directing a "conspiracy" against his enterprises.

In Washington the representatives of the press were intrigued by the great man from California and described his off-the-record conferences as a mélange of foxiness and indiscretion. A "cabal," he charged, had been formed against him, and its machinations reached from the highest places in Wall Street to San Francisco and back to Washington. Of the New Deal administration he said, "I'm cured and disillusioned—through with it." It was run by "young whippersnappers who know nothing about the realities of business life." Washington was distracted for a week by Giannini's "war against the United States." He himself persuaded the friendly Jesse Jones to plead his case before the President, in vain. Through California's members of the House and Senate and those from other Pacific Coast states, he almost brought about a legislative investigation of the SEC and the Treasury Department as well. Meanwhile his lawyers won a temporary injunction restraining the SEC from having Transamerica stock delisted.

At one point, unable to have the prosecution of the Transamerica case called off, he suddenly changed his aggressive tactics, spoke with seeming ingenuousness, and invited the SEC's investigators to come to California and examine all his companies' records. He said feelingly: "I have nothing to conceal, my life is an open book, I've never gone to jail and I don't believe in speculation or entangling alliances by officers of a bank." The hearings were suspended while everybody concerned trekked out to California.

There was a cynical philosopher in Giannini who knew men and politics much as Machiavelli and Guicciardini understood them in the Florence of the Medicis. He was reported on one occasion to have said: "There are only three kinds of politicians: those who can be persuaded, those who can be intimidated, and those who can be bought." He also admitted frankly that he tended to "cut corners" in his business, avowing that he didn't care if it was "improper" to do something he wanted to do: "If I know I'm right and can justify myself to go ahead, I take a chance." One of his bright lieutenants on being ordered to undertake a risky assignment, remarked "I may have to go to jail for this." A. P.'s answer was, "Well then, I'll go with you." He was an autocrat, but one with strong paternal feelings. The elephantine Bank of America was always his "baby," its hard-working staff of executives were his "family." In his youth he had shown responsibility in working to support his widowed mother and his brothers and sister. Now, in the hearings for the Transamerica case, when the chief counsel for the SEC, O. John Rogge, pressed him with questions as to what he was lobbying for in Washington, he replied "I am merely a watchdog here to see to it that you boys in Washington don't rob my boys and girls of their institution." His bluntness of speech itself was disarming.

"They've always tried to regulate us, or criticize us," he said of his adversaries in and out of Government, "but in the end we were proved right." Much of his branch-banking program was eventually sanctioned by law. The politicians changed; they came and went; but the banking bureaucracy Giannini had founded stood fast.

The Transamerica case sputtered on and off like an unstopped phonograph record for fifteen long years. During the war the suit of the SEC to delist it from leading stock exchanges was suspended, but it dragged on afterward, ending in 1947 with a gentlemen's agreement whereby the holding company would distribute to individual shareholders most of its remaining stock in the Bank of America. Earlier Mario Giannini had also settled the dispute with the Treasury Department and the Controller of the Currency, when the Bank of America agreed to increase its reserves by about thirty million dollars through an issue of preferred stock to the RFC (which was later fully retired).

But the Federal Reserve Board still wanted the holding company to divest itself of all its remaining Bank of America shares, for even when these were reduced to a small fraction (7.66 percent), Transamerica held working control of the bank, and they had identical officers. The holding company also continued to buy up heaps of banks in five Western states. Therefore the Federal Reserve Board, under Eccles, opened suit against both the holding company and the bank, this time under provisions of the Clayton Act, prohibiting "potential monopoly."

President Truman and the new Treasury Secretary, John Snyder, however, proved to be friends-in-office to the Giannini group, whose very large postwar acquisitions of branches were sanctioned by the Government. The case of the Federal Reserve against Transamerica protracted itself over the years until 13,000 pages of testimony had been compiled. A. P. Giannini died in 1949, and two years later his son also died, but the case dragged on. It was lost in 1952, but won back in 1953 in the U.S. Court of Appeals. By then the last interlocking director was dead, and Transamerica sold off its remaining shares in the Bank of America. But the two corporations have continued to live as Siamese twins, although Transamerica has finally spun off all its various bank holdings in five states and has in its $3 billion portfolio a diversity of investments, of which life insurance is the largest.

Today the outsized institution called Bank of America has assets of more than $32 billion, and exerts a world-wide influence. It was shown to have gathered together nearly 40 percent of the deposits and almost 50 percent of all borrowings in five Western states, including populous California. Not only Eastern finance but important California rivals supported the long campaign, first of the Roosevelt Administration, later of the Federal Reserve, against the "monster chain." Yet in modern times the public seems to have become reconciled to it in its less overtly aggressive and more conventional guise. At all events the power of resistance shown by the bank and the Transamerica group illustrates the extreme difficulty faced by government in containing the species monopoly once it has become rooted in the national economy and grown to the size of a government in itself.

In his later years the aging A. P., aware of his son's frail health, conceived of a useful bureaucratic device that would achieve continuity of management for the world-wide affairs of the Bank of America: a management committee consisting of ten veteran executives. Carl Wente was chairman and Clark Beise was named vice chairman. Giannini's surviving daughter, Mrs. Claire Hoffmann, has been the only member of his family included in the Management Committee, which has ruled over the whole banking empire up to the present day.

The spirited antimonopoly crusade of the later New Deal called the public's attention to the overpowering presence of the supercorporations and to their steady trend to concentration. That little was gained and very little changed by the antitrust suits is suggested by the 1941 TNEC report showing that one thousand leading industrial concerns controlled 60 percent of the nation's manufacturing assets. Even the identity of these corporations had changed little since 1930, when *Fortune* magazine gave its roster of the leading industrials. Generally, the Government's antitrust suits terminated in a peaceful cease-and-desist agreement, the monopolists promising to behave. With the coming of World War II, moreover, the crusading of Arnold and his young lawyers came to a halt.

It was the leading finance capitalists of the nineteen twenties who (with the exception of a Giannini) suffered a severe shake-up under the New Deal; the industrial monopolists were left undisturbed in their possessions. In the nineteen thirties the dominant corporations discovered no new figures of heroic stature to compare with those of Morgan's and Carnegie's day. The giant concentrations (though soon destined to enjoy a tremendous expansion) saw their management becoming more and more bureaucratic and hierarchical. In the later period the public no longer remembered the names of the presidents of the various billion dollar corporations.

The new masters of the great corporations were primarily "organization men" as William H. Whyte, Jr., has named them.[4] Their future depended upon the high salaries, social security, and valuable stock options with which their organizations could reward them. These men of the so-called managerial class were seldom "neutral" in profit seeking, or indifferent to the stockholders' interests, as James M. Burnham and other expounders of the "managerial revolution" have suggested. On the contrary the executive elite tended to work closely with controlling stockholding groups and took their reward in the form of incentive shares or valuable stock options, which added capital gains, at low tax rates, to their high salaries. The old-time "robber baron" could take it or leave it, so far as his company was concerned; or could profit by calculated mismanagement, as did Jay Gould and others. In a word, the old-time tycoon dominated his corporation; but in later stages the corporation dominated the Organization Man; he relied upon it for his expense account, health benefits, and retirement.

Alfred P. Sloan, at the command post of General Motors, the nation's largest industrial concern, was an outstanding administrator, a methodical and colorless man, who became immensely rich through his mounting share of the company's stock. His colleague, John J. Raskob, was the more imaginative type; he had his dream of installment plan selling, and gained much thereby. Yet these powerful executives in the GM clan were destined to be forgotten. William S. Knudsen, decidedly a lesser figure in the GM hierarchy, who became president of the corporation in 1937, was the one who rose to national fame, mainly because of his patriotic services to the government's rearmament program during wartime. In tracing his career briefly we may observe the nature of the adjustments made by his organization in a world undergoing spectacular change, in which GM continued to hold first place.[5]

The nation's largest manufacturing concern had confronted government intervention in the crisis season of the NRA and emerged with its approximately 50 percent share of the automobile market undisturbed, the rest of it being divided mainly between the two other giants, Ford and Chrysler. GM had also balked efforts to introduce independent labor unionism into its plants, with the help of the NRA's regulatory officials. After the Wagner Labor Relations Act was passed, and finally sanctioned by the courts, the unions came forward again, this time employing the stratagem of the "sit-down" strike in the mass production factories. By Christmas week, 1936, GM's Chevrolet plants at Flint, Michigan, were unlawfully occupied by the United Auto Workers. President Sloan called for state troops to eject the men by force, but Governor Murphy, a Democrat, consulted with President Roosevelt and was advised by him to delay using armed troops while trying to settle the affair by negotiation. The barricaded workers meanwhile fought off police who attempted to enforce a local court injunction. Sloan next appealed for help to the President. Mindful of the fact that Sloan had severely criticized him in earlier public statements, Roosevelt refused to see him at the White House, turning him over to Secretary of Labor Perkins. Urged to meet with the strikers or treat directly with John L. Lewis, head of the CIO, Sloan would not yield an inch and broke off contact with the Government people.

William S. Knudsen, the former assembly-line boss at Ford, and for some years production chief at GM's Michigan plants, was under orders not to treat with the union officers. In fact he had made some preparations for the contest by employing labor spies and accumulating a supply of arms and tear gas, at a cost of $995,000, as reported by a Senate Committee in January, 1937. Yet he was a man of different mold from the college-bred Alfred Sloan, having risen high in management status from the ranks of the blue collar workers. Two years earlier he had spoken favorably of the New Deal and gave the impression of being more tractable than Sloan.

He had come here from Denmark in 1898 as an immigrant, but had a fair education and some mechanical skills acquired in a technical school. This barrel-chested giant of a factory hand was no slow coach; employed for some time in a bicycle factory in Buffalo he was soon made foreman of his shop. After his employers began to produce accessories for Henry Ford's T-model car, his workmanship caught the eye of Ford and he was put in charge of the River Rouge assembly lines. In World War I he built "Eagle Boats" en masse for the Government; and after the war he became one of Ford's top production managers. When he ventured to differ with Ford on the latter's policy of continuing the old T-model unchanged, with its primitive gear shift, Knudsen was fired, but he was promptly invited to join the GM staff. His improvement of the formerly ill-starred Chevrolet and his success in organizing its mass production won GM the leadership in the motorcar field. By 1933 he headed the Chevrolet subsidiary—then one of twenty GM divisions— and was the executive vice president of the parent company.

The "Speed-Up King," as he was called, was stern with his men, in the manner of Ford, and terse in speech. Called one day to speak before a convention of Chevrolet salesmen, he limited himself to six words: "You tell 'em, we make 'em!" His life had mainly been spent among his tools, dies, blueprints, and time studies, controlling the rhythm of production. On the day in December, 1936, when the workers seized the Flint plants, he was distraught. The silence of the big factories was for him something catastrophic. Denying the union's charges of constant speedup, he said that the "greatest wrong was to stop production" and that they must set the wheels turning again at all costs. In his days as a young foreman he had been something of a scrapper; now he found it humiliating to be forced to enter the General Motors Building by a rear basement door because of the picket lines.

The sit-down strike lasted forty-four days, the workers declaring that they would die "in the trenches" rather than come out without union recognition. Roosevelt, at the height of his power following the electoral victory of that autumn, intervened actively in the affair, now rebuking Lewis for his extreme statements, or now Sloan for his obstinacy. At length, late in January, 1937, the President persuaded Lewis to go to Detroit and sent a message to Knudsen, "insisting" that he negotiate directly with the United Auto Workers and Lewis, the chairman of the CIO. Governor Murphy, acting as go-between, carried on the bargaining between Lewis and Knudsen, the two parties keeping to separate rooms, Knudsen flanked always by Vice President Donaldson Brown and General Counsel John Thomas Smith. It was then still considered infra dig for GM executives to meet with any union officers in the same room. By this time, however, the GM people felt that they had seen the handwriting on the wall and decided to surrender without delay, granting terms that permitted the unionization of their entire work force of 200,-000. The CIO then moved on to win over other mass-production factories, notably those of U.S. Steel, long an antiunion fortress.

In past times the intervention of the national government in a strike had meant only sending in soldiers to "keep order," and in 1937 most of the press and many members of Congress called for this. But Roosevelt's part in settling the auto workers strike peacefully was decisive, turning the balance toward the CIO. It is not surprising, therefore, that the corporation men at this period tended to call the Roosevelt Administration a "labor government."

Knudsen had walked out of the last conference with Lewis and the union men on February 11, 1937, wearing a broad smile, and saying "Let us have peace and make automobiles." Soon afterward the GM directorate recognized his usefulness by electing him president, while Sloan was named chairman of the board of directors. "Mr. Sloan talks the language of finance, Mr. Knudsen talks the language of the workingman," was the explanation given by GM press officers at the time. Sloan, of course, continued to run the business; but it gave GM a more democratic image to have "Bill" Knudsen, the former mechanic, raised to the presidency of the corporation.

President Roosevelt, in reality, had not given much thought to labor unions, and he had no intention of heading a "labor government." On the one hand he dealt with John Lewis at arm's length, for he regarded him as an arrant demagogue; on the other hand he favored the vigorous repression of business monopolies in order to restore competitive enterprise and "save the capitalists from themselves."

Thus it happened that GM again suffered Government interference in 1939, when they found themselves haled into Federal Court, charged with conspiracy to coerce automobile dealers to contract exclusively for the car financing service of GM Acceptance Corporation at higher rates (up to 24 percent) than others demanded. (In those days General Motors' business relations with its many dealers and subcontractors gave it the repute of a corporation with a marble heart.) During the course of the trial evidence was introduced to show that Knudsen himself, while paying a visit to one of GM's recalcitrant automobile dealers, had threatened him with his big fists. After answering a series of questions put to him by the Government attorney, Knudsen in exasperation rounded on his examiner and said audibly, "I will see you later." At the luncheon recess Knudsen found the attorney in the corridor, gripped him by his coat lapels, and exclaimed: "Young man, this morning you asked me how much I make now. I make one hundred and fifty thousand dollars. When I was your age I make fifteen hundred dollars. That is where *you* are today!"

It seems to us but human that the former immigrant from Denmark should take pride in his success as a managerial expert; he did accumulate an estate of $5 million, and yet he was one of the least of the band of millionaires created by GM.

The antitrust suit ended with GM's agreement to charge no more for installment financing than did other companies. The great corporation thus emerged with little lost save honor.

An aging and eccentric Henry Ford, meanwhile, would

have no truck with either the Roosevelt Administration or labor, declaring that union organization only "leads to evil." For several years longer his armed guards stoutly defended the factory walls at Dearborn, until 1941, when the Government's increased authority and the walk-out of 100,000 men forced him to yield.

The businessman "martyr" of the New Deal era proved not to be Ford, but one who had profited richly through the Government's social welfare program: Sewell Avery, president of the Montgomery Ward mail-order concern. The son of a wealthy lumber merchant, Avery, after graduating from the University of Michigan, entered the building materials business in Chicago and at the age of thirty-one rose to be president of U.S. Gypsum, an amalgamation of numerous companies in its field constituting virtually a trust. During a period of thirty years thereafter, Avery figured as a leader of Chicago's financial world, and in fact a model of the prudent conservative in business management. In the crisis year of 1932, J. P. Morgan and Company persuaded him to assume the presidency of Montgomery Ward, a sickly giant in the mail-order and retail field, employing 80,000 people. Within a year the company was making high profits again, but actually this was due in great part to the New Deal's strong aid to farmers, Montgomery Ward's chief customers. Nevertheless Avery made bold to reject the NRA code and its Blue Eagle, which he declared "was blighting the sunrise of a great new era of prosperity." Thereafter Avery fought long-drawn-out court suits to exclude labor unions from his company, or he would harass them after they had succeeded in winning union elections held by his employees. This tactic he continued, displaying legal ingenuity in fighting the Government's lawyers, even in the midst of the war. In 1943 he undertook to sever relations with the CIO's Retail Workers on technical grounds and in defiance of orders of the War Labor Board and a Federal Judge, holding that Montgomery Ward was a civilian business and should not be deprived of its freedom.

Roosevelt was determined that in the war economy there must be no exceptions to the accepted fair-labor practices. Moreover certain of Ward's subsidiaries were filling war materials contracts. Whereas in earlier times the President of the United States could be persuaded to call out the army to put down a strike, Roosevelt now used his emergency powers to put down a strike by an obdurate and refractory capitalist. Amid a great public sensation he ordered in soldiers to eject Mr. Avery from the Montgomery Ward headquarters and had the Department of Commerce take over the company's management. Thus we have frozen in our memories the newspapers' photograph of the slender, white-haired Sewell Avery being carried out of his office on the arms of two uniformed soldiers, the first such instance in American history. Avery's fellow executives heartily applauded his actions and even lionized him but found it advisable to avoid his example. The affair provided a most troubling image of what might befall even the head of one of our richest corporations when he chose to defy his government in a time of national emergency.

After seven years of the New Deal, the leaders of big business and banking were no happier over the government's interference in their affairs than they had been at the beginning, and they longed to see Roosevelt succeeded by a President after their own heart. Therefore in 1940, when war threatened the nation, and it was suspected that Roosevelt might run for a third term, men in the highest circle of Wall Street made a supreme effort to provide an opposition candidate who would have a strong chance to win the presidential race. It was Thomas W. Lamont of Morgan's and Leon Fraser of the First National Bank who fixed on Wendell Willkie, certainly one of the most talented men in their own camp, as a Dark Horse candidate for the Republican presidential nomination.

Willkie, the corporation lawyer who hailed from Indiana, had labored well in La Salle Street and Wall Street. Recently he had been the president of Commonwealth and Southern Corporation, one of the largest utility holding companies, which owned electric power subsidiaries in the Middle West and the South. In his five-year-long fight against the "death sentence" for such pyramided holding companies, he had not only shown marked ability as an advocate, but had always stood on high ground. While defending the rights of corporations he managed also to represent himself to the public as a sincere and humane liberal, ready to defend the constitutional rights of dissidents. By managing to effect long delays in the liquidation of Commonwealth and Southern he won far better terms from the government for his own and similar companies than anyone expected; the gains added up to many millions of dollars more than the TVA had originally intended to pay for certain subsidiaries of his power company. This hard-driving lawyer was not only eloquent in speech but also astute. The daily newspapers and news magazines built him up as the ablest spokesman in America for a libertarianism that opposed Government interference with the individual man of business—in the classical terms of John Locke—and the New Dealers feared him because he was both able and had a winning personality.

Among the Republican Party regulars, Governor Dewey of New York and the newly elected Senator Robert Taft of Ohio were the leading candidates for the presidency; neither man inspired waves of enthusiasm. The men of Wall Street saw in Willkie a colorful and magnetic personality who might appeal to crowds and beat Roosevelt at his own game.

In the autumn of 1939 Willkie had been promoted to a higher rank in the financial hierarchy by being elected a director of the First National Bank. This was one of the mos

prized directorships in America because of its board's inter-
locks with America's major corporations, such as AT&T
and U.S. Steel. Leon Fraser had been president of the bank
since 1936, when he succeeded Jackson Reynolds. He was unusual among professional bankers, a sophisticate and man of
wit who could cope with the reformers in politics. For a
number of years Fraser's jests at periodic press conferences
about the "gay reformer" Roosevelt were circulated in Wall
Street and were found cheering. Fraser had been friendly
with Willkie, and it was Fraser who had brought him into
the bank's board. At about the same time, in anticipation of
the presidential race the following year, it occurred to Fraser
and his associates (as he related afterward) that Willkie would
make excellent presidential timber and "might offer the same
political sex appeal as Roosevelt."

Assurances of support for his candidacy came from both
the First National and Morgan directors. At any rate, in December, 1939, only a few short weeks after having gained that
prized directorship, Willkie hastily resigned from the First
National Bank's board—plainly to avoid political embarrass-
ment—and set off on a long speaking tour around the country. He addressed many businessmen's and civic groups on
the menace of bureaucracy and the threat of a potential "dictatorship" if, as rumor had it, Roosevelt should run for a
third term. The electric-power lobby had been wont to flood
the press and Congress with propaganda against New Deal
legislation, and Willkie had directed much of this work. In
any case he was a superb propagandist, and soon the whole
country was hearing from him.

The big thrust for the Dark Horse candidate came into
the open rather late in the spring of 1940. In Washington
Roosevelt's lieutenants were seriously disturbed by Willkie's
candidacy; even the doughty Harold Ickes admitted that he
was "an able man who thinks on his feet." Dewey and Taft
started with far more delegates, but most of these were carried

away by the "spontaneous" enthusiasm of the convention delegates at Philadelphia for the former utilities magnate. The professionals saw that much money would be forthcoming from the fat cats of banking and electric power to sweeten the political campaign, and they joined in the stampede.

At the final moment, just before Willkie was to be put in formal nomination by the party's big wheels, a rumor spread that the candidate had been involved years before in some scandalous affair with a woman. One of the delegates, James G. Blaine, president of the Marine Midland Trust, was asked to get the facts of the case quickly. Blaine called Leon Fraser in New York and received assurances that the whole story was a canard. The nomination went through without a hitch.

Roosevelt had definitely decided to run again as early as September, 1939, when World War II opened in Europe, but with good reason he had held back formal announcement of his candidacy until the Republican Convention had made its choice. He was nominated for the unprecedented third term late in July, 1940, and held off campaigning until September. By then Dunkirk and the Battle of France had taken place, and England was besieged from the air; the "phoney war" had become an immense human tragedy. Under the darkening sky of the world crisis, Willkie, who had never run for any office, made a very spirited race. He pledged himself to policies that would avoid involvement of this country in the war (as did Roosevelt), but also supported the current rearmament program begun in May, 1940, as well as the proposed Lend-Lease treaty to aid England. Whereas formerly he had appeared as the advocate of the electric power corporations, he now spoke as the advocate of the plain people, the masses whose votes he needed to win. He declared himself in favor of carrying on with the welfare state and the social security measures of the New Deal, promised more jobs for the unemployed, and made a clever bid for the support of the labor movement. The race threatened to become a close one in the later weeks, though Roosevelt won by a decisive if smaller margin than in 1936. Willkie was certainly one of the strongest contenders the Republicans had nominated in many years.

A fortnight before Election Day, I encountered by chance another of Willkie's Wall Street backers, Sell-Em Ben Smith. "Turn on your radio on Friday night at eight o'clock and you'll hear something that'll curl your hair," he told me, but would say no more. On Friday night, to be sure, John L. Lewis, who had lately resigned as chairman of the CIO over the issue of its support of Roosevelt, spoke in a nationwide radio hookup, calling upon millions of laboring men to vote for the "barefoot boy from Indiana," and warning them that Roosevelt might lead us into war. Lewis's defection came as a bombshell and was well-timed to make it difficult for the Democrats to counter its effect; but it was evidently no secret to the Wall Street grapevine.

The presidential election of 1940 was marked by many manifestations of hatred by various groups of anti-Roosevelt fanatics, though Willkie took no part in this. It was true that the President had assumed enormous powers during the crisis years, more than anything known in peacetime. Many men, whose affairs were now improving, feared the President and feared most of all the power he might wield in a time of war.

In the years that intervened before his untimely death in 1944, Willkie grew in stature as a leader of opinion, and at the same time lost ground in his party. He generated a reasoned public discussion of the issues of war and of the peace and freedom men hoped for after war; he no longer resembled the man Secretary Ickes once described as "unscrupulous" and merely "glib about civil liberties." But as he became more liberal his former friends in Wall Street tended to ignore him. In the spring of 1944 the author of the fa-

mous pamphlet *One World* was brusquely rejected as a pos
sible candidate for the presidency by the Republican Party
organization. Leon Fraser was asked at the time why the big
New York financiers seemed to have lost interest in Willkie
He smiled and said: "Oh well, after a while Mr. Willkie
tried to cover so much territory, he took in so many 'worlds,'
that we could hardly keep pace with him any longer."

10

THE ARSENAL OF DEMOCRACY

World War II kept threatening to erupt in Europe during a period when the United States was pledged to neutrality. A prevailing mood of disillusionment about the consequences of World War I, as well as public exposure of our reputed "merchants of death," helped secure passage of the Neutrality Act of 1935. During the Spanish Civil War the United States embargoed the shipment of arms to the Loyalists; after the frightening crisis over the conference at Munich in September, 1938, when Czechoslovakia was abandoned to Hitler, Roosevelt cabled messages of congratulation to all parties concerned upon their avoidance of a general war. Nevertheless World War II began in September, 1939, with the German invasion of Poland; and during the Battle of France eight months later there came an abrupt shift of American policy from passive neutrality to all-out preparation for national defense and arms production.

In the autumn of 1939 we again had some ten million unemployed, a disappointing sequence to the short boom that had receded two years earlier. The New Deal's opportunistic measures had failed to cure the depression; its deficit spending had never been large enough, perhaps because it reached the limits of what was thought viable in time of peace. Now the war in Europe came to the rescue of our economy; in the closing months of 1939, as the British and French began to buy from us the materials of war, especially ships and aircraft, payrolls and prices of commodities began to rise, and the Federal Reserve index of production was up nearly 20 percent by the end of the year.

There existed on paper a Council of National Defense made up of the Secretaries of War and Navy and four other members of the Cabinet; a scheme for mobilization ("M" Day) had also been drafted. In September, 1939, Roosevelt had appointed Edward R. Stettinius, then the chairman of U.S. Steel, as head of a War Resources Board (linked to the Council of National Defense), which surveyed materials resources and drew up preliminary plans for expanding arms production. The following May, as the victorious Germans drove toward Paris, panic gripped Washington, and many public figures came to the White House to urge the President to start a great rearmament program and place a big business executive at the head of it, as Wilson had done in 1917.

On May 16, 1940, the President made his famous "arsenal of democracy" address, asking Congress for an enormous increase in pending Army and Navy appropriations. The strategy of air war against cities and their civilian populations had come into full use; and he warned the country that bombing planes were now only so many hours away from points in the Middle West as well as the East Coast. He called for "fifty thousand airplanes" as well as an army of

1,200,000—soon increased to 2,000,000—which meant a tenfold expansion of the ground forces. In the several days that followed, the President drafted plans for an emergency defense council according to his own ideas.

Although Roosevelt's speech to Congress called for deficit spending on an enormous scale that dwarfed his earlier deficits for relief, the leaders of conservative opinion no longer reproached him for extravagance, inasmuch as the larger outlays were allotted to the needs of military defense.

One morning late in May, "Big Bill" Knudsen, president of General Motors, heard the telephone ring in his Detroit home and was told it was the White House calling. The President came on and said he wanted Knudsen to join the national defense commission now being set up and take charge of production of armaments. Only a year before Knudsen and GM had been "hounded" in Federal Court on antitrust charges by Roosevelt's lawyers; now he was being called to drop everything and serve his country.

"I was very moved," Knudsen said afterward, "that the President called on me." He couldn't help remembering how he had come to America as an immigrant laborer forty years earlier; now the President of the United States was offering him what seemed the biggest production job in the world. After assuring Roosevelt that he would gladly volunteer his services, he had only one stipulation: "First, I have to talk to my people in New York [i.e., Sloan, Du Pont *et al.*] to see if I can get off." "You're drafted anyway," the President told him.

Those whom Roosevelt called "economic royalists" professed neutrality in politics and indifference to the forms of foreign governments, but some of our large industrial corporations maintained very close working relations with the cartels of Nazi Germany and also shared important patents with the I. G. Farben chemical trust. In this regard the Du Pont Chemical Company and GM were little different from

General Electric, Standard Oil of New Jersey, or Alcoa, which maintained international patent agreements that restricted their manufacture of vital materials, such as artificial rubber and magnesium. One GM executive in charge of their German subsidiary, Opel, had lately published glowing reports of the wonders wrought by the Nazis. Knudsen himself, following a visit to Germany two years earlier, had declared that General Goering had received him with marks of honor, and that economic improvements under Hitler constituted a "modern miracle." He had qualified this statement at the time by adding that he was "not necessarily in sympathy" with the politics of the Nazis. But on April 8, 1940, something had happened to turn his mind very firmly against the followers of Hitler: they had begun the active phase of war in the West by sneaking into Denmark at night and overrunning the small country in which he had been born and which he had never ceased to love. His sisters and his kin were still there. Though his associates at GM were said to have advised against it, he held to his decision to serve under Roosevelt and proceeded to Washington.

The newspapers already knew that the "Speed-Up King" was to head the defense production job and that he constituted an important new adjunct of the Roosevelt Administration. At the airport, before leaving for Washington, a large group of reporters besieged him. "Can you build those fifty thousand planes?" one man asked. "I can't, but America can," he said. On arriving at the White House he was photographed shaking hands with the President, a scene designed to be symbolic of the Administration's shift toward a firm alliance with big business.

Bernard Baruch, the war industries "czar" of World War I, was reported to have remarked that "while Knudsen was a good number two man at Ford and GM, he is not a good number one man." Nevertheless he was to figure as the model of the patriotic business executive in the service of his country in a time of emergency. During the nearly two year interlude of preparedness before Pearl Harbor, Knudsen was to become highly visible as America's most famous industrial manager, and so he would preside over the birth of what President Eisenhower later called our "military industrial complex."

As soon as the photographers had been sent away the two men got down to business. "Mr. President," Knudsen began, "who is to be the boss of this Commission?" referring to the newly announced National Defense Advisory Commission of seven members. "I am," Roosevelt answered urbanely. He indicated however that Knudsen could operate as his lieutenant, could have his ear at any time, and could go into action under direct presidential authority. As things turned out it was never to be as clear and simple as all that.

The President had never wanted a big "poo-bah" in charge of all the nation's defense industries program. Instead he had set up a seven member advisory commission appointed by himself: there was Knudsen, the Commissioner for industrial production; Edward R. Stettinius, for industrial materials; Ralph Budd, the Burlington Railroad's president, for transportation; Chester C. Davis, the agricultural expert, for food and farm products; Professor Harriet W. Elliot of the University of North Carolina, for consumers; Leon Henderson, Roosevelt's economist, for price stabilization; and Sidney Hillman, for labor. The Commission was quite a mixed salad, with capital and labor in the same bowl. Hillman's assignment, incidentally, to help provide manpower for war production and to begin training labor for such work, proved to be one of the most important of all.

From the outset Knudsen ranked high in this Commission—though he did not yet preside over it—but it was not a strong commission. The key word in its title was "advisory." The country was still at peace and absorbed by the circus-like entertainments of a presidential election contest. The NDAC could not give orders, or even buy anything; it was the War and Navy Departments, through their new Under Secretaries, Robert Patterson and James Forrestal, ex-officio heads of the Joint Munitions Board, who did the buying of war material. The larger purchases of more than $500,000 were supposed to be "cleared" with Knudsen and other members of the NDAC, but as often as not the military procurement officers did not bother to seek advice or approval from their civilian colleagues. The NDAC, nevertheless, had the important task of planning, together with the military leaders, a huge expansion of arms production and also managing the adjustment of the civilian economy to such expansion.

In one of his first meetings with his Defense Commissioners late in the summer of 1940, Roosevelt outlined the program in more definite form: the number of ground troops to be equipped was raised, the number of planes for the immediate future fixed at 18,641, and the already large Navy was to be doubled in size. The impact of such a tremendous buildup, involving estimated expenditures of about $35 billion within little more than a year, was expected to create severe social and industrial dislocations in the nation's economy, one of the most difficult problems with which the NDAC and its staff would have to cope. Within a few weeks the new government agency became a bureaucratic establishment with a personnel of 1100.

Under this new setup, the complexion of the Administration at Washington underwent a striking change. Formerly it had been served by somewhat scholarly and sometimes even seedy-looking university professors, several of whom worked under the veteran New Dealers Henderson and Hillman. But these were soon greatly outnumbered by the dollar-a-year men that Knudsen, Stettinius, and Budd brought in: big corporation executives, usually flanked by their Wall Street lawyers, well-groomed and fashionably dressed in $200 suits.* Knudsen had as his deputy commissioner, John D. Biggers, a high-powered administrator and president of the Libbey-Owens-Ford glass company, and his lawyer Frederick Eaton. Other advisers and planners came from the Pratt and Whitney Aircraft Company, from Du Pont, General Electric, and Bethlehem Steel. A U.S. Steel executive cleared the allocation of steel contracts and supplies; a Standard Oil of California vice president, Ralph Davis, became the all-powerful coordinator of the Petroleum Administration, as deputy to Secretary of Interior Ickes. ("Honest Harold" now ate, drank, and slept with the oil people in order to get on with the war).

The NDAC headquarters had been established in a wing of the Federal Reserve Board's new marble palace. Over the door of one of its offices one saw the name plate of a Rockefeller (Nelson A.), acting as Coordinator of Inter-American Affairs, and a Harriman (W. Averell), assisting Commissioner Stettinius. Men who headed big industries and the sons of our "baronial" families put in the shade the remnant of the New Dealers. Although as patriots they gave their services for a dollar a year (supplemented by their corporations), it was plain that they intended to keep an eye on their private business interests. The NDAC was not yet fully empowered, but it was to grow into a full-fledged War Production Board, which as Walton Hamilton phrased it, would compose "a House of Delegates from American industry."

Some of the New Dealers, finding themselves being pushed around by the business contingent, complained at what they regarded as a Trojan Horse maneuver of the dollar-a-year men to capture the government from within. The President himself remarked that there were too many Wall Street fellows around the Defense Commission. Yet they kept coming in "through the windows, through the doors . . . and through the floor." "Well, after all, if you want quantities of

* $200 of the prewar, 1939, U.S. dollars; equivalent to some $500 of 1971 dollars.

smokeless powder, or of shell-casings," one of the business contingent was reported to have remarked, "you can't just go to some New Deal professor to get them."

At the same time Army and Navy officers flooded into the capital city. The presence in the Washington scene of a multitude of men in uniform gave the effect of the players having made a quick change of costume. We had not seen much of the military brass these twenty years. Now the colonels and captains performing administrative services were everywhere, and they could scarcely conceal their pleasure at the promising turn of events. After having been long "starved," as General MacArthur used to complain, they found themselves cherished. "Every twenty years they need us," General Patton exclaimed when he learned, to his great joy, that war threatened. For the professional military it meant unlimited Treasury funds and rapid promotion. A first consignment of more than a million draftees moved into army barracks, and the numbers of the unemployed fell.

Who was to run the war industries? Not the zealots of the New Deal! As Budget Director Harold D. Smith reported in 1942:

> A desperate struggle for position got under way. Industrial and financial groups sought to gain control of the defense program. The War and Navy Departments were mainly allied with them. Other groups fought to retain their gains of the preceding years, and prevent domination of the Government by industrial and financial interests.

The major industrialists were both attracted by the enormous contracts offered them and apprehensive of loss of freedom to the Government. To cite a metaphor used by Winston Churchill (in a different context), the major industrialists gave the effect of an aged man going to the altar with a young bride, with emotions divided between anticipation of future pleasure and fear of incapacity.

The first definite assignment Roosevelt gave Knudsen was to speed up the manufacture of aircraft and provide the additional machine tools that would be needed for this. He was also directed to consult with Army and Navy ordnance officers about having diverse airplane models "frozen" into a small number so that they could be produced in quantity. At first Knudsen worked with masses of blueprints of plane parts and engines, which he laid out on the floor of his office. But Air Corps officers kept changing their specifications on the basis of fresh reports from military observers in Europe. Knudsen and his aides met with serious delays; on one occasion they were forced to wait nearly six months before obtaining from the military procurement officers a detailed list of their requirements. The "desk soldiers" performing administrative services looked busy as they hurried in and out of NDAC headquarters with their stuffed briefcases. Knudsen discovered what "Vinegar Joe" Stilwell found in the labyrinth of the new Pentagon:

> We have been rushing around seeing people and missing people and waiting for people. Getting nothing done. . . . A rush of clerks in and out of doors, swing doors always swinging, people with papers rushing after others . . . buzzers ringing, telephones ringing, rooms crowded with clerks banging away at typewriters. "Give me ten copies of this at once." "Get that secret file out of the safe." "Where the Hell is the Yellow Plan (Blue Plan, Green Plan)?" Someone with a loud voice and big stick ought to appear and yell "HALT. You crazy bastards. SILENCE." . . . Then they could burn up all the papers and start afresh.[1]

The civilian planners encountered not only bureaucratic confusion, but also the reluctance of the military to share their added power with anyone but their own kind. Knudsen complained to the President, saying: "Let them make up their minds—I'm no military strategist—but let them tell me what they want and I'll get it for them." With

Roosevelt's help friction was reduced. Later the commanding officers in charge of supply, such as Generals Brehon Somervel and Lucius Clay, got on very well with Knudsen and the other production men.

The most reasonable objections to the military made by intelligent administrators, such as Leon Henderson and Sidney Hillman, was that their understanding of the world outside the military sphere was too narrow for them to be able to deal with the social upheavals set off by the rearmament program. There were delays while statistics had to be gathered; Henderson was worried by the rise in prices; Hillman was concerned with maintaining union standards in the new factories, controlling the migrations of workers, and starting the training of (eventually) 2,500,000 for special wartime jobs. In that first year, 1940, important interests waited to see how the third-term election would turn out.

In August Knudsen set off in an Army plane on a tour of inspection that took him all over the country, visiting seventeen aircraft plants, and what was no less important, checking up on machine-tool facilities. The press made much of him as the "mass production genius" who would help the nation "outbuild Hitler" in military hardware and who was supposed to be passing out large orders to business. Other better informed commentators, however, perceived that Knudsen was actually little more than a figurehead, who was being used by Roosevelt and his aides to win friends and influence people in the heavy industry sector. What Roosevelt had really counted on was Knudsen's ability to persuade his old friends, the Detroit automobile manufacturers (then still bitter at the President), to convert their extensive plants quickly into factories for war material and planes, while cutting down on pleasure cars.

As Roosevelt's emissary, Knudsen did sound out the auto magnates, but they all flatly refused to suspend the manufacture and sale of private cars so long as we were at peace. They were enjoying a boom, turning out more than four million cars a year, as in 1929, and earning profits of 20 percent (after taxes), whereas government arms contracts for ships and war planes were then limiting profits to 8 percent or less. A boom had got under way in nearly all peacetime industries; people were buying all sorts of articles in fear that war might limit purchasing of things they needed. Roosevelt was reported to have said "There will be no millionaires coming out of this defense program." The motorcar manufacturers, finally, had good reason to expect that if war came heavy excess profits taxes would be imposed. It was their contention that the conversion of their specialized automobile plants into aircraft factories would be as costly in time and money as building up new manufacturing space and machinery; and that if they invested in these new facilities they would risk heavy losses later, for such plants would be useless to them once the emergency period had passed. The Detroit magnates made some interesting counterproposals: let the government pay for the new defense plants and lease them, or if private contractors built them, allow rapid depreciation for their cost. Under such conditions they would be more disposed to convert.

When Knudsen got back from one of his trips to Detroit, he went to the President and told him bluntly what the heads of GM and Chrysler wanted. (Ford, at the time, had refused to make airplane engines for the British and seemed loath to convert his plants to arms production under any circumstances.) The President, who was eager to go forward with conversion, agreed to the idea of rapid amortization of special defense plants' costs, to be charged off taxes at the rate of 20 percent a year; and he announced that he would give support to a bill embracing such provisions. This decision marked a turning point in the program. Knudsen beamed as he left the White House, declaring to reporters that the clearing of arms contracts would now be greatly accelerated.

There was a delay of some months while Congress debated the appropriation of billions upon billions and the proposed tax remissions for arms manufacturing. Knudsen appeared before Congress as an earnest advocate of the liberalized contracts and tax procedures. On October 9, 1940, the Excess Profits-Tax-Amortization Bill was finally passed and signed. On that day alone so many defense contractors crashed their way into Knudsen's office that some four billion dollars of Army and Navy orders were cleared.

Big Government had come to the rescue when big business had failed the country in 1933. Now, grown bigger than ever, the Federal Government in the crisis of world war ushered in the "defense economy" and began building up the nation's armor; at one and the same time the Government was becoming the principal customer of our major industries, and their banker as well. Besides offering rapid amortization for conversion into defense plants, new plant space was to be paid for by the Government and leased to contractors, whose orders from the Army or Navy were to be financed through the RFC as "V" Loans guaranteed by the United States Treasury. This meant that the 200 major industrial concerns, who were awarded on the average some 70 percent of the defense business, could, like Standard Oil of New Jersey, set up a plant for making toluol (base of TNT) costing $12 million, and then buy it back after five years at 25 percent of its cost. It meant that U.S. Steel and Bethlehem Steel could obtain efficient, low-cost plants by having the Government pay for 60 percent of the new facilities. Little wonder that the heads of the giant industrial corporations rushed to take up contracts for building plane engines, airframes, ships, tanks, trucks, and gun mounts without waiting any longer for the outcome of the presidential election and without any more "ideological" fear of Roosevelt.

The marriage bonds of big government and big business were quickly sealed in 1940 after Paris fell to Hitler. The prosecution of trusts was quickly wound up. It should be noted that at the time when the new Defense Commission with its all-important business contingent was established by the President, he also chose to introduce the spirit of non-partisanship in his Cabinet by appointing two distinguished Republicans, Henry L. Stimson and Frank C. Knox, as Secretaries of War and Navy respectively. Other conservative figures joining the Administration were James Forrestal, president of Dillon, Read and Company, as Under Secretary of the Navy; Robert L. Patterson, corporation lawyer, as Under Secretary of War; and Robert Lovett, a member of Brown Brothers, Harriman, as Assistant Secretary of War for Air. The last three were men of the first rank in the financial world; they worked closely with the top military leaders— Marshall, King, Somervel, and Clay—and their influence with the brass made them the real directors of the semi-war economy, overshadowing the civilians of the NDAC.

For a year and a half from mid-1940 through 1941 the country passed through a strange interlude, during which we were not at peace and not at war. There was loud dissension among civilian and military planners for the national defense. But considering that ours was a democracy geared to the ways of peace, with anyone free to oppose the head of the state, with Congress more critical than formerly, and New Dealers bickering with dollar-a-year men, there had been a fair beginning of the rearmament drive. The former incompatibles, big government and big business, and now also big labor, were trying to work together harmoniously, though not always with success. Because the ship of state was cumbersome we made some mistakes, but they were never as fatal as those of the swift-moving dictator-states. The United States, which was inherently so rich, developed the will and the organization to turn its economic potential to account, putting on a far better performance under the semi-wartime conditions than the limited peacetime effort of the depression.

Roosevelt had long before formed the habit of creating new presidential commissions (often overlapping older agencies) to handle different problems. After the elections he undertook to improve the seven-man Defense Commission by turning it into a two-headed agency named the Office of Production Management (OPM), with Knudsen and Hillman as its codirectors. Knudsen had shown himself more diplomatic in public life than some had expected though insiders knew that the tough General Motors organization was a school of "business Machiavellis." Sidney Hillman, the Russian-born labor leader, was widely esteemed for his intelligence, imagination, and administrative skill. The "two immigrants" were very different—one a large, ruddy, placid-looking Nordic, the other a small, pale, nervous Russian-Jewish type; but like many immigrants who, as Hillman once said, were "Americans not by accident of birth, but by choice," both were ardent patriots, and if not always in agreement, cooperated with each other in civilized fashion as they worked within their "two-headed monster" of an agency. The two men also embodied Roosevelt's oft-expressed yearning that capital and labor should lie down together like the lion and the lamb. Conservative press opinion, to be sure, objected because Roosevelt had made Hillman coequal with Knudsen, the former president of GM. But there was much fear of labor unrest, and Hillman was supposed to help in that area.

A great deal had been learned already about the "bottlenecks" to be dealt with in converting to a military economy. A

Priorities Board, urgently needed to designate which things came first in the way of war materials, was set up. Donald Nelson, a balding, pipe-smoking vice president of Sears, Roebuck, accustomed to purchasing thousands of different articles each year for his giant mail-order firm, had been placed in charge in October, 1940. Leon Henderson, who was concerned with the inflationary rise of prices already felt in the autumn of 1940, was placed in charge of the important Office of Price Administration (OPA), attached to the OPM. Prices began to rise at the rate of about 10 percent a year during 1941, but at first Henderson could only post up "maximum" prices acceptable to the Government without fixing penalties. In time his power was increased.

Knudsen had ventured some light-hearted predictions about raising the output of military airplanes rapidly by the beginning of 1941 to twelve hundred a month, but it didn't even reach three hundred. Aircraft plants needed machine tools and lathes in order to expand output; some of these tools were large and elaborate instruments were booked to capacity for two years ahead.

Other bottlenecks showed themselves in light metals such as aluminum, needed for the production of planes. But the Aluminum Company of America (Alcoa) had so restricted supplies of aluminum ingots that from the summer of 1941 they would have to be rationed for military use. The Justice Department, which was then suing Alcoa for conspiracy, had also discovered that the lighter metal magnesium —which the Germans were using for pursuit planes—was almost unobtainable here, because the American aluminum monopoly had made a secret agreement with I.G. Farben of Germany to restrict magnesium production and maintain its price 50 percent higher than aluminum. A similar international cartel controlling patent rights had been discovered operating in the synthetic rubber industry, which was now of critical importance because Far Eastern raw rubber supplies were scarce and likely to be cut off by the Japanese any day. Standard Oil of New Jersey had exchanged patents with the German chemical trust and agreed to restrict manufacture of synthetic rubber from petroleum byproducts.

"The Nazis have already invaded America," exclaimed Leon Henderson as the scarcities created by secret cartel agreements were exposed. Roosevelt had begun to call off the various antitrust prosecutions, but in the case of the long suit waged against Alcoa, the action was not ended until a bargain had been struck with the trust. In return for a grant of immunity by the Government, Alcoa agreed to waive its patent rights and suffer the entry of two competing producers of raw aluminum into its monopolized field. These were the Reynolds Metals Company, a processor of aluminum foil, and Henry J. Kaiser, head of an independent West Coast construction-engineering firm, which had made a great start at shipbuilding. Here the Government not only punished a powerful trust but acted as midwife in facilitating the birth of competition in a wholly monopolized industry. The erection of new mills and foundries for Reynolds and Kaiser, financed by the RFC, would take no longer than constructing large additional facilities at new power sites for Alcoa. This was one constructive development of the state capitalist program, as improvised in the eve-of-war period, which would provide more abundant and cheaper supplies of two essential modern metals—aluminum and magnesium.

During the nineteen thirties steel had been a drug on the market, but by 1941 the planners for defense industries forecast a serious shortage which, in fact, was felt throughout the war years. In this industry there were only a few large-scale producers headed by U.S. Steel and Bethlehem. An executive of U.S. Steel serving on the War Production Board (as established in 1942) presided over the allocation of scarce steel supplies. According to the report of the Senate committee under Harry Truman investigating war industries, the allotments of steel strongly favored the long-established customers of U.S. Steel. Moreover President Michael Fairless of U.S. Steel also served as civilian adviser of the Joint Army and Navy Munitions Board, at the top controls of military procurement.

In Germany the Nazis, in building up their arms industry, had found it most convenient to deal with the trusts such as I.G. Farben, Thyssen, and Krupp. Similarly in the United States military supply officers showed a marked preference for dealing with the corporate giants, for they tended to admire the men who commanded the "big battalions" in the business world. General Clay said "You could get results more quickly" through the big companies. The British worked in an entirely different way, scattering contracts in "bits and pieces" among hundreds of small contractors who produced parts of fighter planes or fine electronic instruments with a speed that was said to have surpassed the efforts of the Germans in aircraft manufacture. In Congress, Representative Maury Maverick of Texas urged that the English method be adopted here, and some effort was made in this sense. But in 1941 the military turned over 75 percent of the first $35 billion in military contracts to fifty-six of the largest American manufacturing corporations; this policy was little changed during the next three years. Yet Senator Truman's committee would show that it was such concerns as U.S. Steel and Bethlehem that created shortages by their slowness to increase capacity.

By February of 1941, steel-ingot production had risen from 61 to 99 percent, but still the need was not met, for increasing mill capacity was a time-consuming job requiring much labor and transport. After Pearl Harbor, although the major companies began the task of setting up new mills and furnaces, a severe steel shortage developed at West Coast shipbuilding and munitions centers, where supplies trickled in slowly from Pittsburgh and Chicago by over-burdened railways. In the hope of relieving the situation quickly, the Government's planners brought in Henry Kaiser, already a favorite of the New Deal, and awarded him priorities for material, as well as an RFC loan of $112 million, so that he might create a large new integrated steel plant on the shores of the Pacific.

If there was a businessman hero on the home front of World War II it was assuredly Henry John Kaiser, the bald, hulking, barrel-chested road-and-bridge-builder of Oakland, California. His career is worth reviewing, if only briefly, as an illustration of the method of an able entrepreneur working with capital supplied by the state.

Born in 1882 in a small upstate New York town, the son of German immigrants of the working class, he had been obliged to leave school at the age of thirteen and help his family by taking odd jobs. Within a few years the young Kaiser had set up a successful photographic supply business with branch stores in several vacation resort towns. Seventy years ago this was a new field; it was characteristic of Kaiser all his life that he interested himself in mechanical inventions and innovations.

Though he had a going business of his own in the East he journeyed to the West Coast in 1907 with a view to earning money more rapidly in its growing building trade. A few years after settling there, he had a large sand and gravel business in Oakland, and he also engaged in building roads, bridges, and pipe lines under public contracts. By the early nineteen twenties his construction engineering company was highly regarded on the West Coast; Kaiser had gathered together a team of able engineers and loyal working crews and was known to pay them well. Self-taught, he was something of a cracker-barrel philosopher, who sometimes preached lay sermons in churches on the ethics of industry and labor relations. Around that time he formed a useful friendship with

A. P. Giannini and benefited through the liberal financing provided by the Bank of America chain. In 1931 he was awarded one of the principal contracts for the huge Boulder Dam hydroelectric site, and acted as chairman of the six companies (of contractors) that completed this difficult assignment. Early in 1933, when large public works were being planned by the Federal Government, Giannini wrote President Roosevelt a letter introducing Kaiser as an outstanding figure in California's construction engineering field, and as one of the low bidders for the San Francisco Bay Bridge, for which he built the great piers. Kaiser came to Washington and was awarded contracts by the Public Works Authority for parts of the Grand Coulee, Bonneville, and Parker Dams, which, as Ickes noted, he completed rapidly and at lower cost than other bidders. Although he had never produced cement, he bid successfully for the supplying of the Shasta Dam project and for this purpose quickly constructed the largest cement kiln in the world, the Permanente Cement Company, a low-cost producer. In its construction jobs the Kaiser concern habitually used some of the largest earth-moving or materials-handling machines known. The 240-pound Kaiser was not heavy-footed; he liked to move swiftly about the country by airplane, accompanied by his retinue of engineers and geologists, as he tackled one big job after another. "Problems are only opportunities in work clothes," was one of his sayings. "They tell me I often go out on a limb. Well, that's where I like to be."

As war began in Europe he took up a British Government contract to build thirty small cargo vessels, though he knew nothing of ships. The ships were built in a suprisingly short time at the old Todd Shipyards in San Francisco Bay. After that came much larger orders for 10,000-ton "Liberty Ships" for the U.S. Maritime Commission. He had his team draft novel plans for prefabricating sections of the vessels and moving these by gigantic cranes into the ways of his specially designed shipyards, where they were rapidly welded together. By such assembly-line methods freight ships were turned out in as short a time as four days and fifteen hours. At the end of the war he had constructed a total of 1490 merchant and landing ships, accounting for 35 percent of the nation's wartime ship deliveries, and thus giving powerful support to the Pacific front.

Up to the war period Kaiser had worked with little capital of his own, usually borrowing from banks or counting on government financing. Construction jobs, he said, yielded uncertain profits—"chicken today, chicken feathers tomorrow!" By 1945 his government contracts mounted to a total of about $4 billion, most of it for ships. His RFC loans for developing the Kaiser Steel Company and Kaiser Aluminum added up to nearly $200 million. Kaiser enjoyed working as the partner of the government; and despite excess profits taxes, he and his son Edgar acquired considerable wealth in the form of the common stock of his "war baby" companies, Kaiser Aluminum and Kaiser Steel.

In some ways Henry Kaiser resembled the early, innovative Henry Ford, though unlike Ford he worked with other people's money. He had also a much keener sense of national politics, and he dealt fairly with unions; in fact his "inspirational" methods with wartime labor increased his fame. "Workers are human beings—if you pay good wages you get good men," he said and added, "Labor troubles are eighty per cent of the time management's fault." During the war he introduced the prepaid Kaiser Medical Insurance Plan for his workers, a radical departure that called forth the wrath of the conservative American Medical Association. But he had admirers in the Roosevelt Administration, and it was they who brought him into the monopolized steel business after the Japanese attack on Pearl Harbor.

The two majors of the steel industry, U.S. Steel and Bethlehem, then had only small fabricating units at San

Francisco and Los Angeles. After much trouble in overcoming their objections to his entrance into the field, Kaiser drew up plans to lay down an integrated steel plant at the convenient tidewater base of San Pedro. But naval authorities intervened; claiming that security against Japanese air attack was imperative, they ordered him to move his proposed site to a point in the desert, at Fontana, eighty miles from the sea, where transport would be more costly and water nonexistent. (At that time executives of Bethlehem and U.S. Steel were consultants to the Navy on their industry.) Even so, Kaiser Steel's ultra-modern mills and furnaces, with a capacity of two million tons, were completed in record time, and the vitally needed ingots and sheets came rolling out as required for the last decisive year of the Pacific war, at no greater cost than Pittsburgh steel.

At the end of the war, Kaiser wound up his partnership with the government in excellent shape. He now controlled some thirty-odd corporate vehicles, together with his big steel and aluminum companies, which constituted the postwar Kaiser "empire."

After the war, still eager to give battle to the monopolists, he leased the Government-built airframe plants at Willow Run, Michigan, and undertook the manufacture of automobiles. The Kaiser-Frazer was offered as a family-size car; his chief hope, however, lay in the small economy car called the "Henry J.," which evidently appeared in advance of its time. Capital was raised through the sale of stock to the public by independent underwriters such as Cyrus Eaton. The competition of the "big three" motor companies with their armies of car dealers, however, was very stiff; start-up costs proved large, exhausting capital, and financing troubles also beset the automobile venture, which soon came to an end with heavy loss. Kaiser retained the excellent Willys jeep; and his other important companies were intact. In the nineteen fifties, a decade of war and cold war, he made a phenomenal recovery and knew success again especially in housing and in planned residential developments. At his death in 1967 the Kaiser group's controlled assets were valued at more than two billion dollars. At all events, Kaiser's experience demonstrates the great powers of adaptation of private capital operating in the public sector of the economy. But the question whether such rapid accumulation as his should be permitted, where government not only furnishes profitable contracts but even finances them, is certainly moot.

When the Japanese aircraft carriers made their surprise attack on Pearl Harbor on December 7, 1941, not only did the American military forces go on a war footing, but the civilian defense agencies as well. Decisions on priorities and price controls which had been hanging fire were quickly settled. The OPA began to impose penalties on violators of prices it had posted in order to fight inflation. Early in January a sober-looking group of war-industry planners, headed by Knudsen and Under Secretaries Patterson and Forrestal, flew out to Detroit and met in conference with leaders of the motorcar industry, including Sloan of GM, Keller of Chrysler, and Hoffman of Studebaker. Their companies had just enjoyed the most prosperous year they had known since 1929, and they had not yet stopped turning out pleasure cars. Now they agreed to wind up their private business and convert the great Michigan plants entirely to producing tanks, aircraft, and the munitions of war.

The President had often been urged to place Knudsen in full command of the war industry councils. Instead, Roosevelt—who repeatedly changed his administrative agencies—placed Donald Nelson, recently the Priorities Administrator, at the head of the new War Production Board (or WPB), which was to supplant the two-headed OPM. The shakeup was ordered abruptly, without softening the blow for Knudsen, who had been judged as knowledgeable in production matters but wanting in decision-making strength. However the old assembly line boss was promptly adopted by the Army, which commissioned him a Lieutenant General and used him as a consultant for the duration of the war. Hillman, the old-time privy councillor on labor relations, was then offered some honorific office, but he chose to resign.

The WPB, which tried to serve as the directing brain of the civilian war economy, functioned tolerably well under the mild rule of Donald Nelson, a $50,000 a year purchasing executive, who was an intelligent person of moderate views. Its headquarters, however, sometimes became the theater of intense struggles for power between different classes of bureaucrats serving there: remnants of the New Deal "careerists" who were specialists in economics, statistics, or trade union affairs; the dollar-a-year men who had come from the major corporations, some of whom, like chairman Philip Reed of General Electric, continued to draw annual salaries from their companies of as much as $200,000; and the military officers, of whom a goodly contingent was always present at the meetings of the WPB.

Nelson, a "quiet American," found himself obliged to make decisions of tremendous importance affecting the nation's entire economy. Roosevelt had thrust this responsibility upon him at the outset, assuring him he could write his own ticket as boss of the show. At an early stage of affairs, however, Nelson decided that the actual drafting and signing of contracts for war materiel should be left to the military departments, with the civilians of the WPB retaining only planning and consultative functions and the right of appeal to the President. Such is the account given by Bruce Catton, who served on the WPB as one of Nelson's press officers, in his memoir, *The War Lords of Washington* (1947). The WPB thus began business by renouncing a decisive part of its power. Nelson's stated reasons were that any other plan, requiring a drastic shift of authority already being wielded by the military, would have delayed the war program.

The role of the dollar-a-year men raised serious problems that troubled the Senate's watchdog, Harry Truman. Truman urged that the dollar-a-year men should sever connections with their corporations and work for the annual pay of higher government officials (about $10,000), inasmuch as so many others were making even greater sacrifices to go into the combat services. He also contended that procurement matters should not be entrusted to men who had given "such hostages to fortune." But Nelson insisted that the business executives had become adjusted to a way of living and to financial responsibilities that made it impossible to serve the government as experts unless their previous remuneration were maintained. And so it was the dollar-a-year-men who told the WPB how adequate were the supplies produced by their own industries. Their tendency to self-interested error was summed up by Senator O'Mahoney late in 1942:

> More than a year ago the experts of OPM said that we had enough aluminum to fight the war. They were wrong. They told us we could get enough rubber. . . . They were wrong. They told us we had enough steel to provide for the needs of the nation in the midst of war. They were wrong.

The military, however, preferred to work with the big business contingent. Nelson, though defending the status quo, was intelligent enough to understand that he must rely upon *disinterested* experts, such as the Government's economists, to warn him where the plans for the home front might go wrong; for example, if the skilled miners of a given region were all drafted, then trains and steel mills were left without coal. Such economic forecasting and statistical work was in charge of a group of former New Dealers under Robert Nathan, and Nelson treated them with consideration. He also gave earnest attention to the proposals of Walter Reuther and Philip Murray to introduce labor-management councils in the war industries in order to raise morale and improve output, though this scheme was rejected as "sovietizing." At any rate the WPB became the scene of a hidden palace struggle with the military and business group on one side, the former New Dealers on the other, and Nelson in between. Yet his detachment troubled the military. From high Navy quarters came a sudden thrust to oust Nelson and have him replaced by the hard-nosed Wall Street banker Ferdinand Eberstadt. After serving as a naval officer in World War I, Eberstadt had gone up in Wall Street, becoming a partner of Dillon, Read, and an associate of James Forrestal—through whose influence he had been named deputy to Nelson. On learning that a cabal led by the ubiquitous Bernard Baruch was exerting pressure on the President to have him supplanted by his deputy chairman, Nelson anticipated events by brusquely dismissing Eberstadt and obtaining the services of President Charles Edmund Wilson of General Electric as his deputy and chief of production planning. "Engine Charlie," as he was called, managed these affairs with great vigor and also held the respect of the military procurement officers. The WPB continued thereafter under a system of divided authority, but it was able to meet shortages or other industrial problems with some skill in improvisation, even after Roosevelt, in November, 1942, confused matters further by naming still another man to high authority in this field.

This was the former Senator James F. Byrnes of South Carolina, who had recently been appointed an Associate Justice of the Supreme Court; he resigned from the bench to become Roosevelt's overall Director of Economic Stabilization. An experienced politician stemming from the Southern wing of the Democratic Party, Byrnes was known as an anti-New Dealer and as such was well regarded by big business interests. He was also believed to be Bernard Baruch's friend-in-office.

Now well into his seventies, yet well-preserved and vigorous, Baruch still yearned for high public office; though frustrated in this ambition, he assumed the air of one who was a "power behind the throne." The press and the news weeklies touted him as a wise old man of money who had great knowledge of war mobilization problems and enjoyed the confidence of the big business community. Roosevelt, however, mistrusted him, while making a show of consulting him. Baruch was often to be found on a bench in Lafayette Park looking toward the White House and imparting to favorite newspaper correspondents such as Arthur Krock of *The New York Times* some of his wisdom and inside knowledge. There was also an informal "Bernard Baruch Club" that convened in an apartment at the Ritz Carlton Hotel. Here, during the war, generals and admirals, war contractors, lobbyists, press agents, and newspaper reporters gathered at the end of every afternoon to partake of free sandwiches and cocktails, and to carry on the discussion of human affairs. These informal gatherings, over which the venerable Baruch presided, became the occasion for many "contacts"; they also disseminated much Capitol gossip, but probably they wrought little harm and helped relieve tension.

After Germany's defeat in 1918 Ludendorff in his memoirs attributed the result to the intervention of the Americans, and principally their "gigantic and pitiless war industries" that served the Allies. It was not surprising that this nation's fighting men acquitted themselves well in the more protracted combat of World War II. Our ground and sea forces and air squadrons met the enemy with a massed firepower hitherto unknown; they were rich in everything, thanks to a lavish government and the achievements of its surging war industry on the home front. Compared with the Government's efforts to cope with depression in the nineteen thirties, it may be said that the war economy of the nineteen forties was a tremendous "success." The gross national product soon rose to more than double that of 1929, and 50 percent of it was diverted to the needs of war (twice the ratio in World War I). Our military became the world's biggest buyer for the world's biggest consumer, and the industrial corporations filling war contracts kept in step with the demands of Army and Navy procurement officers.

To the civilian experts of the WPB the behavior of those quartermaster and supply officers often suggested the delirium of grandeur; they seemed intoxicated by their immense new economic power. Senator Truman reported that the military professionals "seldom had any idea of the value of money, they did not seem to care what the cost was." They accumulated material for the present and even for future ages to come! "The time for squabbling over dollars has passed, when it comes to winning the war," the Air Corps commander General H. H. Arnold said to a committee of Congress. Admiral S. A. Robinson declared it was impossible for the Navy to consider comparative costs as was done in private industry; and General Lucius Clay admitted that the Army did not even keep track of redundant military supplies at behind-the-front depots or in transit. Another high officer admitted that there was an instinct in quartermaster personnel that made them "squirrel away" articles of every kind in quantities to provide for unknown contingencies. Yet there was no need to have filled whole islands in the Pacific with great parks of abandoned trucks and tanks that could be seen by Congressmen flying over them, nor was there any justification for the accumulation of flush-bowls, flown over the Pacific for MacArthur's staff officers, in a jungle site of New Guinea and abandoned after the headquarters moved on. And why should one Navy depot have accumulated eleven million oyster forks, virtually a corner of the world supply, acquired during the dark days at the beginning of the war? With so much equipment Navy messes would be prepared to consume shellfish delicacies for a century to come!

The Air Force was the *nouveau riche* of the military departments, increasing its personnel from a few hundred flyers to 2.4 million and expending $8 billion for planes in the single year 1944. Corporations like Curtiss-Wright, Boeing, Douglas, and Consolidated-Vultee each grossed a billion dollars or more in sales during the war years. Fees were now fixed at 5 to 8 percent, but the cash flow was enormous; plants were 90 percent supplied by Government, and the annual profits of contractors on their paid-in capital ranged from 25 to 34 percent. Even after high excess profits taxes, corporate gains increased more than 100 percent during the war years, compared with the partially depressed year of 1939. The stock market remained low and dull until 1944, when more active speculation for the rise prefigured the victorious consummation of the war.

The sum total of outright graft and plunder was not large in World War II. It was apparent that the Army and Navy, with the help of civilian lawyers and accountants, extended themselves to keep the record clean. Old-line munitions concerns, which had been doing business with the military services for fifty years or more, behaved correctly enough. The corporate profits of the war years were quite legal. It must be remembered that the actual gains of many corporations were augmented by very liberal contract provisions for rapid tax depreciation for war plants. Still greater were the gains harvested by corporations doing a large-volume business in basic industries, where prices were stabilized at favorable levels, as in petroleum, chemicals, rubber, steel, copper, and aluminum. In many cases also, bounties or subsidies were paid by the Government to cover "high-cost" extraction of scarce metals or minerals. Such profitable affairs, leading to inordinate gains, were sometimes contrived by great feats of *manipulation* in political, military, and big-business circles (accomplished under the cloak of wartime secrecy), rather than by overt fraud. European observers noted that American industry and management were very "well-paid" to do their job during the war.

To be sure, a few petty racketeers here and there among inspection officers were caught levying toll upon some of the smaller war contractors. Their winnings, however, were paltry compared with the lawful profits of the "majors" in motors, chemicals, metals, oil, electronics, machinery, rubber, and aircraft. More than elsewhere, however, scandal attached itself to the Army Air Force procurement staff and to the "war-baby" industry of aircraft manufacturing, which was almost entirely Government subsidized.

Most of our flying officers were honorable men who risked their lives repeatedly in air combat. But there was among them a little group of chairborne airmen at the AAF procurement bureaus who were in the war neither for love of country nor of honor, but as the military analyst Hanson Baldwin has phrased it, as "empire builders" on their own. It was they who awarded the "cushy" contracts while dealing across the table with tycoons in billions of dollars worth of aircraft and electronic equipment; and it was not surprising that some of them, as in the case of Major General Bennett Meyers, deputy chief of procurement, should became drunk with power. Meyers, it was reported, used to boast of his purchases of "a hundred thousand airplanes." At the same time he managed to divert a small part of this business with aircraft manufacturers to a sub-contracting company of his own, controlled through dummy directors. His profits from such fraudulent transactions were estimated by Treasury authorities later to have amounted to about $140,000.

What is of special interest in the case of General Meyers (brought to trial and sentenced after the war) is its illustration of the disintegrative effect of the free wartime spending and the big military deals upon the standards both of the military institution and of the business system. It was the upstarts, the light-waisted speculators in war contracts who pressed their attentions upon officers like General Meyers and who devoted thousands of dollars of their expense account funds to wining and dining them. The desk generals and colonels were poor fellows, financially speaking, earning only $8000 to $10,000 a year in salary, while surrounding them were civilians whose pockets bulged with easy money.

Howard Hughes, for instance, a millionaire glamor boy of the oil trade and the motion picture industry, had gone into military aircraft manufacture at the beginning of the war, establishing the Hughes Aircraft Works in California. He proposed building improved reconnaissance planes for the Air Force, and in the course of his negotiations he and his representatives had a number of private interviews with the deputy chief of procurement. The records of both Congressional hearings and the subsequent trial of Meyers show that much political influence was brought to bear on the Air Force in favor of the Hughes reconnaissance plane contract. Yet endless delays were encountered. Hughes and his public relations agent found, as they admitted, that it was very important to kowtow to Air Force officers and procurement chiefs. One aspect of this relationship was that the Hughes Aircraft Works from time to time provided sums of $1,472 to $3,242 a week for the entertainment of General Meyers and his cronies or girl friends at hotels and nightclubs in Los Angeles during the war.

At the interviews between General Meyers and Hughes a certain pattern developed in their relationship, which was to become all too familiar in military procurement business. Hughes mentioned the fact that he might be needing a new executive manager at the growing Hughes Aircraft Works. At this General Meyers remarked "with a cute little smile," as Hughes recalled, that he himself might be interested in such a job. He then proposed that Hughes sign a contract with him, to begin at some date in the future, and allow him an advance payment of $50,000 against his future earnings.

But this sum, on the advice of his lawyer, Hughes prudently refused to hand over. Thereafter, Hughes Aircraft encountered new delays in its negotiations.[2] The contract was eventually won, but the development of the new "recon" model, unfortunately, met with technical difficulties—a serious risk in aircraft research—and the Government ended up with a loss of some $22 million.

Disquieting rumors concerning General Meyers's unsoldierly conduct and his sybaritic life reached the Air Force General Staff in 1943 and 1944. It was learned that Meyers had been speculating in the securities of leading aircraft companies, with which he was on terms of confidential business relations as the Government's agent, and that some other senior Air officers did likewise. When the Air Inspector General warned Meyers and other procurement officers at Wright Field that they ought to stop such market operations, they simply shifted their securities to brokerage accounts held in their wives' names.

The investigation and trial of General Meyers in 1947 revealed more than the sorry record of his fraudulent deals with aircraft contractors; it was shown that war contractors made approaches to military procurement officers over long months and years, holding out the bait of future lucrative employment. A $125-a-week procurement officer was forced to wrestle with himself in a "conflict of interest" between his impartial judgment of the good of the service and his future employer's advantage. The Air Force General Staff, though informed about Meyers's misconduct, treated such reports as military secrets, evidently fearing that a public scandal would injure service morale. In 1945 Meyers was retired with decorations and a lifetime pension of $5,532 a year, only to be tried two years later and sentenced to a long term in prison for income tax evasion. Yet some of his superior officers in the Air Force—whose conduct was legally correct—also maintained long and friendly relations with big war contractors

with whom they found employment, after the war at salaries
of $75,000 to $100,000 a year.

Despite the palace struggles going on in Washington,
the Arsenal of Democracy was being built up to its fullest
capacity. After all, both factions, "New Dealers" and "militarists," worked toward the same goal. Wilson, a driving man,
exerted himself to coordinate production schedules; he also
found that it was best to "go along" with the military. On
the home front, meanwhile, the American people, by their
labor in factory and field, were carrying on with a magnificent job of war production, at first setting out plants and
tooling up for expanded capacity in 1942, then building up
a torrential output of $60 billion of war materiel in 1943. In
fact industrial production approached the ceiling of current
capacity by the end of that year, the assembly lines turning
out 30,000 tanks, and aircraft output reaching a rate of
96,000 planes (including training planes), early in 1944. This
was before the landing in France. Both in the Atlantic and
Pacific Theaters, however, the tempo of the American military offensives was, up to 1944, somewhat slower than anticipated. There was never any question of the GIs not having
enough. ("President Roosevelt gave us everything we asked
for," General Marshall said afterward.) Tremendous surpluses were now piling up and they presented problems.

The first phase of expansion, the steep upward climb of
output in 1942 and 1943, was like pushing a great stone up a
long hill. At this stage the civilian experts and managers
were concerned chiefly with how to maintain the upward
movement without letting the stone slip back or lose momentum. But once you reached the crest of the hill, the peak of
output under current capacity (almost 90 percent above the
production rate of 1940), you approached definite limits. The
hope of victory grew in 1943, perhaps prematurely. Now to
the civilian authorities the important thing was to make sure

that the stone would be under control as it rolled on the downward slope. The changeover from an all-out war economy to peacetime activity would be, at best, a difficult affair offering danger of either inflation or economic collapse, and promising serious dislocations in employment for 30 million men and women war workers.

The first thoughts of planning for peace were privately discussed in the WPB agency toward the end of 1943, after a succession of Allied victories in Italy, in Eastern Europe, and in the Pacific suggested a decisive turn in the fortunes of war. The civilian planners felt that the problems of industry's reconversion, and of demobilization of the military forces, would need to be prepared for in orderly fashion, instead of permitting the nation to drift or crash into peace.

Late in November, 1943, WPB Chairman Donald Nelson wrote a letter to President Roosevelt in which he pointed out the need for planning a program of partial reconversion early in the next year. Many surpluses were beginning to pile up, and some companies were already cutting back on their inventories as if anticipating cancellations of orders. Numerous workers were "jumping" jobs, some leaving aircraft factories to look for work that would continue in peacetime. It would create confidence if the Government announced that the changeover to a peacetime economy would be carried out in good time in orderly fashion, with the Government giving assistance both to business concerns and labor for readjustment. Civilian workers had been hard-driven for years; restrictions on many articles for consumer use were airtight; and many laborers in war plants literally had no place to lay their heads at night. Nelson, therefore, made a concrete proposal: in order to improve workers' housing he recommended that restrictions on housing supplies be relaxed wherever surplus materials, such as aluminum and copper (now in abundant supply), were available without interfering with the munitions program.

At the mere rumor of such planning for peace, the heads of the armed services, from Secretary Stimson and General Marshall down to the generals and colonels in the Quartermaster Corps, reacted angrily against their civilian colleagues. There must be no lifting of restrictions on consumers' articles. On New Year's Day, 1944, all the newspapers featured "a long, impassioned and somewhat startling interview with an impressively unidentified 'personage high in the councils of the United States and the United Nations.' " [3] This anonymous personage (said to have been General Marshall) warned the country of the dangerous mood of laxity and optimism spreading among the people. A number of small-scale labor disputes then going on were characterized by him as "the damnedest crime ever committed against America"; they threatened to prolong the war by six months, he declared, and bring about the loss of hundreds of thousands of American soldiers' lives.

The interview was the first move in a series of propaganda maneuvers directed from the Pentagon against any preliminary steps toward reconversion. The next move was Stimson's appearance before Congress early in January, 1944, to berate the citizens, and especially the workers, for "slacking," and to call for the extreme measure of a universal service law on the ground that men behind the front should enjoy no more privileges than those fighting for their country on the battlefronts. A bill calling for a form of wartime labor draft was in fact introduced into the House as part of the strategy of "psychological warfare" waged against the American people behind the front.

There were, at this time, many special business groups lobbying in Congress for relaxation of wartime controls, often in the name of small business. Roosevelt now assailed these and other elements in a speech demanding that there be an end to bickering and dissension behind the front. He also gave some tentative approval to the proposed labor draft, though in guarded terms, also suggesting harsher measures against more privileged groups, such as raising income taxes for the higher brackets. As he foresaw, nothing came of these proposals.

The curious thing was that loss of time through strikes was all but nonexistent, and efficiency, or man-hour production, was rising all through 1943 and 1944. On February 3, 1944, Secretary of War Stimson himself announced that a cutback in the military procurement program had been ordered in the amount of $12.8 billion. Senator Harley Kilgore of West Virginia, commenting upon the contradictions between such cutbacks and the complaints of slacking by labor, wrote to Mr. Byrnes: "Two different military departments shut down their plants in my state at the same time, and they not only wrecked a town, they wrecked every citizen in it." With our entire national economy geared for war, peace evidently offered many dangers.

Stimson admitted later that his complaints of January, 1944, had been deliberately exaggerated because he feared that too many persons believed the war was nearly won, when, in fact, we were still faced with the unknown consequences of the scheduled landing in France.

D Day arrived on June 6, 1944; the American-British forces were successful in making good their landing in Normandy thanks in great measure to the enormous weight of armor and fire-power that American labor and industry had provided. After two months at the beachhead, there followed the breakout of the Allied Armies, and France was quickly overrun. In August the War Department estimated that the war in Europe would be over by November, 1944.

To the people at home victory now seemed near, and a faction among the civilian experts in war production (in

July, 1944) resumed their efforts to plan for reconversion. At the WPB a small team of economists under Professor Stacy May, former director of the Rockefeller Foundation, now chief of the WPB's Statistical Bureau, had been engaged in charting flow of production, locating shortages or surpluses and reporting their findings confidentially to the members of the Board and the Pentagon.

The regular monthly progress report for July, 1944, as approved by Chairman Nelson, showed that large stockpiles of surplus war materiel were being accumulated on the one hand, while on the other some shortages were evident in items such as heavy artillery, radar equipment, and rockets. For example, there were stores of trucks, trailers, Navy mattresses, and uniforms, as well as training planes and small arms enough for five years ahead. The report included proposals aimed both at relieving the shortages in military goods and diverting surplus material and manufacturing capacity elsewhere in order to furnish some badly needed civilian goods. Since the Army either did not keep full records, or made a secret of its shipments of war materiel in transit or at depots behind the fighting front, the economists' report was actually an underestimate, for its figures were based only on supplies visible in the United States, which they deemed sufficient for eighteen months of war in two hemispheres. Part of the problem was the allocation of manpower; in some regions thousands of workers made idle by cutbacks were not migrating from their homes to scarce-labor areas such as California as the military hoped they might be forced to do. The report (after some news of it leaked out) thus gave confirmation as *The New York Times* Washington correspondent wrote:

> . . . to the widely held belief that the Army's own methods of allocation are, in part, responsible for the shortages in some areas and gluts of some supplies in others.[4]

A key passage in this "classified" statistical survey had drawn the conclusion that:

> The turning point of direct requirements for manpower has been passed. With the forces at peak strength, large releases from the munitions industries in prospect will be available for civilian production.[5]

The report of the WPB statisticians had, according to the rules, been cleared for factual accuracy by General Clay's own staff before being circulated as a restricted document among the WPB members and military staffs, and it was only as an afterthought that the Army brass took exception to it.

Nelson, having studied the figures, was fully convinced that cutbacks and gradual steps toward partial reconversion to consumer goods production were feasible at this stage of the war. Hundreds of thousands of workers at defense plants located, in many instances, in remote sites were living wretchedly in trailer parks, under bad sanitary conditions, without commercial laundries, without drug stores, and sometimes without means of public transport. It was growing difficult to hold labor together at such "war facilities" centers. Nelson, therefore, tried to work out a plan for "spot authorization" allotting surplus metal and manufacturing capacity to some housing and consumer goods firms.

However, General Clay, as the operating boss of the Army Services Forces, rounded upon the officials of the WPB and protested that he had not been consulted before the bulletin was issued. It was "not factually correct," he held; it made "improper assumptions" regarding the supply situation and would lead to "misinterpretation" of the Army program. The whole report was a "wrong action," he charged, and he insisted that it be withdrawn, suppressed, or at least deleted in great part.[6]

The conflict between the professional military men and the civilian economic experts was now broadened so that it involved Nelson and his chief deputy, Wilson. Wilson declared that he was inclined to agree with the Army view and supported their objections to any reconversion plans. The members of the War Production Board, with the dollar-a-year men preponderant, by a majority vote rejected Chairman Nelson's plan for "spot authorization" of civilian goods manufacture. Meanwhile the military insisted that the offending passage in the report concerning surplus Army goods be deleted. On this issue Nelson himself (though holding the economists' survey to be accurate) retreated without much resistance because, as he explained afterward: "We didn't want to get into any fights with the Army—we are there to help them." [7]

At about this period (July 4, 1944), Secretary of the Navy Forrestal wrote in his diary of the Nelson-Wilson controversy, noting with satisfaction that "Wilson now reflected the views of the services as against any broadscale resumption." Reconversion, Forrestal remarked, "would be dangerous . . . because of the indirect psychological results that would flow—namely the assumption that the war was in the bag." [8]

The two young economists who had but done their duty and written their report truthfully, on being repudiated by their superiors, handed in their resignations in the first week of August. News of the affair was whispered about in Washington, until it reached a well-known radio commentator who broadcast the story of "two able and conscientious members of the WPB statistical staff" having been driven from their jobs by the Army brass because of their accurate report of alarming surpluses of war supplies and of blunders by military procurement officers. Must it always be kept secret when the military went wrong? Must those who honestly criticized the military authorities be destroyed? [9]

However, on the day before the clash between WPB officials and the Army and before the story of the two statisticians was on radio and in the newspapers, a special release was issued from the Pentagon by General Brehon B. Somervel whose purpose was plainly to counteract such news. It was headed:

PRODUCTION LAG ALARMS WAR LEADERS

The rumors of a behind-scenes struggle between the "New Deal" and the "militarists" now created a live public issue. Some newspaper columnists assailed Charles E. Wilson, the reputed "dynamo" of the war industries program, holding that he had become the pawn of the military brass. Other press comment defended the military and demanded the dismissal of Donald Nelson, which was certainly the Army's objective.

At this stage, former Representative Maury Maverick of Texas, an ardent New Dealer then serving as chairman of the Small War Plants Corporation, delivered himself of strong public attacks upon the big corporations that had the lion's share of the war contracts. These, he charged, opposed even a partial reconversion to civilian goods output because they were determined to hold on to the same share of their markets that they had controlled before the war. What the big corporations feared most, he said, was that while they worked to complete their war contracts new competitors would become entrenched in their consumer industries. Therefore, Maverick continued, the big war contractors joined forces with the military block in resisting relaxation of wartime controls.

"I do not believe you can have democracy and at the same time forbid new competition," Donald Nelson wrote in a letter to Senator Francis J. Maloney of Connecticut at about this period. And Senator Truman who was soon to run for the vice presidency, issued a statement charging that a gradual reconversion program was resisted not only by the Army and

Navy leaders but by "selfish business groups that want to see their competitors kept idle until they finish their war contracts." Truman declared that twelve hundred ordnance plant workers had already been dismissed from their jobs in St. Louis and yet no reconversion program was being started to take up the slack. A popular newspaper columnist also warned the public that the "militarists" and "the big munitions manufacturers" were acting in combination to hold up reconversion until they were ready for it.[10]

There was always a core of Populism in the New Deal, reflected in its protective attitude toward small business and in its antitrust activity. In the conflict within the War Production Board, Nelson, perhaps through no wish of his own, embodied these New Deal aspirations, while Wilson of General Electric seemed to speak for the heavy-industry-Pentagon combination. Charles Edmund Wilson had, after all, devoted most of his life to the service of the country's third largest industrial concern. In the WPB he had assumed an ever greater influence while gaining the support of the professional military leaders. "Wilson could understand the problems of the big corporations; he could understand the problems of the Army too," one of his admirers wrote.[11]

The Senate Committee on the National Defense Program, taking note of the growing public controversy about surpluses of war materiel and efforts to suppress news of them, promptly called both factions to appear before it. Was it not true, Nelson was asked, that more munitions than were needed were being accumulated? Were not the reports of the WPB's Division of Statistics correct?

MR. NELSON: *There was nothing wrong, sir, with that report, statistically.*
SENATOR FERGUSON: *But doesn't this report indicate that we have surpluses and are still producing the same articles?*
MR. NELSON: *That is right . . .*

Nelson, however, remarked apologetically that "surpluses are part of the cost of war," though the American people "would holler a lot about paying for dead horses." Under questioning he admitted that it was General Clay who had "requested" that offending passages in the report be deleted from the WPB record, and that Wilson had agreed to this.[12] Some of the Senators had been visiting the war front and seen with their own eyes the immense stockpile of supplies going to waste. "Is not civilian judgment essential?" Senator Homer Ferguson asked anxiously.

At his appearance before the committee General Clay began by speaking softly. It was true, he admitted, that there was an oversupply of military hardware in some areas. But, he argued, the Army could not afford to "gamble with human lives" by figuring whether the war would end one month sooner or later. Blandly he defended his action against the WPB's statistical report. Warming to his subject, General Clay said proudly:

> We are running the largest business that the world has ever seen. We have a department store that has more items than all the department stores in the Unted States combined, and we have our customers to satisfy, the men fighting at the front.[13]

Nothing was to be denied by America to her fighting men; and nothing was done to bring civilian business judgment to bear upon the military supply problem. Nelson's plan to release 700,000 workers from munitions factories was dropped, and Nelson himself was "liquidated" (as the military leaders wished) in the usual Rooseveltian manner, being sent off by the President as his special envoy to China for a period of six months. In any case the work of scheduling war production was managed in routine fashion thereafter, real control passing in the autumn of 1944 to Director of Mobilization Byrnes, who appointed General Clay as his Deputy

Director for War Programs. In the end, the military, who were so persistent in pursuit of their objectives, had made fast their control of the war economy.

The liquidation of Donald Nelson and the dismissal of his young statistical specialists seem but a minor episode in a war approaching its horrible end with the two atomic bombs dropped on Japan. Yet it signifies a great deal: when the military made mistakes these must be kept secret for "reasons of state," even in the matter of wasting supplies. The habit of military secrecy had existed before; it would become stronger than ever in the long decades of cold and hot war that followed 1945. The President and his advisers, commanding an intermittent military action in many quarters of the world, would also become imbued with the tradition of secrecy and of deception, as revealed so plainly by the publication of the "Pentagon Papers" in 1971.

In November the Battle of the Bulge overturned previous estimates of the duration of the war in Europe. During this interval of military reverses, General Clay and Byrnes closed down horse racing and nightclubs and tightened draft deferment, while reopening some munition plants. These measures were mainly for psychological effect, since new supplies ordered in December, 1944, could not reach the fighting front for nine months. After Germany capitulated in May, 1945, the military permitted only a moderate reduction of 20 percent of the current war program, though it was known that Japan was making overtures for peace.

Following the surrender of Japan, peace and conversion came with little of the planning and order Roosevelt's civilian advisers had originally urged. Industry and price controls were eliminated in haste, while the pent-up demands of millions of citizens who had long been starved for some of the necessities as well as the comforts of life, and who had much money in their pockets, now flooded into all the markets. But there was no sufficient stock of consumer goods on hand.

A bureau such as the OPA, without effective controls, could do nothing to check the spiraling force of inflation. Commodity prices soared to a level 90 percent above the 1935–1939 (wholesale) average, and wages went up in their train, so that within two years of the war's end the American dollar had lost almost half its value.

EPILOGUE: THE WAY WE
ARE NOW

The partnership of government and business in the United
States goes far back in time to the days of the canal builders
and the railroad builders who were largely subsidized by
Federal and local government. Woodrow Wilson, the his-
torian-President, held that the government had generally
acted as the junior partner of the concern, while "the combined capitalists and manufacturers" were the senior partners
and the decision-makers for our national economy. It was all
written, Wilson said in a 1912 speech, in the records of Congress as well as those of conferences at the White House, that
"the suggestions of economic policy come from one source,
not from many sources," and that source was the "combined
capitalists."

All this was drastically changed, as one shrewd commentator has remarked, by the Great Crash at the end of the 1920s:

> Business did not and will never recover from its 1929 failure. ... It had all the power it needed and all the freedom in the world to use it—but the hand was overplayed. Nineteen twenty-nine was the melodramatic end of effective private government in the United States.[1]

In the prolonged crisis the banks, the railroads, the farmers, and the unemployed all appealed to the national government for help. The banking system was rescued, the farmers were relieved, the unemployed were somehow fed, and even homeowners were protected from their mortgagors. The depression made our people accustomed to look to the national government as the responsible, directing force in American society, in a period when private enterprise had lost control of the situation. The public also came to accept the augmented power of the government and the proliferation of Federal agencies and controls which accompanied the intervention of the state in the economy. Meanwhile what had been a regime of restricted and divided governmental powers became one dominated by the executive branch, the Presidency. Under Roosevelt the President's office and power were enormously expanded, while the legislative and judiciary branches grew weaker. Business feared greatly that such power would be abused, but proved impotent to change this. Tens of thousands of added functionaries worked within the new administrative-regulatory commissions thrown up by the crisis and controlled by the President, and many millions more were employed through the WPA. The national government had become Leviathan by the time World War II was upon us.

The overseas war in two hemispheres, employing 12 million in the armed forces and many more in the production of war material and instruments of advanced technology, saw the government assume control of virtually the entire national product, using 50 percent of productive capacity for war. With its expenditure of unimaginable sums of money and its tremendous war taxes, the Federal Government was deep in everybody's business, while its borrowings surpassed $200 billion—sums that would never be repaid. The war advanced further the centripetal tendency of the Government.

The relationship of private capital to the wartime administration became, in truth, that of a junior partner. The great banks, which were wont to impose their will on the Federal Government, now went along selling war bonds to the public and financing government-guaranteed loans, or "V loans," to contractors for war materiel. As Randolph Burgess, then vice chairman of the National City Bank, remarked to the writer, the money-center banks were occupied principally as fiscal agents of the Federal Government, and he feared that they might possibly lose much of their knowledge of the private banker's art of judging credit-worthiness! Interest rates were kept low, yet the banks had no recourse but to buy war bonds and help distribute part of the load to the public as a means of enforced savings; but as the money supply doubled and redoubled, the banks earned more, floating easily on the higher flood of paper money.

America's industrial entrepreneurs had long cherished their freedom of enterprise; now in wartime they were duty bound to serve the government and supply the needs of the military services. They found that despite some initial confusion over the restriction of profits, controls, and priorities, it was pretty good business. We have noted how the heavy industries of steel and nonferrous metal prospered thanks to their military contracts and government-financed defense plants, as in the case of Henry Kaiser and countless others. The aircraft industry was a relatively new field, a huge "war baby" made up of recently created corporations which now achieved major size, such as United Aircraft, Boeing, Lockheed, and Douglas. The government-paid research and development work in wartime brought forth important new inventions designed for high technology warfare in the field of space, electronics, optics, and computers for fire control. (The emergence of International Business Machines as a giant corporation dates from the war.) Major industrial concerns became happily wedded to the government's gargantuan military establishment.

An interesting example of the warplane contractors' experience is that of Stuart Symington, who headed one of the medium-sized manufacturing companies making parts for the Air Force. His is a success story of our armament economy period and entirely at variance with the old rags-to-riches myth of business success.

Born in 1901, the scion of an old New York State and Maryland family that controlled long-established railway equipment concerns, Symington was educated at Yale, where he rated as a harum-scarum student but an attractive personality. After graduation he married an heiress, the daughter of James Wadsworth, then he struck out for business, beginning at the top of the ladder in one of the Symington companies at Rochester, New York and moving on a while later to head the small Colonial Radio Company at Rochester. In the hard times of the depression Symington won no signal success as an executive, but he was promoted in 1938 to the presidency of the Emerson Electric Company of St. Louis, which manufactured, among other things, radios and phonographs. Its business and sales were modest until the war came. In 1941 Symington went to Washington and came back with an Air Force contract for $113 million of bombing-plane turrets, a sum two or three times greater than Emerson's annual volume of sales up to that time. The company expanded its factory space, hired thousands of laborers, and they were off.

Symington managed the defense jobs well; he maintained excellent relations with his unionized labor force and was also commended by the AACP for his treatment of black workers. War taxes limited profits and cut salaries, but Emerson, like other companies; awarded liberal stock options to its executives, which at the end of the war yielded Symington $5 million in capital gains. Before this he had apparently never seen any big money of his own.

His social prominence and political contacts in St. Louis, as well as his good reputation as an administrator, led Symington's Missouri compatriot, President Harry Truman, to appoint him Administrator of Surplus War Materials. In 1948 he supported Truman's campaign for reelection and afterward was named Secretary of the Air Force, in which office he made himself known as a "hawk" and a cold warrior, demanding ever more and bigger bomber planes. His views were undoubtedly colored by his close contacts with the Strategic Air Command, led by General Curtis LeMay. After he became a U.S. Senator from Missouri in 1952, he played a leading part in preparing legislation for military appropriations, although his ardor for war in Vietnam cooled in later years. But throughout his career in the Cabinet or Senate he expounded his faith in a form of partnership between the state and private business that closely resembles state capitalism.

In the spring of 1960 when Symington was briefly a contender for the presidential nomination, he declared in an interview that he wanted the Democratic Party to embrace in its platform what he called:

> . . . this one fundamental concept of government being a partner of business, a partner of labor . . . and of the farmers too. This Republican talk of pulling the government out of business is not only stupid, it's . . . dangerous. . . . Look, you get up in a plane, you want to make sure it lands safely— we can't give up the Federal Aviation Authority. You buy

a bottle of medicine in the store, you want to be sure . . .
we can't give up the F.D.A. You buy stock in a mine . . .
you need the SEC. You tune in your radio—you don't want
five stations on the same channel—we can't give up the FCC.
This silly Republican prattle of pulling Government out of
business. Absurd! This country's become strong because government is a partner of everybody, and we have to recognize
that kind of strength is our only hope . . .[2]

Even greater than the flood of business orders from the
military services was the impact of research in the technology
of weaponry upon the future of the industrial giants. The
scientific knowledge needed was already in the possession of
our university theorists, as of the men in the laboratories of
firms like GE, Bell System, Du Pont, or Eastman Kodak; but
their industrial research activities were very limited. Only
the Federal Government could expend $4.5 billion for long-
term development work on a secret weapon that would un-
leash the energies of "a thousand suns," and on a variety of
new industrial products leading to the formation of new
industries.

Secretary of War Stimson, the corporation lawyer from
Wall Street, was put in charge of the elaborate atom bomb
project, using an army of technicians under the direction of
General Leslie Groves and Professor Robert Oppenheimer.
At the War Department an Interim Atomic Energy Commission was created to supervise the work with Stimson as
chairman; Commander (later Rear Admiral) Lewis W.
Strauss represented the Navy in this inner circle; while Van-
nevar Bush, Karl T. Compton, and James B. Conant were
the scientists on the Commission. Strauss, who had served in
the Navy in World War I, had been a partner of the investment banking firm of Kuhn, Loeb since then. The Government was spending many billions on industrial research, and
yet about 90 percent of the patent rights for new products
devised was to be distributed gratis to the private corpora-

tions associated with the arms research projects. It was not surprising therefore that far-sighted financial men would be interested in such affairs.

As Stimson was feeling his age, he invited one of his trusted friends, George L. Harrison, who had not only administrative experience but the habit of secrecy, to act as alternate chairman of the Interim Atomic Energy Commission. Harrison had recently resigned from the Federal Reserve and become the $100,000 a year president of the Morgan-controlled New York Life Insurance Company, from which office he was borrowed by the Government. When he first learned in 1943 of the huge secret organization preparing to make atomic missiles, as he told of it later, he felt "staggered at realizing that a project of that kind and of such a magnitude had been carried on without people like me knowing anything about it." He was even more astonished when he realized what kind of an infernal machine they were perfecting.

The ubiquitous Harrison, who enjoyed what C. P. Snow calls "the corridors of power," turned up again at one of the big moments of history to work over the A-bomb with a tight-lipped group of military officers and scientists, a select group indeed—in which Wall Street representation was not lacking. They deliberated day by day over all the problems— military, political, and scientific—presented by the development of the bomb; they drew up public statements to be issued after the first bombs were to be dropped, drafted a bill for the domestic control of atomic energy, and outlined recommendations for its international control. Stimson has stated that while he was the chairman of the Interim Committee, "the principal labor of guiding its extended deliberations fell to George Harrison, who acted as Chairman in my absence."

Harrison was in charge of the Interim Committee when the successful test took place on July 16, 1945, in New Mexico, Secretary Stimson having gone with President Truman to the Potsdam Conference. "I had agreed to keep in close touch with Mr. Stimson and President Truman," he relates. When the first reports of the unimaginable effects of the bomb came in, Harrison started to hurry off a message by radio to Stimson. But then the caution of the central banker asserted itself. To preserve secrecy as far as possible, he set up a code after his own fancy, paraphrasing the language of his message as he had often done in confidential business cablegrams.

His historic radiogram sending first news of the atom bomb in action has an unintendedly comic tone:

DOCTOR HAS JUST RETURNED MOST ENTHUSIASTIC AND CONFIDENT THAT LITTLE BOY IS . . . HUSKY. . . . THE LIGHT IN HIS EYES IS DISCERNIBLE FROM HERE TO HIGHHOLD AND I COULD HAVE HEARD HIS SCREAMS FROM HERE TO MY FARM

Stimson knew that the Harrisons' farm at Upperville, Virginia, was 50 miles from Washington, while his own in Long Island was 250 miles distant. Thus he quickly gauged the distances and the range of the bomb, and brought word of its effectiveness at once to President Truman at the opening of his conference with Stalin and Churchill.

The dictatorial powers of the President in wartime was in accord with long-established precedent and law. In modern times military strategists tend to assume that aggressive war against the United States would begin as a surprise attack (on "fifty Pearl Harbors") with no time allowed for debate. Therefore Congress vested sole authority to use the nuclear arms in the President, leaving its usage to his judgment of what constituted a sudden war emergency. It constituted the power of instant nuclear warfare.

As the war in two hemispheres drew to its end many expected that a postwar depression would set in as before, with the defense plants closing down and millions of workers and servicemen being discharged. Henry Kaiser, foreseeing difficulties in reconverting to peacetime industry, proposed that after the war there be formed a "reconversion credit pool . . . with such aid from the government as private industry cannot give." The famous war contractor indicated the yearning of many of his fellows for the continuance of the state-financed security from risk, which capital had enjoyed for four years. Something of the sort has certainly eventuated: a form of capitalism enjoying powerful Government support has persisted throughout the generation that has elapsed since the day of Hiroshima.

During the decade of the nineteen thirties, free capitalist enterprise in the United States had certainly made a sorry showing, with the total of goods and services, or GNP, falling in 1933 by 62.5 percent from the level of 1929. In the thirteen years up to 1943 unused capacity and idle labor cost the nation some several hundred billion dollars in goods and services. According to econometric calculations made recently, the total productive wealth lost might have supported 5 million families in comfort through all that time, if the private economy had been producing full tilt and keep up its average rate of growth. The long stagnation of industry was habitually attributed by spokesmen for laissez-faire capitalism to Government "meddling" under Hoover and the New Deal. But when war came there was far more extensive intervention by Government in fixing prices and controlling the allotment of material and production, while some twelve million citizens were transferred to combat and other military services. Thereafter all unused capacity was taken up and new production capacity added until the GNP climbed by 90 percent above the prewar peaks. Hence men asked themselves: if we could make such a magnificent showing in expanding our economy, under Government control in time of war, why should we tolerate disuse of our machinery and labor in peacetime and allow a part of our population to rot in urban ghettoes or rural slums?

In 1946 Congress passed a resolution committing the Government to assure employment for all who were able and willing to work. The "full employment" resolution—though that term was not used—signified the shift toward the cradle-to-grave welfare policy already espoused by England. It meant that the United States would not revert to a laissez-faire economy; it meant deficit spending for the sake of employment. Men would differ about what kind of a mixed and paternalistic economy it was, some calling it, with Galbraith, the "affluent society," while others, in ironic spirit, called it the "warfare-welfare state." At all events the state-sponsored economy of the postwar era has certainly been nothing at all like the free enterprise system our grandfathers knew.

The problems of converting to peace were managed simply enough. For one thing the public, having lived for four years under a scheme of enforced savings and deprived of consumer goods, had money to spend and were of a mind to buy freely. A postwar boom followed, accompanied by rapid price and wage inflation. (The U.S. dollar lost about 50 percent of its 1939 value.) In the second place, the fears of some that arms production would be stopped with the coming of peace were set at rest when it turned out that there would be no real peace, and only a brief slow-down of arms-making. The demand for the maintenance of a powerful military establishment was pressed on Congress by America's famous "war lords," Secretaries Stimson and Forrestal, Generals Marshall, Arnold, and Doolittle, and Admirals Nimitz and Leahy, as well as Charles E. Wilson, the production chief of the WPB, who openly called for a "permanent war economy." The spokesmen for great aircraft manufacturers such as Boeing and Douglas, as well as other important suppliers of materiel, all testified along the same lines. Among civilian experts on foreign policy, George Kennan, chief of the State Department's planning division, urged that the United States assume world leadership and impose a *cordon sanitaire* around Soviet Russia. In addition to the fact that Russia had a form of government abhorrent to most Americans, it was regarded as the only power strong enough to challenge the United States. These were reasons enough for selecting the USSR as The Chosen Enemy. In any case it has never happened in all history that a great nation furnished with the world's most powerful arms should refrain from using them or threatening to do so.

Early in 1947 came the promulgation of the "Truman Doctrine," by which the United States proposed to help "free people" everywhere against those who would impose totalitarian regimes upon them. Thereafter the cold war was pursued aggressively against guerilla or insurgent factions, not only in threatened Greece, but throughout the Near East, whose vast oil reserves now came under the dominance of American oil interests. The nuclear missile race with Russia had begun; and our standing military establishment maintained three million men under arms, ten times the prewar size of the armed services. For our politicos the most appealing and most patriotic form of public sector spending has been that for the national defense.

How greatly our peace-loving republic had changed its style—our generals and admirals were not put on the shelf, as in 1919. President Truman appointed a number of professional military men to high civilian and diplomatic office, one of them becoming Secretary of State. On the other hand many high Army and Navy officers made haste to retire with full pensions and take up executive positions in the giant corporations that continued to supply arms, tanks, aircraft, and ships for the Defense Department. General MacArthur, for example, assumed the chairmanship of Sperry-Rand at $100,000 a year; General Clay became chairman of Continental Can at "over $100,000" and also a director of General Motors; General Levin Campbell, former chief of Army Ordnance, joined International Harvester and Curtiss-Wright; while many a lesser general or admiral, colonel, or commander, some 1400 in all as of 1959, retired to take the pay of the 100 largest defense contractors. There was complaint in Congress that officers who had directed so much military spending in wartime were now being hired by the contractors to "peddle" their influence in military circles, and as a result regulations were issued in the late nineteen fifties to discourage somewhat the stampede of military brass into the defense supply corporations. But for a while a kind of inverse Gresham's law worked, with the "good money" of the corporations ($50,000 to $100,000 plus stock bonuses) working to draw the military leaders away from the "poor money" of the Government (pensions at $8000 to at the most $20,000).

Were the military brass invading and capturing the industrial corporations controlled by the Rockefellers, Morgans, Whitneys, Mellons, and the like? In reality a very small number of the military men proved to be strong executives in business; most of them were used either as window-dressing or for their contacts. Besides it was the corporate elite, after all, that hired the admirals and generals upon their retirement in middle age, and not the other way around.

At all events the decades of cold war did witness a prolonged love feast between the military and the industrialists, attended with a continual barbecue. By 1951, during the Korean War, the Federal Government's budget for the services had risen to $48 billion a year, and was to rise much higher thereafter to as much as $80 billion. *Fortune* magazine commented that the national government had become the employer and purchaser of "nearly one quarter of the goods and services produced by the U.S. economy." Today the ratio in time of "peace" is nearly 23 percent. Adding state and local expenditures the full government share of the GNP comes to more than 31 percent. High military expenditures and government financing of defense projects, together with the boon of accelerated tax write-offs, made for

the "expansionary economy" of the nineteen fifties and nineteen sixties. The country had entered into what Eliot Janeway, the economic consultant, defined as a "permanent defense cycle," which, he remarked approvingly, added a
"built-in stabilizer" for our economy. By the purchase of
many airplanes and missiles we had "bought ourselves a
boom." "Defense looms up as a major and permanent new
business for American industry," he wrote.

Like the motorcar manufacturers of Detroit who have
found that changing models each year speeds up the obsolescence of their product and raises profits, the Air Force has
profited through the built-in obsolescence of its warplanes,
purchased by the Government at a cost averaging $7 billion
a year during the nineteen fifties. These planes used to be
disposed of in dumping grounds spread wide over our deserts.
After World War II the tourist driving across Arizona could
see from the high road at some distance a remarkable mirage;
thousands of giant military planes which had been left to
molder away in desert dumping grounds. Since then a
"guillotine" has been devised to reduce this cast-off aircraft
to scrap. That "guillotine" no doubt has played an important
part in our economic boom.

In his historic farewell address in 1960, President Eisenhower alerted the nation to the dangers of the "military-
industrial complex." He overlooked, however, a third member of this potent group: the politicians who sit in both
houses of Congress and enjoy their own full share of the
Pentagon's business. During World War II the military procurement chiefs, Generals Somervel and Clay, repeatedly
testified at hearings in Congress that they were under the
severest pressure to allocate cantonments and arsenals, or
other facilities, to the district or states of influential Congressmen, some of whom were members of key committees
controlling military appropriations. In very few of these instances was the suggestion of any form of bribery involved;

the politicians were generally bent on obtaining business and jobs for their constituents. But still, when there was a campaign for the reelection of the incumbent Congressman or Senator—as in the recent case of Thomas J. Dodd, of Connecticut—grateful contractors who had won orders from the Pentagon would contribute funds for the helpful politician's war chest, or subscribe to dinners at $100 or even $1000 a plate.

Senator Dodd proved negligent in accounting for the large donations he received and used for his personal expenses; and so he incurred the rare censure of the Senate and suffered defeat in the next election. He used to boast openly of how much Pentagon business he had brought his state; so did a hundred other politicians whose procedure was more correct. For example Senator Henry M. Jackson of Washington has often been called "the senator from Boeing," though he has had no business connections with that company. But Boeing Aircraft has employed 60,000 workers at its Seattle plants; not only the military contractors, but the United Auto Workers Union, led by Walter Reuther, have supported Jackson's policies. In 1971, following Senate debate over a proposed government loan to Lockheed, the peace-minded Senator Metcalf of Montana cast the deciding vote in its favor, saying, "I am not going to be the one who throws 40,000 people out of work in California." Thus each politician rolls the other's log. When military appropriations are to be voted upon, the Congressmen feel themselves under a double pressure: to get their constituents jobs and to help military supply contractors who will employ their people and also provide money for the Congressmen's election campaigns; and so they vote en masse for military appropriations.

Meanwhile the most conservative financiers have become thoroughly accustomed to the *collectivistic* character of our present-day economy. In the case of the near failure of the Lockheed Aircraft Corporation in 1971, payment of bank loans amounting to $400 million were falling due, but could not be met. A representative of the bankers' consortium to whom the money was owed, Chairman W. H. Moore of Bankers Trust of New York, directed a strong lobby which won the support of President Nixon and Congress for a government loan to Lockheed. Mr. Moore declared:

> We have now come along to the time when the government and the private sector, for the good of the United States, are going to have to join hands in many projects. . . .
> Basically there isn't a private enterprise company or organization that isn't now receiving help or about to get help (from the government).[3]

In 1941 the eminent sociologist Dr. Harold Lasswell prepared a "construct" of recent politico-military developments entitled *The Garrison State,* in which he forecast for America a system resembling Mussolinian fascism. The country, he held, might be turned into a militarized state in which "businessmen . . . tend in fact, if not in form, to become the hired administrators of government programs." What Lasswell feared was that the more absolute the military authority became, the more dangerous it would be for the business elite, as in Hitler's Germany and Mussolini's Italy. It is true that in the United States the business class has been drawn into a close alliance with the military class, which has achieved an outsized organization and has assumed an ever larger political influence. Yet our military, though accustomed to what may be called a socialistic way of life as government functionaries, tend to show profound respect for the men who command the heavy artillery of money and property, the rulers of the giant corporations. Military leaders have been seen lobbying on Capitol Hill for appropriations important to them "by using the pressure of firms with which the services had contracts." That is, the Pentagon would first circulate rumors in military journals about some big scheme like Nike-Zeus, involving future expenditures of up to $20 billion, and so inspire the corporations to help them. When the corporations began lobbying, then the Congressmen would speak forth in droves.[4] No, our military men may be rough-handed betimes, but they have been imbued with faith in our representative system for two hundred years and loyally support our capitalist democracy; only a few hare-brained among them would dream of seeking to change it to some other, perhaps dubious, scheme of government. Our government may have behaved abroad much as other military empires have behaved in past times, but our own "emperor" is an elective monarch, subject to a plebiscite every four years. Power is still much diffused in our Leviathan-like state—and men are still equal before the law—although many believe that the major corporations are "more equal" than others.

During a whole generation after the New Deal, we attempted to reform and regulate our business society; the Department of Justice has kept its surveillance of monopolies unabated. The economic landscape, nevertheless, is dominated by giant concentrations in industry and finance looming above us like the giant redwoods of California. The corporations that divide up the markets as oligopolies, if not as monopolies, have become so enlarged in assets and revenues that the Steel Trust of 1901, founded by J. P. Morgan and Carnegie, appears in comparison a modest family enterprise. Today the typical billionaire corporations in telephones, motorcars, petroleum, metals, chemicals, and electrical equipment or the gargantuan banking units resemble bureaucratic institutions rather than business concerns. They are directed by management teams which are self-perpetuating, like that created for the Bank of America, teams composed presumably of managerial experts, headed by a chairman of a board of directors or president whose name no one seems to remember unless he is familiar with the business. These people, established in their executive suites high up in aluminum-and-glass cages, are "faceless people," as Professor Andrew Hacker has styled them.

A common pattern of concentration has shown itself in all the major fields of manufacturing industry, transportation, utilities, and banking according to a recent staff report of the House Banking and Currency Committee, as of the end of 1967. "There is always a top one or two that towers over the rest of the crowd. In industrials, General Motors, number one in *Fortune's* list of the top 500 industrials, is nearly twice the size of its next competitor, Ford. Ford is twice the size of Chrysler . . . Standard Oil of New Jersey is twice the size of Mobil Oil. General Electric is about three times the size of its next competitor, Westinghouse." Among banks, the three superbanks, Bank of America, First National City, and Chase Manhattan, each more than twice the size of the nearest competitors, show the same pattern of oligopoly. A survey of the 49 major banks in 10 cities has also shown that these banks held 768 interlocking directorships with most of the 500 largest industrials; and in these major banks there were held 60 percent of the more than $1 trillion in assets owned by all the institutional investors in the United States. The great banks thus hold working control (5 percent or more) in the major part of the nation's largest industrials, utilities, and insurance companies.[5]

American Telephone's regulated monopoly, for example, has been likened to a government in itself, for it has 3,100,000 stockholders as well as 830,000 employees, its gross revenues surpass those of many sizable nations, and its weekly meetings of executives have been called by insiders "cabinet meetings." In the same spirit, the board meetings of the multinational Standard Oil of New Jersey are likened to the councils of the rulers of the "Roman Empire." The two hundred leading industrial corporations now account for two-thirds of all

America's manufacturing capacity; to the one hundred corporations largest in point of assets were awarded about two-thirds of the Defense Department's contracts for supplies during the nineteen fifties decade embracing the Korean War.

What do the directors talk about at their "cabinet meetings"? At a recent board meeting of Standard Oil of New Jersey 85 percent of the time was devoted to the discussion of politics, according to the findings of Professor Robert Engler of the City University of New York, who had access to their minutes.* The question of Federal taxation looms large in these discussions; a tax reduction or abatement of the incentive type designed to encourage capital investment, may be translated directly into profits. Often the corporation's public image is a principle theme, as well as its relations with its stockholders, customers, and governments at home and throughout the world.

Today the annual reports issued by leading corporations are beautifully presented, for they are designed to win the hearts and minds of 200,000 stockholders for Consolidated Edison, or 800,000 for Standard Oil, or 1.4 million for GM, or 3.1 million for American Telephone. In short the task of the chief of our oligopolistic organizations in these days is largely political. Their reports deal with the company's concern with air and water pollution or with bettering the condition of ethnic minorities in the ghettoes by charitable investments in housing for the poor. Though actual philanthropies are quite limited, such are the themes stressed in recent annual statements to stockholders from First National City Bank, Gulf Oil, Consolidated Edison, and many others. For these are parlous times with "strike committees" campaigning in democratic style for stockholders' proxies. At all

---

* His conclusions in a paper read before a symposium on management held at the Columbia School of Business in 1971 were corroborated by a vice president of Standard Oil who happened to have been in attendance.

events the executive types of today, the managerial elite, have adopted a social welfare vocabulary befitting the era of the "people's capitalism," as they term it, and contrasting broadly with the spirit of the Vanderbilt who once said, "The public be damned," or of J. P. Morgan, who when questioned about his policy by the press, exclaimed, "I owe the public nothing."

Corporations with masses of stockholders are vulnerable to movements of public opinion. Their apparent change of heart has been inspired by the crusading press, by congressional reformers, and notably by the vigorous campaigning of Ralph Nader, the young "people's lawyer" who serves as leader of a consumers' movement concerned with ecology, public health, and the exposure of unethical business conduct in corporate management. These companies are supposed to be regulated by diverse government agencies that have long been established; but Nader's Raiders have argued in carefully documented publications and reports that such regulatory agencies tend to become slack or corrupt. The ICC, supervising railroads since 1887, has had a long and undistinguished record; nine of the 11 recently retired Commissioners were found to have begun a new life as lawyers or executives for the very companies they had just finished "regulating." [6]

It has been said that the corporate chairmen and presidents are much occupied in acting as arbiters or magistrates (e.g., committee chairmen) within their elaborate organizations, while delegating buying and selling and the much-systematized promotion programs to department chiefs. Under such circumstances the ruling interest of the top executive group is to avoid bold adventures, and keep the ship moving smoothly. In the case of the major companies, sales operations are generally carried on with noncompetitive pricing in "administered markets," while the public is saturated with high-powered television advertising. In analyzing a survey of the roles of 1500 executives made some years ago, C. Wright Mills concluded that as many as 44 percent of them were not engaged in entrepreneurial activities involving risk-taking. This ratio has probably not changed significantly in the years that have followed. For concerns doing part of their business with the Defense Department or other branches of the public sector, the element of risk is now further reduced; contractors have been given their fair profit even for producing defective warplanes, as in the case of the Navy's F3H jet fighters of 1955.

The men in the executive suites enjoy salaries ranging from $100,000 to $250,000, which are subject to high Federal taxation. But there are other important perquisites: the expense account way of life, private plane travel, company automobiles, retirement benefits, and best of all stock options awarded as incentive bonuses which are taxable as capital gains. A high executive officer, though owning but a tiny fraction of one percent of the capital of his corporation, may within five years or so salt away a competence of several million dollars. This may be very useful as management teams are shaken up more often than is generally believed, some observers of the business scene judging the frequency of shake-ups to be about once in five years.

Your Plucky Dicks of Horatio Alger's old business romances, your ragged farm boy or newsboy filled with the "pure" entrepreneurial spirit, has become a rare bird in the executive suites of today. Analysis of numerous biographies of Organization Men has shown that 85 percent of them stemmed from the educated middle or wealthy class. Today the majority of the top executives of the 100 largest industrial corporations hold the degree of Bachelor or Master of Business Administration from one of the older universities or the B.S. of engineering schools such as M.I.T. A number of such top executives claim that they actually started "at the bottom of the ladder" in a factory, but that is generally because father placed them there after their graduation from Harvard's or Chicago's School of Business. The "Algerian" hero of today is the one who, like Stuart Symington, brought home the bacon in the form of a Pentagon contract for millions, or billions; or snagged a Government loan for a faltering corporation. Less and less does he resemble Adam Smith's classical free enterpriser. "Many of the people in business have become caretakers . . ." was one of the blunt statements made by an aggressive new operating chief, on taking over the sales headquarters of Mobil Oil and beginning to clean house.[7]

A. P. Giannini, called "the greatest banker after J. P. Morgan," was certainly the most competitive of commercial bankers of his day. Since his time a self-perpetuating management committee has run the gigantic institution he founded, with passable success. Recently, however, a veteran vice president who was one of the old Giannini group resigned his post in anger, taking his retirement pension several years before his time; on this occasion he permitted himself some plain statements to the effect that the bank no longer competed with others by cutting costs of financial service to the public, and that its management had lost "the Giannini approach." The Bank of America was larger than ever; but its business policies had become more conventional, much like those of the old Eastern institutions, and have come under the attack of consumer groups in California.

If our telephone monopoly could be likened to a government, what could one say of a colossus like General Motors? That it was an industrial empire, formed originally out of an amalgamation of twenty-one automobile manufacturers, control of which was sold to the Du Ponts after World War I. Today its gross revenues surpass $25 billion annually and derive from over two score diverse industries besides that of motorcars, which it clearly dominates. Following government suits to force divestment of GM holdings by the Du Ponts, control of the company is now still apparently lodged in the Du Pont and Morgan money pools, functioning through 967 trust funds and 1,371,000 stockholders. The actual management of the company is in the hands of a self-perpetuating directorate that is reputed to be powerful, secretive, and ruthless. GM's impact on the U.S. economy is such that its theoretic removal would be equal to winding up some large foreign war, as in Korea or Vietnam! When GM came out for large wide cars with protruding fins, that was the style the American consumer had to accept in the nineteen fifties; the more costly and oversized cars made a boom for the moribund steel industry between wars and brought fantastic profits to GM, while congesting all the cities of America and polluting their air. The matter of human well-being and environment simply did not come under consideration by the GM command. This attitude, however, encouraged strong competition in the form of imported German and Japanese cars; and also an insurrection on the part of the consumers led by the disinterested and reputedly ascetic "consumers' lawyer," Ralph Nader.

The serious threat posed by the economical Volkswagens and Toyotas was countered by President Nixon's New Economic Policy initiated in August, 1971, placing a 10 percent surcharge on imports and eliminating the 7 percent automobile excise tax. At the same time a freeze of wages and prices was decreed. Thus the Administration, in seeking to spur the faltering U.S. economy, gave first aid to our largest manufacturing industry, half of which was accounted for by GM. Overnight the 285 million shares of the company's stock surged in Wall Street, gaining about $3 billion in value. GM's president, James M. Roche, though disliking price controls by government, expressed deep satisfaction at the Government's intervention.

It proved less easy, however, to deal with the increasingly popular consumers' "crusade" that had got under way in earnest toward 1965. In a polemical paperback book read by millions, Ralph Nader had assailed General Motors' cars as "unsafe at any speed." He also directed a vigorous lobbying campaign before Congress in favor of laws requiring pollution-free car engines and added safety devices. Many lawsuits had been instituted against GM by customers who claimed their lives were endangered; in Michigan the blacks waged a resounding campaign for fair employment of their brothers. President Roche responded by ordering a stout legal defense of the corporation; and the company's lawyers engaged detectives to investigate young Mr. Nader. Finding himself followed, spied upon, and harassed, Nader protested GM's alleged persecution before a subcommittee of the Senate and also instituted a suit against the corporation for damages sustained. Now in 1966 there occurred a remarkable confrontation between Roche, the executive head of GM, and the crusading lawyer, Mr. Nader.

In the old days the rulers of our giant corporations, when under attack for some action that seemed wrongful to the public, remained silent, or denied everything. James M. Roche was no Rockefeller or Morgan, but an archtypical Organization Man, a veteran "staff man" as Peter Drucker called him, product of forty years' service in what has been described in the press as GM's "army style bureaucracy." His supercorporation seemed to have come under fire from all sides. In this crisis over questions which had hitherto been given only slight consideration—whether Chevrolet customers might be killed through faults of their machine, or whether people in the cities might be strangled by polluted air—Roche underwent a sudden and surprising change of heart. He determined to go to Washington, appear before the Senate Committee preparing laws regulating motorcar manufacture, and apologize to Mr. Nader in behalf of GM. (Moreover Mr. Roche carried his board of directors with him and soon afterward was promoted to the place of chairman). The corporation, hitherto governed by motives of profit and growth of profit, bent itself in submission before Mr. Nader and an aroused public opinion, and avowed acceptance of its *social duties*. The suit with Mr. Nader was settled out of court with a payment of $425,000 that went to the consumers' movement; GM also began to increase the number of black workers employed. In short, the policy of the company was turned around completely so that it might assume the image of a benign bureaucratic institution concerned for the environment and the health and safety of the people. To be sure, it was made plain that the added costs of such improvements were to be passed on to the public.

GM's change of front and its confession of wrongdoing ensured the passage of the Highway Safety Act in 1968. It constituted a notable victory for the consumers' movement. Mr. Nader's "crusade," which resembles that of Justice Louis D. Brandeis in his early days as the "People's Lawyer," may not change the world quickly, but it may work some good while we wait for the world to be improved.

The industrial monopolies and semi-monopolies have lately been under a surveillance that seems progressively mild and tolerant. It is now clear enough that in several important American industries, Federal and state regulation has tended, for various reasons, to preserve the monopoly condition governing supply and even pricing. Unlike the angry Populist masses of an earlier period, the people also seem now reconciled to living with the monopolies, while tolerating the most extreme inequalities of fortune.

No field of business has been under more extended surveillance than that of the securities exchanges and their brokers. But has there been *effective* regulation? Has investment become safe under the new order in Wall Street?

The SEC now maintains a force of 1500 to keep watch over the nation's principal securities exchanges and the unlisted or over-the-counter markets. There has been improvement in enforcing the rule of "truth in securities" by the requirement of exact and pertinent information to accompany the registering of corporations with the SEC, or the issuance of new stocks or bonds. But there has been criticism of the SEC bearing on its tendency—as in other government regulatory agencies—to adopt "sweetheart" relations with the regulated. For fear of upsetting important financial applecarts the Commissioners have too often tended to make their punishments milder than befitted the crime.

Outright fraud, for example, is not hard to detect and punish through the courts. But in the gray area of proper business conduct in market operations, it is more difficult to spot and curb unethical conduct. The Board of Governors of the New York Stock Exchange has been loath to take action in such affairs even when complaints are lodged with them, while the Commissioners of the SEC have proceeded on the assumption that public exposure alone may discourage unfair or unethical business conduct.

The rules governing the transactions of "insiders"— that is executives or directors—in their own company's stock have been in force for many years; they are well understood, and yet may always be difficult to enforce. A recent case was that involving the largest brokerage firm, Merrill, Lynch, Pierce, Fenner and Smith, in actions to conceal from its huge clientele of small traders advance information about a certain corporation's earnings, while communicating this information exclusively to a few large-scale operators, the managers of mutual funds. These favored clients, dealing in blocks of ten thousand to a hundred thousand shares, were the happy few who were able to sell McDonnell-Douglas Aircraft a few days before its report of declining earnings came out, while the common herd of customers were being encouraged to hold or even buy this same stock! At hearings before the SEC the Merrill, Lynch firm admitted its fault, but placed the blame on some over-eager underlings, who were suspended. The actual punishment of the firm seems to have been innocuous (a branch office closed for a few days); and while the SEC's public censure was no doubt painful, it was soon forgotten.

In a similar case of insiders using advance intelligence, Thomas S. Lamont (son of Thomas W. Lamont), who was a vice president of Morgan-Guaranty and a director of Texas Gulf Sulphur, was a principal figure. On learning at a directors' meeting of TGS that its engineers had discovered an enormous copper lode on the company's lands in Canada, Mr. Lamont quickly placed orders for ten thousand shares of TGS stock for certain trust estates held at Morgan-Guaranty, before news of the mining strike was effectively released to the public by the press. Thereafter TGS swiftly rose about 200 percent in market value. When the story came out, the SEC held hearings and derivative lawsuits were entered by injured stockholders, who claimed that Mr. Lamont had not waited for "a reasonable amount of time" to elapse before taking action. It was a most unhappy and protracted affair for Lamont, who previously had had an honorable record at Morgan's, and a rather spectacular lesson. But Wall Street's denizens hold that hundreds of borderline transactions that are unethical or unfair go undetected.

The mutual funds, of the open-end or closed-end type, have proliferated in the prosperous postwar years, gathering in millions of small or middle-class investors as their clients. They are also closely regulated by the SEC. Nevertheless, several years ago a leading manager of mutual funds, Lowell Birrell—and a minister's son at that—was able to abscond to Brazil with several million dollars of investors' money.

The striking change in the Wall Street market is that the sheer scale and numbers of everything involved have become so large that they assume geometrical proportions. Formerly a few thousand of the rich preyed on each other in the stock market; by 1929 something under a million margin accounts showed that a part of the middle class had entered the lists. But now there are said to be 31 million persons directly or indirectly involved in the fluctuating securities market, through mutual funds, pension funds, and trust institutions, which taken together held a stake of about $72 billion, mostly in equity shares, in 1970. Thus the funds' day-to-day bulk transactions in the markets, to the tune of tens or hundreds of thousands of shares, cause extremely sharp fluctuations, so that the small trader finds it dangerous to operate in the same arena with such gigantic and informed adversaries. The bulk traders for mutual funds or trust institutions also enjoy lower brokers' commissions, while the small fry pay the highest charges. The small dealers who used to contribute to the fluidity of the securities markets find present-day conditions discouraging. The funds, meanwhile, have urged the public to seek safety in their hands, by exchanging their cash or shares for certificates representing their diversified holdings selected by committees of expert "money-managers." The mutual funds, in short, tend to "bureaucratize" stock speculation. They are so large that with their one billion to five billion dollar portfolios they can, in favorable seasons, assure "the fulfillment of their prophecies." Their bulk operations even threaten the hegemony of the 1500 New York Stock Exchange members as a monopolistic "private club": on the one hand they are seeking membership in it to avoid paying commissions; on the other hand they make bulk deals in Big Board stocks on the so-called "Third Market"—outside the New York Stock Exchange—with over-the-counter dealers who arrange "net" prices between parties without commissions. (The Exchange's members are forbidden to deal in this "outside" market which now threatens the Exchange's monopoly of the listed stocks.)

The affluent nineteen sixties were featured by a fairly sustained inflationary rise of stocks, which in the later stages was evidently fueled by the Vietnam War. In 1962 a craze developed for stocks of small unlisted companies serving the new technological industries; this movement was interrupted by a sudden collapse of the unlisted market that wiped out many thousands of speculators and also severely affected the Big Board. Thereafter the better grade of securities recovered nicely and moved up from the Dow-Jones index of about 600 for its thirty industrials to a peak of 995 in November, 1968. The role of the mutual funds and the new conglomerates was evidently preponderant in this long advance, as well as in the steep descent that began in 1970 and brought precipitous declines in the Dow-Jones averages of from 20 to over 30 points in a single market session. These violent changes have been attributed to the money-managers of mutual funds and conglomerates, who have tended to move in herdlike fashion, selling as prices declined, buying as they rose.

When the masses of the funds' clients redeem their certificates for cash, as they may on demand, the money-managers are obliged to liquidate portions of their portfolios. The year end of 1970 saw the value of all but a few mutual funds, including the largest and long-established ones, fully reflecting the decline of the stock market; the "hot" funds, formed entirely with expectations of quick capital gains, showed losses exceeding the Dow-Jones averages by a wide margin. While the more conservative "balanced" funds, which include bonds as well as stocks in their portfolios, may have brought some peace of mind to clients, most of the others have not spelled real safety.

The conglomerate corporations, such as Gulf and Western, Ling-Temco-Vought, International Telephone and Telegraph, or Litton Industries, have appeared as the natural children of our old friends the holding companies that were once headed by Insull, Kreuger, and the Van Sweringens. Unlike the "vertical" trusts, such as U.S. Steel, or the "horizontal" Standard Oil trusts, they promise to diversify their investments for all seasons so that when business in tin cans is slack in summer they can sell ice cream; and when the demand for ice cream falls in winter they will make steel. At their head were the new "miracle makers" (or Pied Pipers, if you will)—Harold S. Geneen of ITT, Charles G. Bluhdorn of Gulf and Western, or James Ling of LTV. Ling, for example, working in the field of electronics and military materiel, built up Ling-Temco's assets in nine years from $93.5 million in 1960 to $2.9 billion in 1969 by a process of rapid acquisition of many large corporations. This had an intoxicating effect on the bull market of the nineteen sixties when combined with similar action by other conglomerates. The rise of Litton, Gulf and Western and ITT was no less spectacular than was their fall.

In 1970 the antitrust subcommittee of the House Judiciary Committee, with the veteran Representative Emmanuel Celler as chairman, undertook a lengthy investigation of the conglomerate corporations and their tendency to "concentration of economic power." The subcommittee's report was not released until September, 1971; it said its best in general terms for some of the financial managers examined, such as Harold Geneen of ITT, but its tables and compilations of facts and figures gave an effect of *déja vu*, of having turned back the pages of history to the sorry record of the Van Sweringens, Insull, and Kreuger, when holding companies, to recall the memorable words of the old Stock Exchange expert Hoxsie, were a "temptation to defraud the public." The figures show that LTV became a colossus by paying ever higher prices than their asset value for the companies it acquired, until by 1970 its long-term debt exceeded its salable assets by $170 million. When it was unable to meet interest charges on the pyramid of debt, the new "miracle maker" James Ling was forced out of the concern. Even the relatively successful ITT was shown to have paid a total of $1278 million for a collection of companies whose combined net worth when acquired was actually $534 million according to the estimates of the Congressional committee. ITT tended to conceal its overpayments and to "pool" accounts, so that much "growth" was reflected. But if excess investment were properly accounted for and amortized, the committee held, "ITT's reported net income for 1968 would be overstated by 70.4 percent." Other conglomerates used similar methods for overstating earnings and profits. They made two and two equal seven or ten! The technique of mergers offered large opportunities for paper profits in anticipation of the foreseen event; and some of the conglomerates, as in the nineteen twenties, resorted to "internal trades" between subsidiaries that gave the effect of rapid growth and rising profits— which all too suddenly seemed to vanish when the market collapsed in 1970.[8]

The records compiled by the Congressional committee show that our great banks, the commercial and investment banks, such as Chase Manhattan, Lehman Brothers, and Lazard Freres, vigorously encouraged the growing "craze" for conglomerates and their mergers or "takeovers" of industrial corporations. Thus one finds Chase Manhattan lending $83 million as a collateral loan to the conglomerate Gulf and Western so that it might take over New Jersey Zinc, a large old metal company, at $40 a share, though it was selling for 33. A consortium of banks also advanced as much as $600 million to Ling-Temco-Vought so that it might buy Jones and Laughlin, America's fourth largest steel company, a corporation even bigger than LTV. (Soon Jones and Laughlin experienced adversity, so that LTV quickly lost 80 percent of its market value, while Gulf and Western also suffered a similar fall.) The banks' overgenerous lending for many mergers and takeovers contributed to a scarcity of credit, and dear money, ranging to 8 and 9 percent, heralded a great new market crash.

In 1970, a year of disaster that may be likened to 1929, losses on listed corporate stocks totaled over $300 billion, about tenfold that of 1929; the dollar was cheaper, the size and numbers of everything much bigger. One hundred and fifty member firms of the Stock Exchange went into liquidation, a good many of them being merged with other stronger firms to avoid insolvency. Only a handful of the member brokers, though it included the huge Goodbody and Company with 200,000 accounts, actually became insolvent; up to a certain point the securities and cash owing customers were protected by the special insurance fund the Stock Exchange itself held in reserve and increased by levies on all its membership. When, however, it appeared that the Big Board's brokers would be unable to guarantee the public against further losses through shrinkage of capital or failure by members of the Exchange, the New York Stock Exchange, which had so long proclaimed its will to remain autonomous, appealed to the Federal Government for help. Congress quickly enacted the Security Investors' Protection Act of 1970, patterned after the Federal Deposit Insurance Corporation law, which established a government fund insuring investors' accounts with Stock Exchange brokers against loss through failure or embezzlement to the extent of $50,000. Thus the Government went in with both feet to stand as partner and guarantor in the Wall Street business. The hallowed Stock Exchange at New York had long held out for self-regulation as the best way for the brokers to safeguard the public's interest. But its own surveillance was, if improved over the nineteen thirties, very slack; in the confusions of 1968–1970 the paper work of brokers went wildly askew, so that transactions and deliveries of stocks could not be completed, and masses of securities were actually lost or stolen. At one point in the earlier 1968 breakdown, the huge investment bank of Lehman Brothers "actually lost accountability of some $700 million worth of securities," while conducting business as usual; the Exchange authorities simply cautioned Lehman to curb its promotion advertising until the problem was resolved! [9]

The SEC still has not achieved primary responsibility for regulation in this field. The New York Stock Exchange's obsolescent trading mechanism has been under increasing pressure from the big institutional investors (mutual funds and pensions); the Exchange has been drawing up its own elaborate plans for reorganization, but as announced, these have appeared inadequate in the face of growing demands for a radically new nationwide securities market.

The saga of the ITT engrossed and amused the American public in the late winter of 1971 and on into 1972. A syndicated newspaper columnist, Jack Anderson, had seized upon what was said to have been a confidential message of one of the ITT's public relations agents indicating that the corporation was acting as guarantor, in an incredibly generout fashion ($400,000), for the Republican National Convention at San Diego. A few months before this, the Justice Department, under President Nixon, had finally negotiated a settlement out of court of the antitrust suit instituted to block ITT's merger with the Hartford Fire Insurance Company, resulting in a compromise by which the government sanctioned that merger. In 1969 Ralph Nader, the consumers' advocate, had tried to enjoin the merger plans of ITT in courts, without avail. Now in 1972 it appeared that ITT was committed to paying an unduly generous part of the expense of President Nixon's campaign for reelection.

Serious opposition to the plans of the huge conglomerate and its chief, Harold Geneen, for unbounded mergers in all directions had arisen in the bosom of the Nixon Administration itself; yet this was overcome. The ITT paid a very high price to absorb the Hartford Fire Insurance Company, perhaps twice as much as some leading insurance companies were selling for. It was by such extravagant overpayments of their stockholders' money that the Van Sweringens and the Insulls came to grief after 1929 and inflicted losses upon many thousands of investors.

The conglomerate corporation denied all charges of having used undue influence by offering large donations to the Republican Party in return for immunities; but its denials were produced belatedly and awkwardly. President Nixon's newly nominated Attorney General, Kleindienst, who was accused of having treated secretly with the ITT's executives while serving as Deputy Attorney General, came to his new office under a cloud.

The Senate's Judiciary Committee investigated the affair at length to discover if improprieties had been committed. While the Justice Department refused to disclose its documents, and the ITT executives destroyed ("shredded" was the word) its own papers bearing on the same affair. The public nevertheless caught lurid glimpses of what appeared like the crudest wheeling-dealing between great corporations and high Federal office holders. The ITT had grown, within a few years, to enormous size under Mr. Geneen, boasting assets of more than $7 billion; but the bigger it grew the cruder became its political operations. Big Government under conservative Republican leadership was increasingly collectivist; it administered welfare with more largesse than ever, but many believed Mr. Nader's contention that its richest favors or immunities were being granted to the giant corporations.

Who Rules America? The question is repeatedly asked, lately again in a book of that title. Is it still the "sixty families" of Ferdinand Lundberg's study of 1936? The militarized "power elite" vaguely limned by C. Wright Mills? A "technocracy" of managerial experts and technicians remote from ownership? Or is it still that "spider web" of banking power and money pools said to be dominated by the Morgan and Rockefeller interests—according to the Marxian economists P. A. Baran and P. M. Sweezy, and Victor Perlo?

I am disposed to believe that there is no one spider or many-tentacled octopus controlling the whole American economy with a single head that might be taken off at one blow.

The old power centers are there in Wall Street, holding their strategic positions and interlocking corporate controls; yet they no longer rule through that tight "community of interests" J. P. Morgan once fashioned. Combinations and alliances are more fluid, dividing the prizes of industry and finance, functioning separately, but united in time of danger to confront the government and win its help.

There are seasons when the managerial groups directing the supercorporations appear strongly mounted, though they do not "own" much stock in their organizations. So long as their operations show *growth* and yield dividends, they are safe. But when there is crisis, when money is lost, and the need of liquid capital becomes urgent, then we find that the great trust companies, insurance companies, investment bankers, and mutual funds, who do hold the controlling interest or working control in the affected corporation's stock, may move in on the situation with great speed, oust the management, and replace it. It is only then that the dominant role of the great pools of money and credit becomes clearly visible. Such was the case of the $2 billion Ling-Temco-Vought conglomerate, from which the "brilliant" James Ling was rudely ousted several years ago. Next the vast Penn-Central Railroad conglomeration, whose Philadelphia "main line" managers seemed to be running it for quick capital gains in diverse non-railroad fields, found itself unequal to paying interest on 500 million dollars of notes owing a banking consortium. The giant railroad and its bankers closed ranks and besought the Government for loans, but this time they were refused, and the greatest bankruptcy in history followed in 1970's catastrophic springtime. In the rescue operation for Lockheed a year later, where the business was almost 90 percent in military aircraft and space contracts, it was the group of Wall Street banks that led the successful lobby for Government help. It is well never to underestimate the power of the bankers.

In June, 1970, for example, the Chrysler company, the

nation's sixth largest industrial, appeared to be in serious trouble. But the Manufacturers Hanover Bank of New York moved in quickly and put together a consortium of Eastern banks that raised $400 million to loan Chrysler on a crash basis—"to avoid a serious financial panic," as it was said at the time, according to *The New York Times* of July 7, 1970.

The TNEC Committee as of 1939 reported to the nation on the constant trend to ever greater economic concentration. More than thirty years later little or nothing had been done about this question which has so long concerned the Congress and the people. At the end of 1971, at any rate, a ginger group in Washington headed by Senator Lee Metcalf of Montana was offering a resolution for the authorization by the Senate of a "new TNEC investigation" of industrial and financial monopoly in its modern forms. Senator Metcalf in a speech of July 8, 1970, declared:

> Since World War II the nature of the problem has changed considerably . . . because of the dramatic growth of institutionally managed funds, including mutual funds, insurance funds, employee benefit funds, and private trust funds held by banks. It appears that the trend identified in the 1930s, of major corporations being controlled by management because of the wide dispersal of stock ownership . . . may now be giving way to a new trend toward control of these vital elements of our economy . . . through . . . the voting of large blocks of stocks in these corporations held for beneficiaries by a relatively few giant financial institutions.[10]

Where in all this, we may ask, are the grand old family dynasties who ruled the economy of America fifty or more years ago, sometimes appearing as a "duumvirate" of Morgan and Rockefeller? Where are the other families making up a "baronial" caste, an aristocracy of money: the Harrimans, Mellons, Du Ponts, Whitneys, Guggenheims, and Fords, most of whom made their ascent in the latter part of the nineteenth century? The Morgans appeared to lose much of their power in the nineteen thirties, but still hold a strategic position as a banking and investment combine in the Eastern money center. The grandsons of the dashing "robber baron" W. C. Whitney—John Hay and Cornelius Vanderbilt Whitney—have been more public spirited and charitable than their feckless ancestor; though they did not appear to be formed for business careers, their combined inheritance, an estate reckoned at $90 million in 1906, has risen through skillful investment during two world wars to a total sum estimated at $400 to $500 million, much of it placed in high-technology industry. The Du Ponts, a clan with a thousand trust funds, have remained the allies of the Morgan group; while the Mellons, in control of their own large banks, as well as the super rich Alcoa, Gulf Oil, Westinghouse, and Koppers Coke companies, have become one of the two or three wealthiest families in the world. The Vanderbilts and Goulds have become atomized as financial powers.

The industrial empire created by Henry Ford has undergone a vigorous revival under the command of his grandson Henry Ford II, sharing the "oligopolist" automobile market with its larger rival, the colossal GM, and its smaller rival, Chrysler. In paper dollars, the Ford empire is worth some $6 billion, or about six times larger than Henry Ford left it in 1944. The seven Guggenheim brothers, the sons of old Solomon Guggenheim, who once reigned as king of copper and silver, have many heirs, but no one of their name sits on the boards of their corporations. The family, however, like the later Fords, has become notable for its philanthropies in the cultural field. No Rockefeller rules all the world's empire of oil; the Rockefeller Brothers Fund of today, while maintaining a working control of the immense Standard Oil group, is much diversified in urban real estate developments and in the new "growth industries" of space, optics, and electronics. (The old dynastic families, such as the Rockefellers, Whitneys, and others, are engaged in a frantic chase for capital gains, for the "quick buck" to escape from crushing taxes.) To be sure, one of the younger brothers, David Rockefeller, after lengthy preparation, presides as chairman of the twenty-one billion dollar Chase Manhattan Bank, one of the key positions in the realm of money. Nelson, however, has for many years made politics his métier, not only as Governor of New York but also as leader of the Eastern bloc of the Republican Party—a persistent candidate for the presidency of the United States.

In earlier times the plutocratic grandees of America used to forbid their sons to enter public life, holding that politicians were the kind of people one "bought." But the enormously increased power of the Federal Government vis-à-vis the business world has altered their ideas. The spectacular public careers of the new-rich Kennedys, though darkened by tragedy, have also focused the attention of other and older families of wealth on the political scene as their future purlieu. Up until recently there were as many as four Rockefellers in public office, two of them, Nelson and Winthrop, serving as governors of states. The Harrimans and Whitneys have also held high elective or appointive office; and the Lodges, Tafts, Romneys, Percys, and Stevensons are no poor men either. Never have so many of the rich pursued political careers so insistently as at the present time; and, coincidentally, the costs of campaigning and electioneering by television have become so fearfully high that only those who can muster a cool million or two for the preliminary nominating contest, and much more thereafter for the full election campaign, may hope to become Senators or governors, let alone President. If it ever comes to pass that our leaders in politics should be chosen mainly from the dominant financial institutions and families, then ours will resemble the old Venetian Republic where the oligarchic families sat down together at the council table of the Grand Doge to rule the state between them.

As long ago as 1936, Werner Sombart, the German historian of capitalism (an anti-Marxian), wrote a prophetic paper on the changing economy of the advanced industrial nations, concluding that their specifically capitalist and entrepreneurial elements were gradually being dissolved. In their heroic years capitalists were distinguished for their independence of mind, their daring decisions, even their defiance of all restraint; but the later capitalism has been featured by mixed public and private undertakings, by state and communal public works managed as cooperative enterprises. The major industrial concerns have standardized productive and selling methods, depersonalized credit relations, and tended to fix or administer market prices for a captive public. Their sales campaigns, Sombart noted, are all mapped out and budgeted, the management becomes routinized, and ceasing to be capitalistic, resembles more and more that of a regulated public corporation, virtually an arm of the government. Management and workers alike pursue a routine like government functionaries, assured of promotion, fringe benefits, and pensions. To his regret Sombart concluded that "late capitalism" was gradually turning into state capitalism. At the end of World War II Joseph Schumpeter, a learned commentator who also admired the pristine capitalist system, in his book, *Capitalism, Democracy and Socialism* (1950), forecast a gradual evolution of America's economic society toward a more collectivistic order.

Decidedly we now have a mixed economy with an enormous public sector (31 percent of the GNP) functioning side by side with elements of small competitive business and of noncompetitive corporate giants. Some observers hold that we are moving toward a loose democratic form of the "corporative state"; others say that we are becoming a nation of government-supported monopolies, who for size and power, dominate our economic life. The monopolies, it has been observed, have become like governments themselves; while the Federal authority, Big Government, even under conservative auspices, constantly extends its controls over ever larger areas of what were the untrammeled fields of private business. In our struggle with the difficult social welfare problems in America, we have come already to the solution of the "guaranteed income." Economists have held that private capital loses energy, once the state accounts for more than 25 percent of the GNP; in the United States, the Government share was up to 31 percent in 1970.

Bureaucracy, political and economic—and I do not mean it in a pejorative sense—looms large in our future. Something of this sort came into being years ago in the older business societies of England and Sweden. There the owners of capital for many years have contented themselves with a smaller take, leaving a larger share for the increased public sector and its welfare services. A similar evolution in the United States, in which capital contented itself with a substantially lower net profit *after* taxes than formerly, might maintain for years to come our mixed economic system as a more or less benign bureaucracy, leaving property relations only moderately changed, while equating a society devoted, more than in the past at any rate, to the welfare of all its citizens.

NOTES

FOREWORD

1. Russell Lynes *Confessions of a Dilettante* (New York, Harper & Row, 1967), p. 145.

PROLOGUE

1. "In 1924 Matthew Josephson, late of Columbia University and the Paris surrealist circles, went to Wall Street and became a customers' man. Josephson admitted that he knew little of what was going on and relied more often than not upon rumors for the advice he gave clients." Robert Sobel, *The Big Board* (New York, Macmillan, 1965), pp. 241–242.

2. According to the diaries of Clarence Barron, James R. Keene was once engaged to direct the pool of the so-called "whisky trust"; at the time when the pool was being organized the question was raised "whether individual members could also operate on their own account." Mr. Keene said, "Certainly, operate all you want to; buy it

and sell it . . . but just understand that I will get the best of you all in the business and I invite you to trade with me." . . . Then Mr. Keene began. Ten thousand shares went out one day and were bought back . . . He kept it swinging back and forth. Then when the whole public was trading in whisky stock with a great big swing to the market, Keene "landed the entire stock of the pool on the public." Clarence Barron, *More They Told Barron* (New York, 1932), p. 11.

3. Studs Terkel, *Hard Times* (New York, Pantheon, 1920), p. 65.
4. Lucien Romier, *Who Will Be Master—Russia or America?*, trans. by Matthew Josephson (New York, Macaulay Co., 1928).

CHAPTER ONE

1. Forrest McDonald, *Insull* (Chicago, 1962), p. 145.
2. Carl D. Thompson, *Confessions of a Power Trust* (New York, 1932), p. 101.
3. McDonald, *op. cit.* p. 185.
4. *Ibid.*, pp. 203–204.
5. *Stock Exchange Practices*, Part 3, Hearings of Senate Committee on Banking and Currency (June 27, 1933).

CHAPTER TWO

1. Boston *Transcript* (June 5, 1928).
2. *Time* (February 8, 1937), citing hearings of the U.S. Senate Sub-Committee on Railroads.
3. Marquis and B. R. James, *The Biography of a Bank* (New York, Harpers, 1954), p. 230.

CHAPTER THREE

1. Carl D. Thompson, *Confessions of a Power Trust* (New York, 1932), p. 248.

CHAPTER FIVE

1. Marquis and B. R. James, *The Biography of a Bank* (New York, Harpers, 1954), p. 303.

CHAPTER SIX

1. *The New York Times* (April 28, 1935).

CHAPTER SEVEN

1. Richard J. Whalen, *The Founding Father; The Story of Joseph P. Kennedy* (New York, 1961), pp. 107, 130–134.

CHAPTER EIGHT

1. Frank Bailey, *It Can't Happen Here Again* (as told to Hannah Josephson) (New York, Alfred Knopf, 1944).
2. Joseph Borkin, *Robert R. Young, The Populist of Wall Street* (New York, 1969).
3. Max Lowenthal, *The Investor Pays* (New York, Alfred Knopf, 1933).
4. Testimony of R. R. Young before the SEC; hearings of February 18, 1954.
5. *The New York Times* (February 3, 1958).
6. Borkin, *op. cit.*, p. 127.
7. Matthew Josephson, "The Daring Young Man from Wall Street," *The Saturday Evening Post* (August 11, August 18, August 25, 1945).

CHAPTER NINE

1. Joseph Schumpeter, *Capitalism, Socialism and Democracy,* Third Edition (New York, Harper & Bros., 1950), pp. 64–65.
2. Oddly enough, Young turned against the Roosevelt Administration because it had become "too bureaucratic," and also because he feared, in 1940, that it was moving into World War II. He supported Senator Wheeler's abortive bid for the Democratic presidential nomination, and afterward contributed to the Willkie campaign. With Wheeler he also joined the America First Committee, and after the war ended he became an ardent supporter of Senator Joseph McCarthy of Wisconsin and of his anti-communist "crusade." Borkin, *op. cit.*, p. vi.
3. David Lilienthal, *The Journals of David Lilienthal,* Vol. I, *The TVA Years* (New York, 1964), p. 712. Abe Fortas, a Tennessean, who afterward was appointed to the United States Supreme Court by President Lyndon Johnson and resigned in 1969 under the cloud of some scandal about his lawyer-relationship to a former client, was another instance of a New Deal official who "built himself up" for more lucrative business that he would handle after leaving the Government service. Fortas, who was a youthful professor at Yale

Law School, served on the AAA in 1933 to 1934 and in other New Deal agencies, rising to be Under Secretary of the Interior in 1942 when he was thirty-two years of age. His service under the exacting Ickes was that of an able administrator, and one who conducted himself with entire probity up to the time of his resignation in 1946. Thereafter, his law firm, in partnership with Thurman Arnold and Paul Porter served some of the clients he had been wont to regulate in the past and became one of the largest and most profitable in Washington.

4. William H. Whyte, Jr., *The Organization Man* (New York, 1958).

5. An industry that was exceptional in that it generated old-style individualistic tycoons was that of oil drilling, especially in Texas. The wildcatters, such as H. R. Hunt, Roy Cullen, Sid Richardson, and Clint Murchison, began their climb during the period after 1940 when war preparations called for increased oil exploration. By perfecting their technique as gamblers or hunters for oil acreage they were able to accumulate fortunes running to more than a hundred million dollars and even up to two hundred million or more in a few years' time. As Professor Robert Engler has demonstrated, the special tax allowance for rapid depletion at 27½ percent a year was what contributed most to the creation of new multimillionaires. These men, he writes, were ruled by a few simple ideas about their "game," which seemed to offer "boundless opportunity for all who would reach out for it." Their ideas derived from their own lucky experiences, and thus harked back to the nineteenth century in America when the frontier offered incalculable subterranean wealth, and government regulation was unknown. Unlike the Organization Men of modern times the oil drillers of Texas were little concerned with the problems of stockholders' rights, unions, welfare, or social duties. Robert Engler, *The Politics of Oil,* (New York, 1957), pp. 351–363. Howard R. Hughes, a native of Houston whose father founded the Hughes Tool Works supplying the oil drillers, is one of the same Texas breed.

CHAPTER TEN

1. Joseph Stilwell, *The Stilwell Papers* (New York, 1948), p. 15.

2. *The New York Times* (excerpts from hearings before the Senate Sub-committee investigating war production) (November 7, 8, 10, 14, 15, 17, 19, 1947).

3. Bruce Catton, *The War Lords of Washington* (1947).

4. *The New York Times* (August 11, 1944).

5. Drew Pearson, the Washington *Post* (August 7, 11, 1944); *The New York Times* (August 8, 11, 1944).

6. Senate Committee for the Investigation of the National Defense Program (August 16, 1944), Part 24, p. 11, 080.

7. *Ibid.*, pp. 10, 893–895.

8. James Forrestal, *Forrestal Diaries,* Walter Millis and E. S. Duffield, eds. (New York, Viking).

9. The Washington *Post* (August 11, 1944).

10. Drew Pearson, the Washington *Post* (August 9, 1944).

11. E. Janeway, *The Struggle for Survival* (New Haven, 1951), p. 157.

12. Senate Committee for the Investigation of the National Defense Program, *op. cit.*, pp. 10, 896.

13. *Ibid.*, pp. 11, 909.

EPILOGUE

1. David Bazelon, *The Paper Economy* (New York, 1963), p. 37.

2. Theodore White, *The Making of the President* (New York, 1961), Appendix.

3. *The New York Times* (July 13, 1971).

4. Julius Duscha, *Arms, Politics and Money* (New York, 1964), pp. 95–97.

5. Senate Resolution 113, To Investigate Economic and Financial Concentration, submitted by Senator Lee Metcalf of Montana, *Congressional Record* (May 5, 1971).

6. "Who Regulates the Regulated?", Leonard Ross, *The New York Times*, Section 7 (August 8, 1971) .

7. "Mobil's New Sales Manager," *The New York Times* (January 17, 1971).

8. "The Economic and Political Menace of Conglomerate Corporations—Scandalous Revelations the Press Ignored," *I. F. Stone's Bi-Weekly* (September 20, 1971).

9. "Wall Street," Chris Welles, *The New York Times* (October 24, 1970).

10. *Congressional Record* (July 8, 1970).

INDEX

Acheson, Dean, 164
Adams, Charles Francis, 136
Adrian H. Muller & Sons, 191–192
Agricultural Adjustment Association
  (AAA), 163, 172, 248
Alleghany Corporation, 82–83, 94, 95,
  96–98, 135, 254
  collapse of, 132–133
  Young, Robert R., and, 190–236, 247
Allied Chemical and Dye Corporation,
  209
Aluminum Company of America
  (Alcoa), 253, 280, 291–292, 355
American Association of Railways, 254
American Bankers' Association, 64,
  167–170
American Can Company, 9, 182
American Commercial Alcohol,
  176–177
American Liberty League, 170
American Medical Association (AMA),
  296
American Sugar Company, 27
American Telephone & Telegraph
  (AT&T), 88, 107, 186, 273, 336
Anaconda Copper Company, 6, 85, 87,
  115, 116, 127
Anderson, Jack, 351
Anglo-California Bank of San
  Francisco, 141
Arnold, General H. H., 303, 329
Arnold, Thurman, 253–254, 264
Associated Gas and Electric Company,
  84
Association of Edison Electric
  Illuminating Companies, 42
Astor, Vincent, 227
Atomic Energy Commission, 258
Avery, Sewell, 249, 270–271
Ayres, Leonard P., 47, 192

Babson, Roger, 87
Bache and Company, 244
Bacigalupi, James A., 63, 70, 74–75,
  138, 144
Baillie, Earle, 218, 220, 221, 222
Baker, George F., Sr., 22, 23, 46
Baker, George F., Jr., 91

Baldwin, Hanson, 305
Baldwin Locomotive Company, 3
Ball, George A., 192, 193, 198, 199,
  223–224
Ballantine, Arthur, 146
Banca d'America e d'Italia of Milan, 74
Bancitaly, see Transamerica
  Corporation
Bank of America, 66, 70, 71, 72, 73,
  75, 79, 124, 137–138, 141–150,
  170, 295, 335, 336, 340
  assets, 263
  founded, 65
  New Deal antitrust crusade and,
  255–257, 259–263
  See also Bank of Italy (before 1929)
Bank of England, 162, 163
Bank for International Settlements
  (World Bank), 157
Bank holiday of 1933, 147–150, 153
Bank of Italy, 34, 49–50, 58–79
  assets, 64, 66–67
  beginning of, 58–59
  California gubernatorial race and
  (1926), 66
  fined, 62
  growth of, 61–67
  Morgan and, 53, 70–71, 72, 76,
  77–78, 79
  number of shares, 77
  renamed, 79
  stock split, 73
  stock value, 67, 73
  See also Bank of America (after
  1929)
Bank of United States, 145, 150
Bank of Visalia, 65
Bankers Trust (New York), 71, 334
Banking Act of 1933, 149, 172–173
Banking Act of 1935, 170, 255
Banque de France, 122, 157, 162
Baran, P. A., 352
Barron, Clarence, 15
Bartow, F. D., 71, 76
Baruch, Bernard M., 9, 10, 20, 27, 28,
  87–88, 178, 248, 280, 301–302
Bear (short selling) operators, 106–129,
  135